That the Scriptures Might Be Fulfilled through Perfect Worship

That the Scriptures Might Be Fulfilled through Perfect Worship

An Investigation of John 19:36–37

NATHANAEL R. POLINSKI, O.S.B.

☙PICKWICK *Publications* • Eugene, Oregon

THAT THE SCRIPTURES MIGHT BE FULFILLED THROUGH PERFECT WORSHIP
An Investigation of John 19:36–37

Copyright © 2019 Nathanael R. Polinski, O.S.B. All rights reserved. Except for brief quotations in critical publications or reviews, no part of this book may be reproduced in any manner without prior written permission from the publisher. Write: Permissions, Wipf and Stock Publishers, 199 W. 8th Ave., Suite 3, Eugene, OR 97401.

Pickwick Publications
An Imprint of Wipf and Stock Publishers
199 W. 8th Ave., Suite 3
Eugene, OR 97401

www.wipfandstock.com

PAPERBACK ISBN: 978-1-5326-6315-4
HARDCOVER ISBN: 978-1-5326-6316-1
EBOOK ISBN: 978-1-5326-6317-8

Cataloguing-in-Publication data:

Names: Polinski, Nathanael R., O.S.B., author.

Title: That the scriptures might be fulfilled through perfect worship : an investigation of John 19:36–37 / by Nathanael R. Polinski, O.S.B.

Description: Eugene, OR: Pickwick Publications, 2019 | Includes bibliographical references and index.

Identifiers: ISBN 978-1-5326-6315-4 (paperback) | ISBN 978-1-5326-6316-1 (hardcover) | ISBN 978-1-5326-6317-8 (ebook)

Subjects: LCSH: Bible. John, XIX, 36–37—Criticism, interpretation, etc. | Worship.

Classification: BS2615.5 P6 2019 (print) | BS2615.5 (ebook)

Manufactured in the U.S.A. NOVEMBER 5, 2019

Nihil Obstat: The Reverend Monsignor Larry J. Kulick, JCL, VG
Censor Librorum

Imprimatur: The Most Reverend Edward C. Malesic, JCL
Bishop of Greensburg
Date: July 9, 2019

The nihil obstat and imprimatur are official declarations that a book or pamphlet is free of doctrinal or moral error. No implication is contained therein that those who have granted the nihil obstat and imprimatur agree with the contents, opinions or statements expressed.

Contents

Acknowledgments | vii

Abbreviations | viii

1. Introduction | 1
    Significance of the Fulfillment Attested by John 19:36–37 | 1
    Preliminary Information on John 19:36–37 and the Overall Gospel | 2
    Overview of the Present Study | 7
    Conclusion | 8

2. John's Presumed Context of Worship in First-Century Judaism | 10
    Temple | 11
    Feasts | 15
    Sacrificial Worship | 32
    Summary | 39

3. John's Proximate Context of Early Christian Worship | 40
    Early Christian Worship as the Proximate Context for John's Gospel | 41
    Worship as an Overarching Theme in the Fourth Gospel | 54
    Summary | 76

4. Ancient Exegetical Methods Relevant to John 19:36–37 | 78

    Biblical Interpretation in the New Testament and Late Second Temple Judaism | 79

    Exegetical Methods Relevant to John 19:36–37 | 84

    Examples of Applications of the Methods Relevant to John 19:36–37 | 92

    Potential Evidence of These Exegetical Methods in John 19:36–37 | 97

    Summary | 100

5. Exegesis of John 19:36–37 | 102

    Analysis of the Text of John 19:36–37: Its Primary Referents and OT Sources | 103

    The Original Contexts of John's OT Sources | 111

    Significant Contextual Elements in the Gospel for Understanding John 19:36–37 | 121

    First-Century Jewish Worship and Its Fulfillment in John's Gospel | 127

    Fulfillment Attested by John 19:36–37 | 131

    Summary | 140

6. Summary and Synthesis | 142

    Summary of the Study | 142

    Synthesis of the Results | 147

    Conclusion | 149

Bibliography | 151

Index of Names | 159

Index of Ancient Documents | 163

Acknowledgments

THE FOLLOWING WORK IS a revised version of the doctoral dissertation that I defended at the Catholic University of America (CUA) in 2017. First and foremost, I give thanks to the Lord for the gift of Sacred Scripture and for opportunity to study and pray with it. I also take this opportunity to acknowledge a number of individuals for their important contributions in bringing my dissertation as well as this work to completion: my dissertation director, Fr. John Paul Heil, S.S.D., who guided and challenged me throughout the process (with astounding responsiveness and unwavering discipline) to direct my dissertation toward academic excellence in a publisher-friendly form, which I appreciate far more now than I did while dissertating (see Heb 12:11); my readers, Ian Boxall, D.Phil. and Edward M. Cook, Ph.D. who collectively provided invaluable guidance based both on the scope and depth of their knowledge in their respective areas as well as the complementarity of their expertise and personal styles; my major superior, the Archabbot of Saint Vincent Archabbey, Rt. Rev. Douglas R. Nowicki, O.S.B., who sent me for studies at CUA; Fr. Thomas Acklin, O.S.B., my spiritual director for many years; Br. Elliott Maloney, O.S.B. and Br. Rafael Quesada, O.S.B., who graciously proofread my manuscripts and provided editorial insights, and the rest of my brother monks at Saint Vincent Archabbey for their fellowship, witness, and support on the journey in countless ways; and finally, my parents Ray and Mary Ann who handed on the precious gift of faith in our Lord Jesus Christ through the sacraments, word, and deed, to me and my brothers Ray and Rich, who along with their families have been wonderful blessings to me.

Abbreviations

1 Apol.	*First Apology*
AB	Anchor Bible
ABD	*Anchor Bible Dictionary.* Edited by David Noel Freedman. 6 vols. New York: Doubleday, 1992.
ABR	*Australian Biblical Review*
Ag. Ap.	*Against Apion*
Alleg. Interp.	*Allegorical Interpretation*
AnBib	Analecta Biblica
ANE	Ancient Near East
Ant.	*Jewish Antiquities*
Anton	*Antonianum*
ApOTC	Apollos Old Testament Commentary
BDAG	Danker, Frederick W., Walter Bauer, William F. Arndt, and F. Wilbur Gingrich. *Greek-English Lexicon of the New Testament and Other Early Christian Literature.* 3rd ed. Chicago: University of Chicago Press, 2000.
BDB	Brown, Francis, S.R. Driver, and Charles A. Briggs. *The Brown-Driver-Briggs Hebrew and English Lexicon.*
BECNT	Baker Exegetical Commentary on the New Testament
Bib	*Biblica*

ABBREVIATIONS

BJS	Brown Judaic Studies
BNTC	Black's New Testament Commentaries
BSOAS	*Bulletin of the School of Oriental and African Studies*
BZ	*Biblische Zeitschrift*
ca.	circa
CBET	Contributions to Biblical Exegesis and Theology
CBQ	*Catholic Biblical Quarterly*
chs.	chapters
CIM	Christianity in the Making
Comm	*Communio*
Decalogue	*On the Decalogue*
DCH	*Dictionary of Classical Hebrew*. Edited by David J. A. Clines. 9 vols. Sheffield: Sheffield Phoenix Press, 1993–2014.
DJD	Discoveries in the Judean Desert
DSS	Dead Sea Scrolls
EDEJ	*Eerdman's Dictionary of Early Judaism*. Edited by John J. Collins and Daniel C. Harlow. Grand Rapids: Eerdmans, 2010.
EncJud	*Encyclopaedia Judaica*. Edited by Fred Skolnik and Michael Berenbaum, 2nd ed. 22 vols. Detroit: Macmillan Reference USA, 2007.
EBib	*Etudes bibliques*
ExpTim	*Expository Times*
FC	Fathers of the Church
HALOT	*Hebrew and Aramaic Lexicon of the Old Testament*. Ludwig Koehler, Walter Baumgartner, and Johann J. Stamm. Translated and edited under the supervision of Mervyn E. J. Richardson. 5 vols. 1994–2000.

ABBREVIATIONS

HB	Hebrew Bible
HCOT	Historical Commentary on the Old Testament
HUCA	*Hebrew Union College Annual*
IDB	*The Interpreter's Dictionary of the Bible.* Edited by George A. Buttrick. 4 vols. Nashville: Abingdon, 1962.
Inv.	*De inventione rhetorica*
JBL	*Journal of Biblical Literature*
JETS	*Journal of the Evangelical Theological Society*
JSNTSup	Journal for the Study of the New Testament Supplement Series
JSOT	*Journal for the Study of the Old Testament*
JSOTSup	Journal for the Study of the Old Testament Supplement Series
Jub.	Jubilees
J.W.	*Jewish War*
KJV	King James Version
LAB	Liber antiquitatum biblicarum (Pseudo-Philo)
Let. Aris.	Letter of Aristeas
LTR	*Lutheran Theological Review*
LXX	Septuagint
MLSB	Museum Lessianum Section biblique
MT	Masoretic Text
Moses	*On the Life of Moses*
NA28	*Novum Testamentum Graece*, Nestle-Aland, 28th ed.
NAB	New American Bible
Neot	*Neotestamentica*
NET	New English Translation
NICNT	New International Commentary on the New Testament

ABBREVIATIONS

NICOT	New International Commentary on the Old Testament
NovT	*Novum Testamentum*
NT	New Testament
NTS	*New Testament Studies*
OT	Old Testament
Pesaḥ.	Pesaḥim
PNTC	Pillar New Testament Commentaries
Pol.	*Politicus*
Rhet.	*Rhetorica*
RSV	Revised Standard Version
SacPag	Sacra Pagina
SBLDS	Society of Biblical Literature Dissertation Series
SBLRBS	Society of Biblical Literature Resources for Biblical Study
ScEs	*Science et Esprit*
SNTSMS	Society for New Testament Studies Monograph Series
STDJ	Studies on the Texts of the Desert of Judah
SVTGAAS	Septuaginta Vetus Testamentum Graecum Auctoriate Academiae Scientiarum editum
Spec. Laws	*On the Special Laws*
Suk.	Sukkot
TDNT	*Theological Dictionary of the New Testament.* Edited by Gerhard Kittel and Gerhard Friedrich. Translated by Geoffrey W. Bromley. 10 vols. Grand Rapids: Eerdmans, 1964–1976.
TDOT	*Theological Dictionary of the Old Testament.* Edited by G. Johannes Botterweck and Helmer Ringgren. Translated by John T. Willis et al. 15 vols. Grand Rapids: Eerdmans, 1974–2006.

ABBREVIATIONS

Top.	*Topica*
TSJTSA	Texts and Studies of the Jewish Theological Seminary of America
TSAJ	Texte Und Studien zum antiken Judentum
VC	*Vigiliae Christianae*
WBC	Word Biblical Commentary
WUNT	Wissenschaftliche Untersuchungen zum Neuen Testament
ZAW	*Zeitschrift für die alttestamentliche Wissenschaft*
Zebaḥ.	Zebaḥim

1

Introduction

SIGNIFICANCE OF THE FULFILLMENT ATTESTED BY JOHN 19:36-37

JOHN 19:36–37 PRESENTS THE final explicit OT witnesses of the Gospel in the form of a double citation of Scripture. The fulfillment attested by the Scripture citations presented by John near the end of the Passion Narrative might seem straightforward and limited, that is, as only referring to what explicitly took place in 19:31–34. Consideration of the testimony provided by 19:36–37, however, in the context of the overall Gospel as well as the contexts presumed by the evangelist provides insight into the depth and expansiveness of their attestation. Such insight into the broader fulfillment attested by John 19:36–37 does much to illuminate the Gospel and, in particular, the culmination of Jesus' passion and death.[1]

By placing them as the final scriptural quotations in his Gospel, John implicitly attaches immense importance to the two OT fulfillment citations in John 19:36–37: "For these things happened in order that the scripture might be fulfilled: '*a bone of him shall not be broken*.' And again another scripture says: '*they shall look to whom they pierced*.'"[2] John provides no

---

1. The reference to the "fulfillment attested by John 19:36–37" (here and throughout) reflects the significant role that the evangelist's presentation of the OT passages in 19:36–37 plays in corroborating the fulfillment that he recognizes in the culmination of Jesus' passion and death (19:25–30) and what takes place afterward (19:31–35). Chapters 4 and 5 address these topics in detail.

2. Unless otherwise indicated, all biblical translations are my own. My aim for these verses and all subsequent translations is to provide literal, exegetical renderings of the

explanatory remarks, however, to assist his audience in understanding the fulfillment of these scriptures as he perceived it at the culmination of Jesus' hour.[3] The absence of such information, however, is undoubtedly part of John's allusive style by which he engages his audience. He often motivates them to discover additional depth of meaning beyond the evident literal sense of the Gospel text through the external contexts (e.g., first-century Judaism, Christian worship) he presumes and the literary context he provides.

By offering no explicit guidance for comprehending the fulfillment of 19:36–37 after the culmination of Jesus' hour (19:25–30) nor of the things that took place following his death (19:31–35), John requires his audience to rely entirely on contextual information. This study considers the collective implications of fundamental aspects of first-century Judaism presumed by John in light of the Gospel's proximate context of early Christian worship to gain greater insight into the fulfillment attested by 19:36–37. The balance of this chapter provides preliminary information about this passage and the overall Gospel based on recent scholarship as well as an overview of the present investigation of 19:36–37.

PRELIMINARY INFORMATION ON JOHN 19:36–37 AND THE OVERALL GOSPEL

Whereas one can perceive a sense of importance associated with 19:36–37 based on its position in the Gospel, occurring just after Jesus' death (19:25–30) and "these things" that subsequently happened (19:31–35), the recognition of insights of recent scholars dramatically increases its significance. Francis Moloney convincingly argues that the evangelist not only considered himself to be writing Scripture, but that the content of his work brings Scripture "to its completion, its fulfillment, its τέλος;" that "the Scriptures have been fulfilled and perfected in the death of Jesus."[4] Moloney's insights on the inherent claims of the Gospel combined with Richard Hays's

---

Greek or Hebrew texts.

3. With the first (and the only other double fulfillment) citation in 12:38–40, the evangelist provides explanatory commentary before (12:37–38a), between (12:39), and after (12:41–43) the scriptural passages from Isaiah. The "hour" of Jesus is a fundamental theme that runs throughout the Gospel of John (2:4—19:27) referring to his "being lifted up" (3:14; 8:28; 12:32, 34) and to his "being glorified" (7:39; 12:16, 23, 28; 13:31, 32; 16:14; 17:1, 5). It is central to the narrative of the Gospel.

4. Moloney, "Scripture," 460.

INTRODUCTION

observations on John's allusive style expand the field of view regarding the fulfillment attested by 19:36–37 and the contexts upon which it draws.[5] Hays observes that John's Gospel explicitly cites Scripture significantly less than the Synoptics giving "each citation that does appear . . . greater gravity as a pointer to Jesus' identity."[6] At the same time, John requires his audience to draw upon the context he presumes in order to obtain information not explicitly provided by him. First-century Judaism, specifically in its worship and Scriptures, is a fundamental part of his presumed context.[7]

Regarding John's utilization of the OT in 19:36–37, Martinus Menken has examined the sources of the Scriptures presented in 19:36 (Exod 12:46; LXX Exod 12:10; Num 9:12; Ps 34:21 [LXX 33:21]) and 19:37 (Zech 12:10) as well as aspects of the fulfillment attested by them.[8] His rigorous textual analyses of each of these verses and of other passages in which John employs the OT have provided substantial evidence about particular passages and the evangelist's capabilities and tendencies.[9] Whereas subsequent textual analysis of 19:37 has generally affirmed evidence presented by Menken, scholars have also posited distinct hypotheses on the manner by which John arrived at the final form of the Scripture presented.[10] In examining 19:36, scholars have made use of the presumed context of first-century Jewish worship, specifically Passover, to consider an aspect of the fulfillment it attests.[11]

5. Hays, *Echoes*, 424–41.

6. Hays, *Echoes*, 284. Hays goes on state, "John summons the reader to recognize the way in which *Israel's Scripture has always been mysteriously suffused with the presence of Jesus*" (289) and that "all of Scripture, rightly understood, can become transparent to the figure of Jesus." Hays also observes, "while John shows little interest in renarrating the scriptural stories, he regularly makes passing allusions to them." (290).

7. More than a decade ago, Brown (*Introduction*, 120–42) indicated, "a large number of scholars are coming to agree that the principal background for Johannine thought was the traditional Judaism of the first century A.D." (132). More recently, Hays (*Echoes*, 287) observes that in John "the identity of Jesus is deeply imbedded in Israel's texts and traditions" and that "it is impossible to understand John's Jesus apart from the story of Israel and the liturgical festivals and symbols that recall and re-present the story."

8. Menken ("Jn 19,36," 2101–18) convincingly argues for John's conflation of the OT source texts listed above in 19:36. Whereas Zech 12:10 is clearly the source for John 19:37, scholarly analysis has focused on the method by which John arrived at the form he presents. See Menken, "John 19:37," 494–511.

9. Menken subsequently published his articles on 19:36 and 19:37 with his other studies on John's OT citations in *Old Testament Quotations*.

10. Bynum, *John 19:37*; Cavicchia, "Gv 19.37," 205–57; 423–74; Kubiś, *Zechariah in John*.

11. Schlund, *"Kein Knochen"*; Hoskins, "The True Passover Lamb," 285–99; Lee, "Paschal Imagery in John," 13–28. Most recently, Porter (*John*, 198–224) incorporates the

3

First-century Jewish worship plays a prominent role in both the structure and content of the Gospel.[12] In terms of the structure, John refers to three different Passovers (cf. 2:13; 6:4; 19:14) to establish contexts from the beginnings of Jesus' public ministry (2:13) through the culmination of his hour (19:14; cf. 19:31, 42) and he utilizes other Jewish feasts to provide the background for a sizable portion of the Gospel (5:1—10:42). In supplying the context for words spoken (e.g., 7:37–39; 8:12) and actions taken (e.g., 19:14–16), the feasts also contribute to the content of the Gospel.[13] The advances in scholarship on first-century Judaism have provided valuable information to illuminate this fundamental part of John's presumed context.[14] E. P. Sanders's *Judaism: Practice and Belief 63 BCE–66 CE* offers extensive information on first-century Jewish worship.[15] He also implicitly provides guidance on the complementary use of the testimony of ancient sources for this purpose.[16] Josephus, Philo, the intertestamental literature (particularly the DSS), the NT (and the OT), and the rabbinic literature collectively illuminate John's presumed context of first-century Jewish worship.[17] The complementarity of such sources provides important information about

---

testimony of 19:37 into this aspect of the fulfillment attested in arguing that Zech 12:10 is "a further passage taken in support of the sacrificial imagery" (223).

12. Yee (*Jewish Feasts in John*) and, more recently, Wheaton (*Jewish Feasts in John*) address the role of the feasts in John in extended fashion.

13. The context of Tabernacles illuminates 7:37–39 and 8:12 as does that of Passover for 19:14–16. Chapters 2 (7:37–39; 8:12) and 3 (7:37–39; 8:12; 19:14–16) address these passages and the contribution that the feasts make to the Gospel's content by providing the context in which they occur.

14. In the early 1990s, Charlesworth (*The Messiah*, xiii) commented on the phenomenal rise in "the data available for studying Judaism" during "the last two decades, and especially the last five years."

15. SCM Press published Sanders's first edition (which is out of print) in 1992. This study supplies page references based on the recently published 2016 edition. Part II on "Common Judaism" (esp. 69–392) provides an abundance of information on first-century Jewish worship that affords significant insight into this aspect of John's presumed context.

16. Sanders (*Judaism*, 6–18) indicates that Josephus is his principal source and provides background information to support this decision (additionally, he notes the importance of First and Second Maccabees for information on the Hasmonean era which preceded and influenced his period of interest). Sanders also draws upon numerous other ancient Jewish and non-Jewish sources in his work.

17. Although Sanders (*Judaism*, 14–17) distinguishes his work from that of Emil Schürer who relied primarily on rabbinical literature, the revised version of Schürer's work (*History of the Jewish People*) provides valuable complementary information.

extra-biblical rituals associated with Tabernacles that illuminates statements made by Jesus in 7:37–38 and 8:12 in the context of this feast.[18]

Along with the OT as an essential part of the Gospel's presumed context, John's presentation of the Scriptures in 19:36–37 displays evidence of multiple exegetical techniques used by ancient authors to incorporate Scripture into their works, indicating the evangelist's presumption of his audience's familiarity with them. Although the earliest extant categorizations of such techniques occur in texts from the second century AD and later, the rabbinic literature attributes the earliest list to a Pharisee (Hillel) from the first century BC.[19] Evidence of such exegetical methods in the DSS, other intertestamental and first-century Jewish texts, and the NT, corroborate the rabbinic testimony by manifesting evidence of the methods with no attempts to explain or justify them.[20] One such method is the presumption of the original context of the OT passages cited by ancient authors. In this regard, recent scholarly work that argues convincingly for the unity of the book of Zechariah as well as for its intratextual and intertextual character provides significant insight into the fulfillment attested by the evangelist's use of 12:10 in John 19:37 as well as to the allusive style that he shares with the prophet.[21]

Whereas John presumes knowledge of the OT and first-century Jewish worship on the part of his audience, substantial internal and external evidence indicates that early Christian worship is the Gospel's proximate context. The Didache, the *First Apology* of Justin Martyr, and a letter from the Roman governor Pliny the Younger to the emperor Trajan are the earliest

---

18. Rubenstein (*Sukkot*, 159) offers the valuable insight that the rabbinical literature provides the details for the rituals attested indirectly in extra-rabbinical literature. The OT provides a basis for such rituals and the DSS contain evidence that suggests their practice (both addressed in the following chapter).

19. Instone-Brewer (*Techniques and Assumptions*, 4) provides three lists of rules in his study and indicates that the earliest contains "the 7 rules attributed to Hillel (1st C. BCE)."

20. Among the ancient witnesses, the testimony of the DSS is especially significant for establishing the use of such methods during the intertestamental period and into the first century AD. In this regard (as well as for evidence on Jewish worship), insights provided along with the DSS translations by Wise, Abegg, and Cook (*Dead Sea Scrolls: A New Translation*) offer value. In his analysis of Paul's use of the OT, Stanley (*Paul and Scripture*) provides a great resource for locating passages that manifest such exegetical methods in the NT as well as in ancient Jewish and Greco-Roman literature.

21. Such scholars include Petterson, *Zechariah*; Wolters, *Zechariah*; and Boda, *Zechariah*.

extant witnesses on Christian liturgy, and they collectively grant invaluable insight into early Christian worship. Moreover, recent scholarship has provided the basis for recognizing that their trajectory runs through NT times with recent estimates dating (all or essential parts of) the Didache, the earliest of these witnesses, to before the composition of the Gospel of Matthew.[22] Thus, the witnesses run from the mid-first (the Didache) through the mid-second (*First Apology*) centuries AD. Together they attest to characteristics of early Christian worship, including the necessity of integrating ethical and liturgical worship. They also bear witness to the fundamental role of baptism, the centrality of the Eucharist, the reading of Scripture (OT and NT) and homilies, and the overall order of liturgical worship. Whereas these features in the NT attest to its use in worship (e.g., Acts 2:37–42; Rom 6:3–11; 1 Pet 3:18–22; 1 Cor 11:23–26), insights offered on the Gospels in recent scholarship provide significant evidence for recognizing their liturgical provenance as well.[23]

Although exegetes have long-recognized elements of Christian worship reflected in John's Gospel (e.g., baptism and the Eucharist in 19:34), few scholars have treated it in an extended fashion. Oscar Cullmann's work entitled *Early Christian Worship* is a notable exception with the majority of the book dedicated to tracing "a distinct line of thought connecting with the service of worship" in John's Gospel.[24] Gerald Borchert and Dorothy Lee have recently written about John's theme of worship in chapters of books on worship in the NT and Johannine spirituality, respectively.[25] John Paul Heil, however, has been the first to address worship in John's Gospel in

---

22. Draper ("Didache," 177–81) states, "a number of recent studies have even argued for a very early date in the mid-first century" (178). Garrow (*Didache*) and Pardee (*Didache*), who posit different hypotheses for multiple stages of the Didache's composition, both indicate that (all or most of) the information associated with baptism and the Eucharist (the information of interest to the present study) is pre-Matthean.

23. Farkasfalvy's (*Inspiration*, 79–86) insights on the Gospels combined with Eric Eve's (*Oral Tradition*) on the transmission of the oral tradition offer compelling evidence for recognizing the liturgical provenance of the Gospels as authentic witnesses to the life and ministry of Jesus.

24. Cullmann (*Worship*, 37) indicates that he intends to demonstrate "how the Gospel of John regards it as one of its chief concerns to set forth the connexion between the contemporary Christian worship and the historical life of Jesus." After an introductory section identifying basic characteristics of the early liturgy (7–36), the balance of Cullmann's work (37–119) addresses manifestations of these features in John's Gospel.

25. In addressing John's Gospel in one chapter of his book, Borchert (*Worship*, 43–57) establishes that his task is simply "to detail briefly how it [John's Gospel] is . . . a magnificent resource for reflections on worship" (43). Lee (*Hallowed in Truth*, 61–84)

a comprehensive manner. Heil's textually-based analysis demonstrates the pervasiveness of worship throughout its length, convincingly establishing worship as the Gospel's theme and proximate context.[26]

OVERVIEW OF THE PRESENT STUDY

As mentioned above, the evangelist presumes knowledge of first-century Judaism, specifically the OT and first-century Jewish worship. This study addresses each of these, including exegetical methods utilized by ancient author-exegetes that are relevant to John's use of the OT in 19:36–37 and their implications on the fulfillment it attests. It also provides evidence to substantiate the abovementioned claim that Christian worship is the proximate context for the Gospel and identifies aspects of its theme of worship that are valuable for understanding the fulfillment conveyed by John through his presentation of the Scriptures in 19:36–37. This study will utilize information from the contexts presumed and provided by the evangelist in light of the Gospel's proximate context of early Christian worship to provide substantial insight into the fulfillment attested by 19:36–37.

The next chapter addresses John's presumed context of worship in first-century Judaism, particularly the fundamental aspects of the temple, the feasts, and sacrificial worship. Knowledge of each of these integrally related facets of first-century Jewish worship supplies important contextual information that affords the audience greater insight into Gospel passages. All three facets provide information to illuminate 19:36–37 and the fulfillment it attests. The final section of the chapter discusses the purpose and characteristics of sacrificial worship, concluding with a consideration of its relationship to the ritual worship of Passover, the preeminent feast, which provides the context for the culmination of Jesus' hour (19:14; cf. 19:31, 42).

Chapter 3 focuses on the Gospel's proximate context of early Christian worship. After reviewing the earliest extant witnesses on the Christian liturgy and the fundamental characteristics of early Christian worship

organizes her survey of worship in John's Gospel based on Jesus as "the locus and object of worship, the source of worship and the true worshipper" (79).

26. Heil (*John*, 3) observes, "the text of John presupposes its audience's knowledge and practice of common forms of Christian worship alluded to elsewhere in the NT, such as baptism, Eucharist, professions of faith, prayers, hymns, etc." and that "like the Jewish scriptures, [John's Gospel] functions as a source for listening to the word of God in Christian worship services."

manifested by them, it utilizes those insights to provide evidence from NT texts that establishes their fittingness for, and implies their use in, the early Christian liturgy. The following section demonstrates that various features of the Gospels suggest early Christian worship as their purpose and provenance. The balance of the chapter focuses on John's Gospel, tracing its theme of worship from the prologue (1:1–18) through the culmination of Jesus' hour and the final fulfillment citations in 19:36–37.

Chapter 4 addresses a topic inherently related to John's presumed context of the OT, namely, the practices used by author-exegetes to incorporate Scripture into their works around the turn of the era that are relevant to the evangelist's use of the OT in 19:36–37. It begins by discussing the biblical interpretation that flourished from the third century BC through the first century AD (and beyond). The following sections focus on seven exegetical methods relevant to the current study, describing the methods and providing examples of their use in ancient Jewish and NT texts. The chapter subsequently presents potential evidence of John's use of each of these methods in 19:36–37.

Chapter 5 initially analyzes the text of 19:36–37, evaluating the scriptural passages to which John refers and their textual traditions as well as his presentation of them. It subsequently addresses aspects of the original contexts of the OT passages that the evangelist apparently presumes and then identifies significant elements of the Gospel that affirm connections present in John's source passages, assisting his audience in properly understanding and more fully comprehending the fulfillment attested. After considering aspects of relevance from the presumed context of first-century Jewish worship, the balance of the chapter utilizes the contexts presumed and provided by John to offer insight into the fulfillment attested by 19:36–37 in light of the Gospel's proximate context of worship. The final chapter provides a summary of the study and synthesizes its results.

CONCLUSION

This chapter establishes the objective of the present study of the final OT fulfillment passages in John's Gospel, the bases upon which it proceeds, and the approach followed. Its objective is to gain greater insight into the fulfillment attested by 19:36–37 through utilizing the fundamental contexts presumed and provided by John in light of the Gospel's proximate context of early Christian worship. It also provided some preliminary information based on recent scholarship as well as an overview of the present study. Chapter 2 will address John's presumed context of worship in first-century Judaism.

2

John's Presumed Context of Worship in First-Century Judaism

As mentioned in the previous chapter, the Gospel of John is firmly rooted in Judaism, presuming knowledge of the OT and worship in first-century Judaism prior to the destruction of the temple. The Gospel presumes this knowledge both objectively and from the reader's perspective. Objectively, the content (e.g., allusions to aspects of the Jewish feasts without any explanation of them) and the structure (with the feasts playing a significant role in the chronology) manifest this presumption. Correspondingly, the depth of insight into the evangelist's intended meaning (both within and between passages of John's Gospel) that knowledge of first-century Judaism affords the reader, provides further evidence of its presumption.[1]

Three fundamental aspects of worship in first-century Judaism were the temple itself, the feasts celebrated there, and its sacrificial worship. These three essential facets of worship were mutually and, to a large extent, inseparably related in the practice of first-century Judaism prior to the destruction of the temple in AD 70. An understanding of each of them is vital for gaining greater insight into John's Gospel.[2]

---

1. In other words, knowledge of first-century Judaism enhances a modern reader's ability to understand John's intended meaning more fully. Hays (*Echoes*, 287) observes, "it is impossible to understand John's Jesus apart from the story of Israel and the liturgical festivals and symbols that recall and re-present that story."

2. Hays (*Echoes*, 287) states, "the identity of Jesus [in the Gospel of John] is deeply imbedded in Israel's texts and traditions—especially the traditions centered on the temple and Israel's annual feasts."

TEMPLE

The OT establishes the fundamental importance of the temple for the people of Israel. There were two related reasons for the primacy of the temple as their unparalleled place for worship. Yhwh had chosen it as the place where he would dwell in a unique way among his people and, consequently, permitted sacrifice there alone.[3] Although the entire temple complex was understood to be the dwelling place of God, the Holy of Holies, which housed the Ark of the Covenant in Solomon's temple, was especially associated with Yhwh's presence (Num 10:35–36; 2 Chr 6:41; Ps 132:8).[4] Even with the absence of the Ark in the Holy of Holies, the Second Temple maintained the status of being God's dwelling.[5] Witnesses within the OT (First and Second Maccabees) and external to it (e.g., Jubilees and the Letter of Aristeas) testify to the temple's continued importance in the centuries just before the turn of the era.[6] Furthermore, this prominence persisted within Judaism through the turn of the era until the temple's destruction in AD 70.[7] During this time period the Jewish people not only considered the temple to be their *"locus sanctus,"* but also the center of the cosmos (Ps 48:2–3, 9–10; Isa 2:3; Mic 4:2).[8] Evidence of the temple's status in the latter years of its existence includes the enormous expansions and modifications

---

3. Deut 12:5–13; 16:2; 26:2; 2 Chr 7:11–16; Ps 132:14.

4. The account of the consecration of Solomon's temple in 1 Kgs 8:3–11 demonstrates this reality.

5. Second Maccabees 2:1–8 acknowledges the absence of the Ark in the Second Temple and provides the background for its absence in the narrative of the purification of the temple and its rededication.

6. First and Second Maccabees narrate events from the second century BC and are dated to the second and first centuries BC, respectively. They are addressed further below (see 31n81). VanderKam (*Jubilees*, 21) dates Jubilees to 160–150 BC and Charles (*Pseudepigrapha*, 1) to 130–105 BC. Charles (87) dates most of the *Letter of Aristeas* to 130–70 BC. He dates the law section (128–71), however, and its final form to the Christian era. Sanders (*Judaism*, 77) states that Aristeas was "an Alexandrian Jew who visited Jerusalem in the first half of first century BCE."

7. The NT (Matt 24:1; Mark 13:1; Luke 21:5) attests to its physical prominence and beauty in the first century AD.

8. Levine, "Temple," 1289. Levine indicates that "by the Second Temple period... [because the temple] was where God dwelled; this was the cosmic center of the universe (*axis mundi*)... that both nurtured and bound together earth and heaven, as well as past, present, and future."

made by Herod the Great which continued well after Herod's death as the NT (John 2:20) and Josephus (*Ant.* 20.211-19) attest.[9]

References to the temple in the NT abound with the terms ἱερόν and ναός collectively occurring over 100 times, and with the vast majority of these occurrences referring directly or indirectly to the temple in Jerusalem. In some cases the terms refer to the temple building proper; in other instances they refer to the temple complex.[10] Jesus taught (Matt 21:23; Mark 12:35; Luke 19:47; John 7:14), referred to (Matt 12:5-6; 23:16-22), and cleansed (Matt 21:12-13; Mark 11:15-17; Luke 19:45-46; John 2:14-16) the temple. That Jesus cleansed the temple in all four gospels underscores its importance.

John, however, conveys the temple's centrality most effectively with Jesus' response to the Jewish authorities who requested a sign to justify his actions. Jesus responded, "Destroy this temple and in three days I will raise it up" (2:19). Although this statement does not appear in the Synoptics, incorrect references to it occur during Jesus' trial (Matt 26:61; Mark 14:58) and at his crucifixion (Matt 27:40; Mark 15:29).[11] Such content (with the core element of the "temple" being destroyed) in both John and the Synoptics attests to the temple's importance which made the event and Jesus' statement memorable to his disciples (John 2:18-22) and his opponents (Matt 26:61; 27:40; Mark 14:58; 15:29; Acts 6:14).

---

9. After Jesus cleansed the temple in the Gospel of John (2:13-17), the Jews declared that it had been under construction for forty-six years (2:20). Josephus indicates that the modifications were completed around the time Caesarea Philippi was expanded in honor of Nero (*Ant.* 20.211, 219).

10. In his analysis of John 2:13-22, Brown (*John*, 1:115) translates ἱερόν (2:14) as "temple precincts" or "the outer court of the Temple." He indicates that ναός refers to "the Temple proper, the building or sanctuary." Ναός only occurs three times in John. Jesus uses it to refer to the sanctuary of his body (2:19, 21) and the Jews use it to refer to the whole complex (2:20). John uses ἱερόν eleven times and always to refer to the temple complex. Although *BDAG* indicates that both ἱερόν (470) and ναός (666) can refer to the whole "temple precinct," it identifies the uses of ναός in John 2:19-21 as calling "for special attention."

11. In the Lukan tradition false witnesses accuse Stephen of making a similar statement (Acts 6:13-14). Although the particular terms in the various Synoptic passages differ, they are all derived from the adjective ψευδής (itself used in Acts 6:13) which has the basic meaning of being "contrary to the truth" (*BDAG*, 1096). Such statements can be unintentional (i.e., simply false statements) or intentional (i.e., lies). The context of the trial narratives in Matthew and Mark suggests that the distortion of Jesus' words was intentional. Distortions could also be due, at least in part, to the failure of the Jewish authorities to comprehend what was said (John 2:20-21).

The significant role that the temple played in the lives of the early Church after Jesus' ascension (Acts 2:46-47; 3:1—4:22; 5:17-25; 21:26-30) provides additional NT evidence of its prominence. Other witnesses indicate that most of the Jewish people revered the temple whether they lived in Jerusalem or in the diaspora.[12] Josephus, who resided in Palestine, demonstrates such reverence (e.g., *Ant.* 3.179-87, 224-57; *J.W.* 5.17; 4.262) as do the diaspora Jews Philo (e.g., *Spec. Laws* 1.66-345; *Embassy* 156-57) and Aristeas (Let. Aris. 83-99).

The collective resources that the Jewish people dedicated to the temple in terms of time and material wealth also indicate its prominence. Both of these resources were expended in the observance of pilgrimage feasts.[13] The Pentateuch (Exod 23:14-17; 34:22-23; Deut 16:16-17) indicates that Jewish men were to make pilgrimages to Jerusalem for Passover, Pentecost (also known as Weeks or Shavuot), and Tabernacles (also known as Booths or Sukkot).[14] Witnesses from the first century AD supply quantitative (*J.W.* 2.280; 6.423-25) and qualitative evidence (*Spec Laws* 2.145-49; Mark 14:12; Luke 2:41-42; 22:7-13) about the resources committed to the temple for Passover in particular.[15] Josephus (*J.W.* 20.515-16) and the NT (Acts 2:5-11) also provide qualitative evidence about the attendance at Tabernacles and Pentecost.

---

12. Sanders (*Judaism*, 76-77) states that "the overwhelming impression from ancient literature is that most first-century Jews, who believed in the Bible, respected the temple and the priesthood and willingly made the required gifts and offerings."

13. Various witnesses establish that the pilgrimage feasts drew large crowds from Palestine and throughout the diaspora in the first century AD (*J.W.* 6.422-26; *Spec. Laws* 1.69-70; Acts 2:5-10). The cost of the time associated with such pilgrimages included the time at the feast, the travel time (particularly significant for those living in northern Palestine or the diaspora), and the normal activities foregone to attend the feast.

14. Since the subject of this study is a NT text, the titles utilized for the feasts are the English terms used in the RSV translation when the NT refers to them (i.e., Passover, Pentecost, and Tabernacles). The following section will address these feasts more fully.

15. In one instance Josephus (*J.W.* 2.280) estimates that there were some three million people in Jerusalem for Passover. He corroborates this estimate elsewhere (6.423-25) based on a count of the Passover lambs sacrificed (256,500) and the requirement that each lamb be sacrificed for a gathering of no less than ten persons (i.e., a minimum of 2,565,000 people). Some scholars have found this number impossible to reconcile with the practical implications of sacrificing so many lambs (e.g., the space available in the Israelite court of the temple). Levine ("Temple," 1290) provides a summary of the estimates of various scholars (as well as his own) on the number of pilgrims in Jerusalem for Passover.

The significant cost associated with the sacrificial system, which was central to the administration of the temple, also demonstrates its importance.[16] This included the cost of the sacrificial animals, of supporting the hereditary priesthood (and their assistants) who offered the sacrifices, and of the ongoing construction of the temple complex during the first century AD.[17] The priests and their assistants comprised a large workforce during the normal operation of the temple which could increase dramatically at the time of the feasts.[18] Jews living in Palestine and throughout the diaspora afford further evidence of the temple's prominence by the support that they provided for its administration.[19]

Finally, the use of temple imagery in the DSS and NT further indicates the temple's importance. A passage in the Community Rule from Qumran asserts that the community is the new temple (1QS 8:5–10).[20] This passage implicitly conveys that the temple is identified as God's dwelling in the midst of his people and, consequently, is the place of sacrifice in Israel. In a

---

16. Schürer (*History of the Jewish People*, 296–308) offers insight into the extensiveness of the sacrificial system with his description of the public sacrifice in daily worship and his concluding observation that, "many though these public sacrifices were, their number was insignificant compared to private sacrifices" (308).

17. Josephus (*Ant.* 20.219) indicates that 18,000 men were left without work when the construction was completed during the reign of Agrippa II. Sanders (*Judaism*, 142) observes that there were also costs related to large quantities of incense burned each morning and evening (Exod 30:6–10), cloth that the temple required, and periodic costs associated with vessels and basins. See Schürer (*History of the Jewish People*, 275–91) for a summary of the priestly offices and associated functions.

18. Ancient witnesses (particularly Josephus [*Ag. Ap.* 2.108] and Aristeas [*Let. Aris.* 95]) indicate that there were some 20,000 priests and Levites during the first-century organized in twenty-four divisions who served in weekly rotations (1 Chr 24:4; *Ant.* 7.365). Sanders (*Judaism*, 132) considers 20,000 to be a reasonable estimate and he observes that "at Passover, all the priests were on duty, not just one course, but we do not know what kind of shifts they worked."

19. The temple tax of a half-shekel, collected from every Jewish male twenty years of age and older based on the Pentateuch's requirement (Exod 30:14–15) to make such a contribution to Yhwh, was a major source of support. The NT (Matt 17:24–27), Josephus (*Ant.* 14.110; 18.311–13), and Aristeas (*Let. Aris.* 40) affirm the payment of this tax. Levine ("Temple," 1289) states that "almost a dozen imperial and local decrees recognize their collection [i.e., the temple tax contributions from the Jews in the diaspora] as a valid and legitimate practice." Schürer (*History of the Jewish People*, 295) observes that the temple tax provided, in large part, for the daily public sacrifices.

20. Sanders (*Judaism*, 79) indicates that the Qumran community did not oppose the temple per se, but its administration. He also observes that they "had withdrawn from the temple, but they looked forward to taking charge of it, building it to their own design and conducting its service correctly."

similar way, the NT speaks of the Christian community as the new temple, affirming the two fundamental temple attributes that have been identified in this study: it is the dwelling place of God (1 Cor 3:16-17; 2 Cor 6:16; Eph 2:20-22) and the place where sacrifices are offered to God (1 Pet 2:4-5).[21]

FEASTS

As the temple sanctified space in Judaism, so the feasts ordered and sanctified time.[22] This ordering and sanctification applied to the week and to the year. Leviticus 23:1-44 begins with the weekly feast of the Sabbath and then progresses through the annual feasts, starting with Passover (23:5-8) and ending with Tabernacles (23:33-43). Numbers 28:1—29:40 provides a parallel list of the feasts with its summary of various offerings required during the course of the day, week, month, and year.[23] I will discuss the Sabbath, the pilgrimage feasts, and the Dedication, based on their significance for the Gospel of John.

The Sabbath

The week climaxed with the Sabbath which was fundamentally different from the other days (Exod 23:12; 34:21; 35:2; Lev 23:3; Deut 5:13-15).[24]

---

21. Dunn (*The Partings*, 100-128) cites numerous other NT passages to make the case that the NT uniformly conveys that the temple was "*passe*, no longer appropriate for the eschatological people of God" (125-26). The NT communicates this in various ways, including the recognition of the divine presence in the mystical body of Christ (Rom 12:4-8; 1 Cor 12:13-31; Ephesians 4) rather than the temple and with references to the heavenly Jerusalem (Heb 11:11, 15; 12:22-23; 13:10-14) which has no temple (Rev 21:22). The frequency of NT references or allusions to the temple and its associated worship affirm its prominence in first-century Judaism.

22. With regard to the pilgrimage feasts, their biblical bases, and their associated symbolism, Abraham Heschel (*The Sabbath*, 7) observes that "to Israel the unique events of historic time were spiritually more significant than the repetitive processes of nature, even though physical sustenance depended on the latter." John's use of the feasts to order his Gospel reflects both the prominence of this mindset in first-century Judaism and his presumption of it on the part of his audience.

23. The summary lists the daily offerings (28:3-8), the Sabbath offerings (28:9-10), the monthly offerings (28:11-15), and required offerings for each of the annual feasts (28:16—29:38). It focuses on the required holocausts (or whole burnt offerings).

24. The parallel nature between the feasts and, in particular, the Sabbath for sanctifying time and the temple for sanctifying space are reflected succinctly in Leviticus where the Lord says to Moses, "my Sabbaths you shall keep and my holy place you shall

Genesis 1:1—2:3 supplies the basis for this distinction. God blesses and consecrates the Sabbath by resting on it when he completes the work of creation (2:3). Yhwh provides this basis when he promulgates the commandment to consecrate the Sabbath (Exod 20:8-11) during the establishment of the covenant at Sinai. When Moses reiterated the commandment in Deut 5:12-15 Yhwh's liberation of the people from Egypt constituted the basis for Sabbath observance. Their freedom had allowed (and the covenant at Sinai obliged) them to set this day apart and dedicate its use to Yhwh.

Sabbath observance combined ethical and liturgical worship, a distinctive feature in the ancient world.[25] Living in obedience to God embodies ethical worship.[26] Sabbath observance offers ethical worship by foregoing profane activities that are associated with the other days of the week in order to consecrate the day to God (Exod 20:8). Ritual words and actions on the Sabbath manifest liturgical worship.[27]

While the Pentateuch provides specific prohibitions against work (e.g., Exod 34:21; 35:3) associated with the ethical worship of the Sabbath, Amos 8:5 and Neh 13:15-22 establish the general principle that conducting

---

reverence, I am the Lord" (19:30; 26:2). Brown (*John*, 1:cxli), Yee (*Jewish Feasts in John*, 30) and Moloney (*John*, 24) are among scholars who recognize the Sabbath as the first feast in the extended section on feasts in John's Gospel (5:1—10:42) and who acknowledge the Jewish feasts as fundamental to its structure.

25. Sanders (*Judaism*, 76) indicates that the regulation of the whole of life by divine law made Judaism distinctive in the ancient world. Block (*Glory*, 93-102) observes that the way Leviticus 19 interweaves ritual and ethical regulations in an apparently random fashion illustrates the mutual and inseparable aspects of liturgical and ethical worship. Block also identifies Deut 6:4-5 and 10:11-12 as the basis for, and the practical implications of, true worship. He states that such worship "involves covenant commitment rooted in the heart and extending to every aspect of one's being" (102).

26. Heil (*John*, 2) provides valuable information about the nature of ethical worship with insights on the ethical worship to be offered by Christians in accord with John's Gospel.

27. The English term "liturgy" comes from the Greek word λειτουργία. H. Strathmann ("λειτουργέω," 4:215-31) observes that the Greek term λειτουργέω (and its cognate noun λειτουργία) initially conveyed the secular meaning of "the direct discharge of specific services to the body politic" (216). He indicates, however, that the LXX (and Hellenistic Judaism) transformed the words into technical terms for the cultic service of Yhwh (220-21). The only exceptions are Ezek 44:12 and 2 Chr 15:16 for the verb, and LXX 2 Kgdms 19:19 for the noun. The cultic use of the terms corresponds with their original meanings since the services rendered to God promoted "national welfare" which depended on his "gracious disposition" (222).

normal business violates Sabbath observance.[28] And Isaiah provides a valuable insight into the purpose of such prohibitions. At the end of a passage contrasting faulty and proper ethical worship (58:1–14), Yhwh indicates that the ultimate goal of Sabbath worship is to refrain from pursuing one's own interests in order to "take one's pleasure in Yhwh" (58:14).[29] Proper ethical worship directed the hearts and activities of the people to Yhwh. Pharaoh's response to Moses' initial request to let the people go on a three days' journey "to offer sacrifices to Yhwh, our God" (Exod 5:3) similarly establishes the Sabbath rest as ordered to the worship of Yhwh. Pharaoh attributes the request to the Israelites being idle and so he instructs their supervisors to increase their workload (5:6–9). By implicitly associating inactivity, or rest, with the ritual worship of Yhwh, Pharaoh's response affirms that worship is the ultimate objective of both the Sabbath rest and the exodus (3:12b).

The Pentateuch specified animal, cereal, and drink offerings (Num 28:9–10) for the Sabbath beyond those that were to be offered each day (28:3–8). Additionally, the twelve loaves of showbread in the Holy Place (Lev 24:8) were changed each Sabbath (1 Chr 9:32) and Levites offered thanks and praise to the Lord in designated numbers at the times of the burnt offerings.[30] Other witnesses testify about liturgical worship offered away from the temple which included the practices of assembling on the Sabbath (*Moses* 2.215–16; *Ant.* 14.226–27, 257–58), reading and studying the Torah and the Prophets (*Ag. Ap.* 2.175; Luke 4:16–17; Acts 13:14–15, 27; 15:21), and praising God (*Ag. Ap.*, 1.209; *Moses* 2.215–16).

Pompey's siege of the temple in the first century BC illustrates the importance of Sabbath observance and the integration of ethical and

---

28. Although Amos 8:4–6 conveys the principle less directly in the context of a summary of abuses of the poor, it is more compelling since it establishes that even those individuals who were regularly engaging in unethical business practices were not conducting their normal business on the Sabbath.

29. Block (*Glory*, 276) observes that "the seventh-day Sabbath served as a constant test of Israel's fidelity to and trust in YHWH. By adhering to the six-plus-one rhythm of life, they declared their dependence on YHWH to provide for them in six days what they would need in seven. Thus the seventh day was both an invitation to delight in YHWH's rest and a challenge to submit to him with reverence and awe."

30. Whereas Levite singers were to offer thanks and praise at these times each day (1 Chr 23:30), the Chronicler indicates that particular numbers of singers were established for Sabbaths, new moons, and festivals (23:31). Although the Chronicler offers no information on whether the order of the liturgy differed on the Sabbath, Psalm 92 identifies itself as a song of the Sabbath (92:1).

liturgical worship. He utilized the Sabbath to construct siege works for a future offensive, knowing that the Jews could defend themselves against attack on the Sabbath (2 Macc 8:24–27; 12:36–39) but could not respond to any other activity (*Ant.* 14.60–64; *J.W.* 1.145–46). The restraint the Jews demonstrated under such dire circumstances provides a profound example of ethical worship. Furthermore, Josephus's observation that the priests continued to offer the prescribed sacrifices during the construction of the siege works (*Ant.* 14.65–68; *J.W.* 1.48) vividly illustrates the integration of ethical and liturgical worship.[31]

In summary, Sabbath observance consisted of both ethical and liturgical worship. Ethical worship involved setting aside one's own pursuits in obedience to Yhwh and it established the temporal space to engage in liturgical worship of Yhwh. Liturgical worship provided the worshiper(s) the opportunity to focus more fully on God through ritual words and actions. Sabbath observance directed the people to worship Yhwh in response to the covenant relationship established at Sinai and, through such worship, to find their delight in him (Isa 58:13–14).[32] The combination of ethical and liturgical worship fostered this relationship through their imitation of, and interaction with, Yhwh.[33] The ethical worship of the Sabbath rest allowed the participant to imitate Yhwh while providing the temporal space to interact with him through liturgical worship.

Passover

The OT, intertestamental, and first-century witnesses (including the NT) establish Passover's preeminence.[34] The OT and subsequent witnesses

---

31. In the first century AD, Agrippa II tried to discourage the rebellion against the Romans by observing that those who chose to rebel would not be able to observe the Sabbath in light of Pompey's earlier success (*J.W.* 2.392).

32. The opportunity for Sabbath observance to foster one's relationship with Yhwh is reflected by the expression "*my* Sabbaths" which occurs on multiple occasions in the Pentateuch (Exod 31:13; Lev 19:3, 30; 26:2) as well as in Isa 56:4, and repeatedly in Ezekiel (20:12, 13, 16, 20, 21, 24; 22:8, 26; 23:38; 44:24). With respect to Sabbath observance and trusting in God see 17n29.

33. Jesus' response to those who objected to his healing the paralytic on the Sabbath (John 5:19–29) demonstrates such imitation of God or, more precisely, participation in the work of his Father.

34. Alexander ("Passover," 1–24) provides a comprehensive summary of occurrences of Passover in the OT; Ciccarino ("Passover," 33–182) offers such a summary for the OT, intertestamental, and first-century literature (including the NT).

consistently corroborate the event preceding the exodus (Exod 12:1—13:16) as the origin of Passover and its associated feast of Unleavened Bread as well as their joint celebration through the end of the Second Temple period.[35] The collective testimony of the OT, intertestamental literature, and witnesses from the first century AD, recognize the origin of these feasts as the exodus from slavery in Egypt which allowed Israel to serve God by worshiping him (3:12).[36]

Some scholars have nevertheless appropriated certain passages about the combined feasts of Passover and Unleavened Bread to develop alternative reconstructions.[37] The OT refers to the combined feasts explicitly (Lev 23:4–8; Deut 16:1–8; 2 Chr 30:1–19; 35:1–19; Ezra 6:19–22) or implicitly (Exod 34:18–26; Num 28:16–25; Jos 5:10–12) on several occasions and in various ways. Some texts blur the distinctions between the respective feasts and their common observance (Deut 16:1–8; 2 Chr 30:1–19; 35:1–19) due to their close association and to authorial emphases. The apparent discrepancies between the passages can be readily explained, however, if the texts are not viewed in isolation, since there is substantial consistency in the treatment of Passover (and the combined feasts) throughout the OT.[38] One example of such consistency is the preeminence that the OT attributes to Passover among the annual feasts. The OT conveys this preeminence (of

---

35. T. D. Alexander (*Pentateuch*, 30–31) observes that "almost every passage [in the OT] that refers to Passover associates it with either the Feast of Unleavened Bread or the eating of unleavened bread" and that "all the Pentateuchal sources link the Passover with the Israelite exodus" (30).

36. Alexander (*Pentateuch*, 30–31) indicates that "the evidence does not support the assumption [of some scholars] that the later writers created a historical etiology . . . [but rather that] the explanation given in Exodus 12–13 . . . is by far the most suitable."

37. Julius Wellhausen (*Prolegomenon*, 65–85) fashioned the first alternative reconstruction of the origin of the feasts. John Van Seters ("History of Passover," 167–82) produces a more recent reconstruction, which he frankly characterizes as "tentative and speculative" (181).

38. Deuteronomy 16:1–8 is a prime example of a passage in which discrepancies have been perceived (both between it and other passages in the Pentateuch as well as within the passage itself). All of the supposed inconsistencies, however, are readily explainable. See Alexander ("Passover," 1–23) for an extensive summary of the purported discrepancies and a corresponding commentary that addresses each of them (11–14, 21–23nn44–69). My own detailed analysis of this passage and each of the other relevant OT texts concurs with Alexander's analyses and his conclusion that "on the basis of the biblical evidence we see no reason to follow the modern view that the Passover and the Feast of Unleavened Bread had separate origins completely unassociated with the Israelite exodus from Egypt." (18).

Passover or the combined feasts) by its position as the first of the annual feasts (Lev 23:4–7; Num 28:16–25) and with recollections of its observance at major transitions between significant periods within the history of Israel and Judah (Jos 5:10–12; 2 Chr 30:1–19; 35:1–19; Ezra 6:19–22).[39]

Although references to Passover and Unleavened Bread throughout the OT are consistent, there was organic development in the celebration of the feasts.[40] Two examples are of particular interest for the present study; namely, the manipulation of the blood of the Passover lamb in the celebrations of Passover during the reigns of Hezekiah (2 Chr 30:1–19) and Josiah (35:1–19), and a sin offering (Ezek 45:21–24) on the day of Passover in Ezekiel's vision of worship in the eschatological temple (40:1—47:12).

The Chronicler's accounts of the Passover celebrations indicate that the priests sprinkled the blood from the slaughtered Passover lamb (2 Chr 30:16; 35:11). Although the accounts do not specify the object upon which the blood is sprinkled, it is most likely the altar. It typically receives such sprinkling in cultic contexts (e.g., Exod 24:6; 29:16, 20; Lev 1:5, 11; 3:2, 8, 13; Num 18:17; 2 Kgs 16:13,15; Ezek 43:18), including in 2 Chr 29:22, the chapter prior to the Chronicler's first of two accounts of Passover observances.[41] Sprinkling the blood on the altar implicitly associates the ritual slaughter of the Passover lamb with atonement (Lev 17:11). Similarly, the addition of a sin offering of a young bull on the day of Passover in Ezek 45:21–24 (although it is distinct from the ritual slaughter of the Passover lamb in this instance) also associates the celebration of Passover with atonement.[42] These details provide important insight into the identification of

---

39. The major transitions were Israel's entry into the promised land (Jos 5:10–12), the reforms of Hezekiah (2 Chr 30:1–19) and Josiah (35:1–19), and the first Passover celebrated in the Second Temple (Ezra 6:19–22).

40. Alexander ("Passover," 18) insightfully concludes that "although the OT does not provide a complete and detailed account of the Passover's origin, development and history for the entire biblical period of over one thousand years, it does reveal a consistent picture, with only minor modifications through time."

41. *HALOT* (1:283) lists 30:16 and 35:11 as instances of sprinkling "blood upon the altar." The only other "object" specified for sprinkled blood in a cultic context in the OT is "the people" sprinkled during the ratification of the covenant at Sinai (Exod 24:8) after the altar had already been sprinkled (24:6). The LXX uses προσχέω to translate the Hebrew verb (זרק) in all of the verses listed here. Jubilee 49.20 stipulates that the blood of the Passover victim be offered on the threshold of the altar. Similarly, the Mishnah (Pesaḥ. 5:5–6; Zebaḥ. 5:8) indicates that the blood was poured out at the altar's base.

42. Both Allen (*Ezekiel 20–48*, 266) and Alexander ("Passover," 16) indicate that the sin offering in Ezek 45:21–24 is an addition to anything specified in the Pentateuch. In contrast, Fitzmyer (*First Corinthians*, 242) contends that Num 28:22 previously specified

Christ as *the* Passover lamb and the understanding of his death as atoning in the NT in general (1 Cor 5:7; 1 Pet 1:17–19; Rev 5:6–13) and, especially, in John 1:29.

Witnesses from the first century AD on the celebration of Passover include the NT, Josephus, and Philo. In the NT, Matthew (26:17–19) and Mark (14:1, 12) refer to the feasts of Passover and Unleavened Bread occurring together and Luke places the titles in apposition: "the feast of Unleavened Bread, the [one] called Passover" (22:1).[43] Acts 12:1–11 narrates Peter's being set free from imprisonment during the combined feast. The Letter to the Hebrews refers to the initial Passover in Egypt and the manipulation of the blood (11:28).[44] The most significant NT reference (outside of the Gospel of John) for this study is in 1 Cor 5:7 where Paul identifies Christ as *the* Passover lamb of Christians and his death as a transformational sacrifice.[45]

Some of Philo's references pertain to an allegorical understanding of Passover as a liberation from the passions of Egypt (e.g., *Heir* 255; *Alleg. Interp.* 3.154).[46] He also highlights the uniqueness of Passover as the one day of the year on which the people are permitted to act as priests by offering

---

a Passover sin offering. Numbers 28:22, however, clearly specifies a sin offering for the feast of Unleavened Bread (beginning on the *fifteenth* day; 28:17–18) rather than for Passover, whereas Ezek 45:21–24 stipulates the *fourteenth* day. Nevertheless, Fitzmyer's subsequent observations (even if they are only based on 45:21–24) that "the celebration of Passover came indeed to connote the wiping away of sins" and that "the Pauline understanding of the feast associates with Passover the expiating character of Jesus' death [in 1 Cor 5:7]" are valid and significant for this study.

43. The Synoptics mention the feasts in providing the context for the Last Supper (Matt 26:17–19; Mark 14:1, 12; Luke 22:1–14).

44. By employing the noun πρόσχυσις (a hapax in the Bible) when referring to Moses' celebration of the initial Passover, the author effectively fuses the feast's initial celebration with its observance in the temple based on the way that the LXX exclusively employs its cognate verb (προσχέω) to specify the cultic sprinkling (or pouring) of blood on the altar (see 20n41), including Passover celebrations in the temple (2 Kgs 16:13, 15; 2 Chr 35:11). The LXX employs a different verb (τίθημι) in the account of the initial Passover (Exod 12:7; cf. 24:6, 29:16, 21) where the treatment of the blood involved placing it on doorposts.

45. John's more "explicit" references (1:29, 36; 19:36) are less obvious unless they are illuminated by the contexts of the overall Gospel and worship in first-century Judaism. First Corinthians 5:7 will be addressed further in the final section of this chapter on sacrificial worship.

46. See Ciccarino ("Passover," 106–9) for a summary of all of Philo's references to Passover.

sacrifices (*Decal.* 159; *Mos.* 2.224–25).[47] In *Special Laws* 2 (2.145–61), Philo provides details on the celebrations of Passover (2.145–49) and Unleavened Bread (2.150–61); he refers to their origins in the exodus and their common observance.[48]

Josephus unambiguously affirms the exodus as the basis for the celebration of Passover (*Ant.* 2.311–14; 3.248; 17.213). Similar to the NT, he indicates that the feast of Unleavened Bread is called Passover (17.213; *J.W.* 2.10) and that the exodus is the origin of both feasts (*Ant.* 17.213).[49] Josephus also bears witness to the centrality of the feast(s) by observing that great crowds attended Passover (*J.W.* 2.280; 6.423–25) and by using it repeatedly as a temporal marker for other events (*Ant.* 20.106–7; *J.W.* 2.10; 7.401).[50]

The OT, Jubilees, and the first-century AD witnesses consistently testify that the origin of the combined feasts was the exodus from slavery in Egypt. Their testimony on the importance of the combined feast and its observance also affirms that worship was the ultimate end of the exodus. Although there was some development with the addition or explication of certain features of the Passover observance, such development corresponds with elements present in the earlier texts and is congruous with the trajectory set by them.

---

47. Philo's observation refers to the offerer slaughtering the Passover victim, an act he presumed that only priests could perform in all other instances. Sanders (*Judaism*, 189 n. 14) indicates the basis for his presumption is that "a rich Diaspora Jew, like Philo, would have reason to slaughter only the annual Passover lamb." Josephus (*Ant.* 3.226–27) and the Mishnah (*Zebaḥ.* 3:1), however, testify that the offerer could slaughter the victim for other sacrifices.

48. Jubilees 49 also affirms their origins in the exodus and their common observance. For Unleavened Bread, Philo actually provides two origins. In addition to its association with Passover and the exodus, he indicates that the feast occurs at the time of the vernal equinox which serves as a remembrance of the creation of the world and God's providence (*Spec. Laws* 2.150–55).

49. In 3.248–51, Josephus refers to the feasts individually in providing information about their observance.

50. See 13n15 for further information on the great numbers of people. In *J.W.* 7.401, which marked the date of the slaughter at Masada, Josephus simply provides the date (the fifteenth of Nisan) without explicitly stating that the slaughter occurred during the time of the combined feasts.

Pentecost

The OT refers to Pentecost by different designations, including the feast of Weeks (Exod 34:22; Num 28:26; Deut 16:10), the feast of the Harvest (Exod 23:16), and the Day of First Fruits (Num 28:26).[51] The NT identifies it as Pentecost (Acts 2:1; 20:16; 1 Cor 16:8), which is a translation of the Greek substantive for "fiftieth."[52] In contrast to the other pilgrimage feasts, the OT does not associate Pentecost with any particular event in the history of Israel; it simply marks the end of the grain harvest. The distinctive ritual for this feast consisted of a wave offering of two loaves of bread made from the new grain (Lev 23:15–17, 20).[53] The Pentateuch also stipulates specific animal sacrifices (Lev 23:16–20; Num 28:26–31). The ethical worship included foregoing any "usual work" (Lev 23:21), which effectively made this day a Sabbath.[54]

Limited evidence in intertestamental literature indicates that Pentecost was eventually associated with the giving of the Law and the establishment of the covenant at Mount Sinai.[55] The first-century AD witnesses, however, provide no indication of such associations. The NT references to the feast simply provide contextual (primarily temporal) information. Similarly, Philo (*Decalogue* 160) and Josephus (*Ant.* 14.337; 18.254; *J.W.*

---

51. The term "feast" only occurs in Exod 34:22 and Deut 16:10. Numbers 28:26 refers to is as "your Weeks." The feast occurs seven full *weeks* (and a day) after the sheaf offering of first fruits (Lev 23:15–16).

52. In the NT, it occurs as a feminine substantive (πεντηκοστή) of the term πεντηκοστός (*BDAG*, 796). This designation refers to the feast's occurrence on the *fiftieth* day after sheaf offering of first fruits (Lev 23:9–10, 15–16). The masculine form (πεντηκοστός) appears in Tob 2:1 and 2 Macc 12:32 in the OT.

53. The wave offering involved bringing a sheaf of the first fruits of the harvest to the priest who would "wave" or elevate them before Yhwh (23:9–11). Hartley (*Leviticus*, 385) states that the sheaf "was probably barley since it ripened first." Elsewhere he indicates that a wave offering dedicated those gifts to God (91).

54. Hartley (*Leviticus*, 366) translates the prohibition as "you are not to do any usual work." Josephus testifies to such a prohibition on "work" in *Ant.* 13.252, where he indicates that the Jewish army under Hyrcanus remained at a particular location for two days because of the consecutive occurrence of the Sabbath and Pentecost with the same travel restriction applying to both.

55. Jubilees associates Pentecost with both the Noahic covenant (6.15–17) and the covenant at Sinai (6.22), and it indicates that Pentecost renewed the former (6.17). Falk ("Festivals and Holy Days," 636–45) also suggests that DSS texts associate Pentecost with a covenant renewal. He proposes that this can "be inferred from disparate data" (639) in 1QS 1:18–2:25; 4Q266 11, 16–18//4Q270 7 II, 11–12. Such an inference, however, seems tenuous.

1.253; 2.42; 6.299) mention Pentecost only briefly and in passing on a number of occasions. In these instances, the absence of any reference to an underlying meaning for the feast is understandable since such information would have been an excursus. There is one occasion, however, in which Josephus implicitly explains the basis for the name of Pentecost and provides detailed information on the required offerings (*Ant.* 3.252-53). Similarly, Philo writes at length about Pentecost in one instance (*Spec. Laws* 2.176-87) and is clearly trying to convey the significance of the feast. He even tries to demonstrate its significance on numerological (2.176-78), natural (the appearance of the first fruits; 2.179), and theological (recognition of God as the provider; 2.180-81) bases. The absence of any reference to the commemoration of the giving of the Law or the renewal of the covenant in these last two passages suggests that Josephus and, especially, Philo were not aware of any such associations.[56]

Tabernacles

Tabernacles is the third and final pilgrimage feast (Exod 23:14-16; 34:18-25; Deut 16:16) and the last feast of the year according to the Pentateuch's lists (Lev 23:1-44).[57] The OT also refers to it as the feast of Ingathering (Exod 23:16; 34:22); it occurs in the autumn after the end of the harvest. Tabernacles was one of the most important feasts from ancient times, significant throughout the OT into the first century AD.[58] The Pentateuch refers to it either by name (Exod 23:16; 34:22; Lev 23:34; Deut 16:13-16) or by the time of its occurrence (Num 29:12). Passages pertaining to the periods of the First (1 Kgs 8:2-66; 2 Chr 5:2—7:8; 8:13) and Second Temples (Ezra 3:4; Neh 8:14-17; 1 Macc 10:21; Zech 14:16-21) recount past or foretell future observances of it.

In addition to the ingathering of the harvest in the autumn (Exod 23:16; 34:22), the Pentateuch associates its observance and, in particular,

---

56. Louis Jacobs ("Shavuot," 18:422-23) observes, "neither Josephus nor Philo refers to Shavuot as 'the time of the giving of the Torah'" (422).

57. Exod 34:18-25 and Num 28:9—29:40 also provide lists. Exod 34:18-25, however, is an abbreviated list which does not address the feasts in chronological order. Numbers 28:9—29:40 is chronological, but it only addresses the holocausts and associated cereal offerings required for each feast mentioned.

58. Falk ("Festivals and Holy Days," 639) claims that it was "the major pilgrimage festival." Sanders (*Judaism*, 232), however, indicates that it was the second most attended pilgrimage feast.

the basis for the ritual practice of dwelling in booths, with Israel's time in the wilderness after the exodus (Lev 23:42–43). The Pentateuch also specifies an extensive list of animal sacrifices to be offered with their associated cereal offerings for each of the seven days of the feast (Num 29:12–34) as well as a practice in which the people were to take certain types of branches as part of a ritual and rejoice before the Lord for seven days (Lev 23:40). When the celebration of Tabernacles was reinstituted in the Second Temple era the people were instructed to gather such branches to make booths in which they were to dwell as part of the observance of the feast (Neh 8:13–18). This change in custom apparently restored the practice of dwelling in booths that had not been observed since the time of Joshua (8:17).

The accounts of the dedication of the First Temple (1 Kgs 8:2–66; 2 Chr 5:2—7:8) link it to the celebration of Tabernacles by indicating that Israel assembled for the feast in the seventh month (1 Kgs 8:2; 2 Chr 5:3) and celebrated it for seven days (1 Kgs 8:65; 2 Chr 7:8).[59] There is no indication why the temple dedication took place on the feast of Tabernacles. It may have simply been the next major feast after the completion of the temple. It seems, however, that the association of Tabernacles with the dedication of the First Temple added to its prominence and related it to the temple in a unique way. An account of its observance in Neh 8:13–18 may reflect such an association by indicating that some of the booths were even constructed in the temple courts (8:16) and the account of the rededication of the temple by the Maccabees (2 Macc 1:9—2:18) refers to the Dedication as the feast of Tabernacles in the month of Chislev (1:9).[60]

The reference to Tabernacles in Zech 14:6–21 is of great significance for this study. It establishes the basis for extra-biblical rituals in the celebration of the feast in the first century AD that provide important contextual information for passages in John's Gospel (e.g., 7:37–39; 8:12) including 19:36–37.[61] Zechariah 14 foretells the initiation of the universal worship of Yhwh by all of the families of the earth and it associates such worship with keeping the feast of Tabernacles (14:16–19). That this will occur in

---

59. Second Chronicles provides the additional detail that the dedication of the altar was celebrated for seven days and the feast was celebrated for seven days (7:9).

60. Rubenstein (*Sukkot*, 43) also asserts that "Ezra 3:1–6 associates the resumption of festival sacrifices with the festival of Sukkot because the founding of Solomon's temple took place on Sukkot (1 Kgs 8)."

61. The following information associated with Zechariah 14 provides valuable contextual information that affords greater insight into Jesus' statements in John 7:37–39; 8:12 and, along with them, into the fulfillment attested by the scriptures in 19:36–37.

conjunction with Tabernacles, a temple feast, the information provided at end of the passage (14:20–21) establishes that such worship will occur in the temple.[62] Additionally, the passage (14:6–21) provides the basis for the association of the celebration of Tabernacles at the temple with the provision of water by Yhwh and, consequently, the basis for the related extra-biblical rituals that developed (i.e., the water-libation ceremony and the ritual of illuminating the temple courts). The text establishes this association with the transition from worship in Jerusalem (14:17) to "the house of Yhwh" at the end of the passage (14:20–21), the connection between worshiping Yhwh on the feast of Tabernacles and rain (14:17), and the earlier prediction that Jerusalem will be a source of living water for the surrounding regions (14:8). Even though the continual flow of the *living water* is more expansive in Zechariah 14 (flowing to the west as well as the east), the eschatological image calls to mind water flowing from the temple in Ezek 47:1–12 that will be a continual source of abundant life for the region into which it flows.[63] This allusion affirms that the temple is the source of the living water foretold in Zech 14:8–10.[64]

Although the earliest descriptions for the extra-biblical rituals are found in rabbinic literature, corroborating evidence supports their existence in the Second Temple.[65] The rituals are the procession around the

---

62. The passage foretells that the people will go up to Jerusalem to worship "*Yhwh of hosts*" (14:17) and to keep the feast of Tabernacles (14:18–19). After a double mention of Tabernacles, however, it immediately shifts focus to "the house of Yhwh" and sacrificial worship (14:20) before concluding with the inclusio (at the end of the passage and the book) "the house of *Yhwh of hosts*" (14:21). In this way Zechariah 14 establishes that the worship of "*Yhwh of hosts*" will occur in Jerusalem in "the house of *Yhwh of hosts*."

63. The swarms of fish that will attract the fisherman (Ezek 47:9–10) and, especially, the trees, upon which the leaves will not wither and which will bear fruit each month (47:12), establish that the flow of water will be continual. Joel 4:18 similarly foretells a fountain of water flowing from the house of Yhwh.

64. Rubenstein (*Sukkot*, 50) observes that "the annual celebration of the festival [of Tabernacles] contained no inherent eschatological aspect. Rather the restored temple [in Zechariah 14] is the key eschatological concept, rebuilt upon the transformed natural order . . . [and it is] because of its strong association with the temple [that] the festival of Sukkot finds a place in the eschatological vision."

65. The specific rabbinic sources are the Sukkah tractates in the Mishnah and the Tosefta. Although the final redaction of the Mishnah dates to around AD 200 and the Tosefta a little later in the third century AD, there is evidence that both contain traditions that originated in the Second Temple period. Baumgarten ("Recent Qumran Discoveries," 147–58) provides examples of texts from Qumran and Josephus to argue that the dating of the final redactions of rabbinic texts should not preclude their use as sources of

altar with leafy branches, the water-libation, and the illumination of the temple courtyard during the nights of the festival that was associated with the water-drawing ritual.[66]

Regarding the ritual procession with leafy branches, Jub. 16.20–31 asserts that Abraham celebrated Tabernacles by taking leafy branches and rejoicing before the Lord for seven days as specified in Lev 23:37–40. It also indicates that he processed around the altar each morning for seven days as he gave thanks and praise to God (Jub. 16.31). There may be implicit references to such a practice in 4Q409 and 4Q502, which are fragmentary texts from Qumran. The first text is a calendrical recital of various festivals that finishes with an exhortation to "praise and bless and give thanks . . . give thanks with tree branches" (4Q409 1 I,10–11).[67] Although it does not explicitly specify a procession, it conveys a more orderly and intentional use of the branches than simply rejoicing before the Lord (Lev 23:40). The second text (4Q502) appears to be a description not only of *a* liturgy, but arguably part of the ritual worship of Tabernacles, and it plausibly contains a non-biblical term (*lulav*, "bouquet") used in the descriptions of the ritual with the branches in the rabbinic texts (m. Sukkah 3:1; t. Sukkah 2:10—3:1).[68]

Josephus refers to Tabernacles in numerous places in his works. The most significant passage for providing evidence of the performance of the extra-biblical rituals, however, is *Ant.* 3.244–47 where he mentions the

---

information on phenomena from an earlier period. Sanders ("The Pharisees," 183–353) utilizes archeological evidence to demonstrate the same point.

66. The water-libation ritual provides the context for John 7:37–39 and the illumination of the temple courtyard for 8:12. The anticipated flow of living water from the eschatological temple associated with the water-libation ritual illumines 19:36–37. The procession with branches will be addressed due to its association with the other rituals in the rabbinic texts as a means of supporting the veracity of their testimony about the existence of these extra-biblical rituals in the Second Temple.

67. Abegg ("A Liturgy," 476) states that "preserved portions [of the text] include or imply . . . the Feast of Booths, the fifteenth day of the seventh month."

68. Falk ("Festivals and Holy Days," 640) observes that a *lulav* is "a bouquet . . . of palm, willow, and myrtle branches" and that coins from the time of the first revolt in AD 70 depict this festal bouquet. Although only two of six letters of the plural form of *lulav* are clearly present in fragment 99, Baillet (DJD 7, 494) characterizes one additional letter as probable and two as possible, including the first *lamed* about which he observes "Sur le bord droit on devine le contour du premier *lamed*" (i.e., five out of the six letters are accounted for). The most extensive references to Tabernacles in the Qumran texts occur in the Temple scroll which refers to the biblical rituals of sacrifices offered on particular days of the feast (11QT 27:10—28:11) and the construction of booths in the temple complex (42:7–17).

species of branches indicated in the rabbinic literature (m. Sukkah 3:1–11; t. Sukkah 2:7—3:1). Josephus states that these branches are to be held while the sacrifices are offered. Although he does not explicitly observe that a procession took place, he implicitly associates holding the branches with attention directed toward the altar of sacrifice around which the Mishnah states that the procession took place (Sukkah 4:1).[69] Pseudo-Philo (*LAB* 13.7) indicates that the people were to bring four species of branches to God to observe the feast; no other actions are specified. Finally, Plutarch, a Greek biographer from the late first century AD, observes that the Jews performed a procession with branches in conjunction with the celebration of Tabernacles.[70] Although the information provided by these witnesses about the extra-biblical ritual of the procession with branches around the altar is very limited, it affirms that some development had taken place by the first century AD that went beyond the biblical instruction associated with the branches (Lev 23:40). The information provided by these witnesses is consistent with the detailed information found in the Mishnah and Tosefta.[71]

In the case of the water-libation ritual and the associated illumination of the temple courtyard there is notably less textual evidence.[72] The OT provides the basis for these rituals, however, by establishing the relationship between the temple and Tabernacles with the provision of water by Yhwh (Zech 14:6–21).[73] Given such a basis, consideration of an ancient

---

69. Josephus also refers to Tabernacles as "a most holy and most eminent feast" of the Jews (*Ant.* 8.100), paraphrases biblical accounts associated with its celebration (8.100–123, 225–31), and mentions the custom of dwelling in booths (*J.W.* 1.73). The preceding citation from Josephus is from Whiston's, *Works of Josephus*.

70. Plutarch, Quaestiones Convivales, IV, 6.2. See Stern, *Greek and Latin Authors*, for both the original Greek text (553) and an English translation of it (557).

71. There is a complementarity between the limited information provided by these witnesses and the detailed information contained in the rabbinic texts. Rubenstein (*Sukkot*, 159) insightfully observes: "If extra-rabbinic sources depict the forest, rabbinic literature illustrates the trees. When extra-rabbinic sources do mention or hint at specific rituals, there is typically substantive overlap with those of rabbinic literature."

72. Rubenstein (*Sukkot*, 121) observes that "no non-rabbinic source explicitly mentions the libation."

73. John's Gospel implicitly affirms this relationship when Jesus (the new temple [2:18–22]) identifies himself as the source of living water during the feast of Tabernacles (7:37–39). Commentators generally recognize the water ceremonies of Tabernacles to be the context for Jesus' statement in 7:37–39. See Brown, *John*, 1:326–29; Beasley-Murray, *John*, 113–17; Köstenberger, *John*, 239–41; Byrne, *Life Abounding*, 137–40; Heil, *John*, 59–60n25. Keener (*John*, 1:722–24) indicates that the water-drawing and associated

worldview consistent with the OT provides a plausible explanation for the development of the water-libation ritual.

The rains were understood to come from channels that transported the waters of the primordial Deep into the heavens through a natural process that was ultimately under the control of Yhwh.[74] The account of the primeval flood illustrates such an understanding: "All the fountains of the great deep" (Gen 7:11) were opened at the beginning of the flood and closed when God remembered Noah and caused the rain to cease (8:1-2).[75] Since water libations were a common practice in the ancient world, it follows that such a cultic rite would have developed to ritually implore Yhwh for the blessing of rain during Tabernacles, as established by Zech 14:16-19 in the place where he chose to dwell (Deut 16:11) to which Israel was to go to celebrate the feast with joy (16:10-15).[76]

The third ritual, the "rejoicing at the place of water-drawing," began at the end of the first festival day with the illumination of the Court of Women and ended with the water-drawing and subsequent water-libation ceremonies (m. Sukkah 5:1-5).[77] The Mishnah (5:3) associates it with incomparable rejoicing. The Tosefta affirms that rejoicing was characteristic of this part of the celebration (t. Sukkah 4:1, 5) and also indicates that there had once been a problem with irreverence in past festivals that led to

---

water-libation ceremonies were "probably established in Maccabean times." He provides numerous references to testify to the existence of these ceremonies in the Second Temple.

74. See Rubenstein, *Sukkot*, 122-31 for additional information on the biblical worldview associated with the water-libation ritual. The Tosefta provides evidence of the belief that there was a channel in the temple through which the water (and wine) libations poured out at the altar would reach the Deep (Sukkah 3:15). Bienaimé (*L'Eau dans la Tradition juive ancienne*, 214) states that "le souvenir d'une double symbolique qui, dès une date ancienne, était attaché au rite de la libation." He indicates that water ritual was associated with both the water from the eschatological temple (Ezek 47:1-12) and the well in the wilderness (Num 21:16-20), and that together they evoked "les eaux originelles" (i.e., the primordial Deep). The Tosefta (Sukkah 3:3-15) associates all of these aspects with the water-libation ritual.

75. The term (מעין) translated as "fountains" here (in accord with the RSV) has the basic meaning of "place of origin, source" (*HALOT* 2:612). Thus, the narrative implicitly identifies the primordial Deep as the source of the rain.

76. Rubenstein (*Sukkot*, 122) provides an extensive list of sources for information on the "water libations, found in many religions, [which were considered] rain-making rituals."

77. Schürer (*History of the Jewish People*, 296) provides comments on the position of this court and indicates that its designation is "not because women alone were admitted there, but because women could enter as well."

modifications of the temple court to prevent men and women from mingling during the water-drawing ritual (Sukkah 4:1). The implication that the mingling of men and women was once permitted suggests the existence of an exceptional situation for temple worship in Judaism. A fragment of 4Q502, mentioned earlier in the discussion of the ritual with the branches, also provides evidence of a ritual in which men and women worshiped together.[78]

Zechariah 14:6–21, which connects the temple and the celebration of Tabernacles with Yhwh's provision of water, also speaks of a continuous day (14:7), providing a scriptural basis for the development of the ritual of the nightlong illumination of the courtyard that was integrally associated with the water-drawing and water-libation rituals. The Mishnah's description of the ritual, which indicates that the illumination at the temple was so great that it illumined every courtyard in Jerusalem (m. Sukkah 5:1–5), suggests that it was an attempt to simulate the continuous day foretold in Zech 14:7.[79] Jesus' statement during the celebration of Tabernacles in John 8:12, declaring that he (as the new temple; 2:19–22) is the light of the world, is consistent with the context of the extraordinary illumination described in m. Sukkah 5:3.[80]

Dedication

The Dedication differs from Passover, Pentecost, and Tabernacles in that it was not one of the pilgrimage feasts and in being of relatively recent origin for first-century AD Judaism. Accounts of the origin of the Dedication are

---

78. Fragment 24 of 4Q502, which arguably describes a liturgy during the feast of Tabernacles (see 27n68), suggests that men and women were worshiping together. Cook ("A Liturgy of Thanksgiving," 519) states that "this fragment indicates that women also took active part in the liturgy of thanksgiving." Rubenstein (*Sukkot*, 145) suggests that Hellenistic all-night festivals, which "were exclusively celebrations of great joy" and typically included cultic processions, influenced the development of the nightlong temple ritual.

79. Neusner (*Mishnah*, 288–89) uses the term "candlesticks" for the devices that were said to illuminate all of Jerusalem. These "candlesticks," however, which were fueled with gallons of oil each night by men using ladders, were apparently immense. Rubenstein (*Sukkot*, 148) indicates that torches and lamps were characteristic features of the Greek festivals, but that they simply served a utilitarian purpose and had no ritual significance.

80. Examples of scholars who consider the illumination of the courtyard during the celebration of the feast of Tabernacles to be the context for this statement include: Brown, *John*, 1:343–44; Beasley-Murray, *John*, 127–29; Köstenberger, *John*, 253n6; Moloney, *John*, 266; Heil, *John*, 63n36.

provided in 1 Macc 4:36–59 and 2 Macc 1:1—2:18; 10:1–8. The accounts are congruent while also providing complementary details about the events associated with the origin of the feast.[81]

The title for the Dedication (or Hanukkah, which is a transliteration of the Hebrew term), found in First Maccabees, refers to the Maccabees' purification and dedication of the sanctuary (4:36; 5:1) and altar (4:54, 59). The integral roles of the altar and the sanctuary in the temple, as well as the interwoven nature of the narrative of the dedication of each of them, establishes that the Dedication celebrates the *re*dedication of the temple to Yhwh with the newly constructed altar dedicated through sacrificial worship.[82] Similarly, Second Maccabees narrates the purification of the temple and the construction of another altar (10:1–8). Pagan worship instituted by Antiochus IV (1:41–60) profaned the temple and the Dedication celebrated its cleansing and consecration for authentic worship (i.e., the worship of Yhwh rather than idols).[83]

Second Maccabees associates the Dedication with Tabernacles, referring to it as "the feast of Tabernacles in the month of Chislev" (1:9).[84] The account in Second Maccabees implicitly affirms the close association of the two feasts with the temple by referring to the previous dedications of the First Temple by Solomon (2:9–12) and the Second Temple by Nehemiah (2:13). Subsequently, Second Maccabees connects the two themes of the Dedication (i.e., the celebrations of the feast of Tabernacles in Chislev and the restoration of authentic worship in the temple) in 10:1–8. The author does this by implying that the rededication of the temple allowed the

81. Attridge ("Historiography," 157–84) characterizes both works as historiographies, categorizing First Maccabees as being "within the tradition of biblical historiography" and Second Maccabees as "written in the traditions of Greek historiography" (157). He indicates that scholars generally date First Maccabees to the late second century BC (171) and the final redaction of Second Maccabees to the first-half of the first century BC (178). Second Maccabees identifies itself as an epitome of an earlier five-volume work (3:19–32). The events narrated in both works are from the first half of the second century BC.

82. The account begins with the Maccabees saying, "let us go to cleanse the sanctuary and dedicate it" (4:36). The subsequent narrative (4:41–51) recounts their cleansing (4:41–42) and rebuilding the sanctuary (4:48), while the old altar was dismantled and a new one was built (4:44–47). The dedication of the newly constructed altar apparently took place through its subsequent use (4:54–56).

83. The narrative in First Maccabees explicitly states that courts of the temple were *consecrated* (ἡγίασαν; 4:48). The following chapter will address the significance of Jesus' use of this term in referring to himself during the feast (John 10:22).

84. Literally, "*the days* of Tabernacles in the month of Chislev" (1:9).

Maccabees to celebrate the feast of Tabernacles that they had missed due to their being in the wilderness (10:6) while also observing that they restored temple worship on the same day that the sanctuary had been profaned (10:5). The close relationship between the Dedication and Tabernacles explains the reference to the worshipers bearing beautiful branches and palm fronds (10:7) as well as the association of the Dedication with light.[85] John 10:22–42 attests its observance in the first century AD and Josephus recounts the events associated with the feast as the restoration of divine worship (*Ant.* 12.316–26).

SACRIFICIAL WORSHIP

Although John does not employ explicit sacrificial terminology, the centrality of sacrifice in first-century Judaism, its inherent relationship with temple worship, and its association with all of the temple feasts, make sacrificial worship part of the presumed context of John's Gospel and, in particular, 19:36–37.[86] Since offering sacrifices was a prominent feature in the other religions of the ANE and around the Mediterranean, the centrality of sacrifice in the cultic worship of first-century Judaism was not unique.[87] There were unique elements associated with its sacrificial worship, however, that distinguished it from the sacrificial cults of the other ancient religions. The two distinguishing features of Judaism's sacrificial worship of significance for the present study are the restriction of sacrifices to one location and the ritual worship associated with Passover.[88] This final section of the chapter will address the purpose of sacrificial worship in first-century Judaism,

---

85. Josephus refers to the Dedication as the "festival of Lights" (*Ant.* 12.325)

86. The only sacrificial term that John uses (θύω) conveys a non-sacrificial sense in its one occurrence (10:10). Regarding the centrality of sacrifice in Second Temple Judaism, Gilders ("Sacrifice," 94–105) observes that "in its Second Temple era (ca. 520 BCE–70 CE), Judaism was a religion of sacrifice" (94).

87. Gilders ("Sacrifice," 94) states that Judaism, as a religion of sacrifice, "was not in the least out-of-place in the ancient Mediterranean world."

88. Sanders (*Judaism*, 72) indicates that the principal differences between the sacrificial worship of Judaism and the religion of the Greeks were that in Judaism *sacrifice could only occur in one place* and that it was expensive. Selman ("Sacrifice," 88–104) identifies two characteristics of the sacrificial cult in the OT that were distinctive from other Syrian/Palestinian sacrifices: the sacrifices for atonement to address violations of moral standards established by the deity and *the Passover ritual* (101).

characteristics associated with it, and the perception of the ritual slaughter of the Passover lamb as a sacrifice.

The Purpose of Sacrificial Worship in First-Century Judaism

Whereas the pervasiveness of animal sacrifice throughout the ancient world made it a familiar experience at that time, it is a phenomenon that is foreign to most people today. Additionally, neither ancient Judaism nor its contemporaries tend to offer explanations about the purpose of sacrifice.[89] Consequently, Philo's theory on the purpose of sacrifice in first-century Judaism is exceptional and valuable for gaining insight into this topic.[90] It is consistent with the implicit purpose of sacrificial worship embodied in the first two accounts of sacrifice in the OT (Gen 4:3-5; 8:20-21).

Philo observes that sacrifices are to be offered primarily out of honor for God and only secondarily for any personal benefits (*Spec. Laws* 1.195). He also focuses on the integral relationship between the inner disposition of the worshiper and the external actions of the ritual sacrifices. Philo demonstrates this focus with his comments on the whole burnt offering, which he identifies as the most important offering (*Spec. Laws* 1.194).[91] He states that the sacrificial animal must be perfect *and* the worshiper must offer it with "no taint of mortal selfishness" (1.196).[92] Philo stresses the importance of the internal disposition of worshipers by indicating that their souls must be free of vices as "displayed either in word or deed" (1.257). Finally, he demonstrates the importance of the relationship of the liturgical worship offered by individuals through ritual actions and the ethical worship offered

---

89. Selman ("Sacrifice," 89) states that "ancient scribes were much more concerned with giving detailed practical instructions to those carrying out the sacrifice than with explaining the inner meaning of such rituals," with the result "that far more can be said about what was done in sacrifice than about what the rituals meant to those who performed and watched them." Eberhart ("Sacrifice," 17–32), indicates that the absence of any explicit theories on sacrifice in the HB is not unique to Judaism; it is also characteristic of other ancient cultures and religions such as the Romans and the Greeks (19n7). Gilders ("Sacrifice," 95), states that Jewish writers generally "gave no indication that sacrifice itself requires explanation."

90. Gilders ("Sacrifice," 95) observes that "unique amongst ancient Jewish writers on sacrifice, Philo offers what can be termed an explicit theory of sacrifice."

91. Schürer (*History of the Jewish People*, 2:296–99) similarly indicates, "the most important part of worship was the daily burnt offering of the people" (299).

92. The translation provided here and, unless otherwise noted, in any following quotations from Philo's works are from Yonge, *The Works of Philo*.

to God through obedience to his commands by using an analogy about the altar and sacrifices. Philo observes that as the altar plays an instrumental role in supporting the sacrifices, God looks rather to the willingness of the offerer as "the real sacrifice" and the offerer's virtue to ensure the "firmness of the altar" (1.290).[93]

The importance of the relationship between proper external actions (liturgical worship) and internal disposition (ethical worship) for offering pleasing sacrificial worship to God as asserted by Philo's theory is implicit in the first two accounts of sacrifice in the OT (Gen 4:3-5; 8:20-21). In order to apprehend the fundamental truths embodied in these prototypical accounts of OT sacrificial worship, it is necessary to briefly consider the narrative that immediately precedes the first account.[94]

Genesis 1–2 embodies the essential truths that Yhwh created the first human beings (1:26-27; 2:7, 21-23), provided for all their needs (1:29; 2:9-10, 15-16), and honored them by creating them in his image and giving them a share in his dominion (1:28; 2:19-20). There is no mention of any expectation of sacrifice. God had gratuitously honored human beings who, in turn, were to honor God by freely responding to him through obedience (2:15-17).[95] It is only after the man and his wife fail to honor God through obedience (3:1-19) that sacrifice appears in the narrative.[96]

The two subsequent accounts of sacrifice in the Primeval History (the sacrifices of Abel [4:3-5] and Noah [8:20-21]) collectively embody the truths that the proper motivation for offering pleasing sacrifices to God (liturgical worship) is to honor him and that such actions are inseparable

---

93. Perhaps the most compelling OT account that supports Philo's assertion is the *Akedah* (or 'Binding' of Isaac) since the sacrifice initially prescribed never occurred (Gen 22:1-18). Yhwh's recognition of Abraham's willingness to offer his beloved son and the consequent blessings that he bestows upon Abraham for his obedience (Gen 22:15-18) demonstrate the importance of the worshiper's disposition and obedience. Similarly, John's Gospel presumes and conveys the importance of disposition and obedience for offering pleasing worship to the Father. Chapters 3 and 5 will address this topic.

94. The following analysis examines the deeper content embodied in the two accounts of primeval sacrifice. Although these initial accounts of sacrifice demonstrate *a* biblical basis for Philo's theory, the OT conveys the essential truths embodied in them in various ways and texts (e.g., 1 Sam 13:8-14; 15:10-13; Isa 1:10-17; Hos 6:4-10; Pss 40:6-8; 51:15-19; Eccl 4:17—5:1).

95. The commands in Gen 1:28-29 and 2:15-17 implicitly establish obedience as the appropriate response to God to remain in right relationship with him.

96. Selman ("Sacrifice," 101) observes that the distinctiveness of the sacrificial system in Israel was that the purpose of their sacrifices was to maintain "a right covenant relationship with Yahweh."

from honoring God through obedience (ethical worship).⁹⁷ It is the second and culminating account that integrates these truths. Noah's sacrifices offered "*the* pleasing odor" (8:21) to God through distinctive ritual offerings (he offered sacrifices of every clean animal as holocausts; 8:20) and an internal disposition that honored Yhwh (the Flood Narrative recognizes Noah as blameless and righteous [6:9], and consistently demonstrates these qualities by manifesting his obedience to all of God's commands [6:22; 7:5, 9, 16]).⁹⁸ Thus, the prototypical OT accounts of sacrifice demonstrate that its purpose is to honor God through distinctive ritual offerings (liturgical worship) that correspond with the offerer's internal disposition (and actions) to honor God through obedience to all of his commands (ethical worship).

Characteristics of Sacrificial Worship in Judaism

Unlike Noah and Abel (and especially Cain), first-century Judaism had the benefit of knowing the types of distinctive ritual offerings and actions that honored God. Leviticus 1–7 provides the most detailed information on the various types of ritual sacrifices in the OT.⁹⁹ It identifies the five basic types

---

97. The basis for using the plural (account*s*) here, even though the account of Abel's sacrifice does not use the expression for pleasing ritual worship (see 35n98) and the biblical author does not provide as much insight into Abel's character as afforded for Noah, is that Genesis associates the sacrifices of Abel and Noah with one another in two ways. They are the only accounts of pleasing sacrifice in the Primeval History (cf., 4:5) and their essential characteristics, to the extent that such details are provided, correspond with one another (e.g., the special quality of the offerings, the absence of any indication of self-interest on the part of the offerer).

98. The definite article is italicized here to emphasize a unique occurrence of the expression "pleasing odor" in 8:21 (את־ריח הניחח; "*the* pleasing odor"). The HB often employs the expression for fitting ritual sacrifice offered to Yhwh. With the exception of 8:21, however, it always occurs *without* the definite article (i.e., "a pleasing odor"). It appears most often in Leviticus (17 of the 43 occurrences in the HB). In its last occurrence in Leviticus Yhwh tells Israel that he will not smell their "pleasing odor [ריח ניחח]" (26:31) if they do not *obey* all his commandments (26:14). This final use of the phrase (in a text primarily concerned with ritual actions) affirms the integral relationship between liturgical and ethical worship for offering pleasing sacrifice to Yhwh. And its *only* occurrence in the HB with the definite article effectively establishes the integrated liturgical and ethical worship of Noah as the paradigm for offering pleasing sacrifice to Yhwh.

99. Eberhart ("Sacrifice," 20–23) observes that "the most detailed information on ritual sacrifices in the Hebrew Bible is featured in the priestly texts of Lev 1–7" (23), which he refers to elsewhere as "their catalog of sacrifices" (20).

of sacrifices as the whole burnt offering (holocaust), the cereal offering, the peace offering, the sin offering, and the guilt offering. Although each has distinctive features, an important observation for the present study is that "most sacrifices involve the slaughter of an animal and the manipulation of its blood in some way."[100]

The centrality of blood in the sacrificial system and of the value implicitly attributed to it are of fundamental importance for this study. Leviticus 17:11 succinctly conveys the significance of blood in sacrificial worship when Yhwh advises Moses that "the life of the flesh is in the blood and I have given it to you for the altar to atone for your lives."[101] This verse also associates sacrificial blood with the altar; the location for pouring out blood offered for atonement.[102]

Sacrifice and the Ritual Slaughter of the Passover Lamb

This final section will address whether there is sufficient evidence to conclude that the slaughter of the Passover lamb was considered a sacrifice.[103] Such evidence begins with the narrative of the first Passover in which Moses

---

100. Jenson, "Levitical Sacrificial System," 27. Jenson identifies two exceptions to his observation. "The chief exception is the grain offering, which was occasionally offered alone (Nu. 5:15), but generally accompanied blood sacrifices (Lv. 23:13; Nu. 15:1–12)." The second is that "fine flour can substitute for an animal if the offerer is poor" (Lev 5:11–13). He attributes the latter exception to the priority given to atonement which "takes precedence over the good of offering a blood sacrifice" (38n5).

101. Yhwh also states that the blood atones by the life it possesses (17:11). Philo acknowledges the importance of sacrificial blood when he observes that "the blood is the libation of the life" (*Spec. Laws* 1.205). Henniger (*Les Fêtes de Printemps*, 125) indicates that the Semites, in general, attributed the utmost value to the blood: "Chez les Sémites, le *sang* est l'objet le plus précieux du sacrifice" (emphasis original). Carnazzo (*Seeing Blood and Water*, 25–26) observes that the OT associates blood with the purification for sin. He identifies the Day of Purification (Lev 16:15–21) as the most prominent example and also presents the repetitive use of the phrase "blood of sin" (Exod 30:10; Lev 4:25, 34; 5:9; Ezek 45:19) as vivid evidence of this relationship (26n15).

102. Eberhart ("Sacrifice," 27) observes that the "altar [מזבח] is the location where substances from all types of sacrifices—including the cereal offering—are offered to God."

103. There is no consensus among current scholars on this topic. Eberhart ("Sacrifice," 20), who believes that there was debate in ancient Israel over the type of ritual that was properly classified as a sacrifice, is an example of a scholar who contends that the Passover ritual was not considered a sacrifice. Alexander ("Passover," 6–7), an example of a scholar who argues that it was considered a sacrifice, observes that "the detailed instructions for this ritual parallel closely those relating to sacrifices" (6).

instructs the Israelites to explain the ritual to future generations by stating that "it is the Passover sacrifice to Yhwh" (Exod 12:27).[104] The instructions for the ritual slaughter also indicate that it was a sacrifice by the verb used to specify the action (12:6).[105] Similarly, the detailed instructions provided in Exodus 12 for the treatment of the blood, flesh, and bones of the victim convey a sacrificial understanding. Furthermore, Yhwh refers to the Passover victim elsewhere in Exodus as "my sacrifice" (23:18; 34:25).[106]

The requirement that the slaughter be performed in the temple in the First and Second Temple periods, *the* place of sacrifice for the religion of Israel and, subsequently, for Judaism, affirms a sacrificial understanding of the ritual. The consistent evidence in the First (2 Chr 30:16; 35:11) and Second Temple periods (Jub. 49.20; m. Pesaḥ. 5:5–6; Zebaḥ. 5:8) that the blood of the sacrifice was brought into contact with the altar also demonstrates that the Passover slaughter was considered a sacrifice.[107] Furthermore, the first-century witnesses, important for this study, repeatedly indicate that the Passover ritual was a sacrifice. For example, in some instances Philo implicitly affirms that the slaying of the Passover lambs was considered a sacrifice (*Decal.* 159; *Moses* 2.224–25; *Spec. Laws* 2.148) and in others he explicitly refers to it as a sacrifice (2.226; *Alleg. Interp.* 3.94, 165; *Moses* 2.226, 228). Philo also observes that it is the sacrifice offered that provides for the feast (*Spec. Laws* 2.148). Josephus repeatedly attests that the Passover

---

104. Both Alexander ("Passover," 7) and Eberhart ("Sacrifice," 20) refer to this statement. Eberhart's subsequent attempt to dismiss it, by attributing it to later redactors (enabling him to maintain his position), demonstrates its significance.

105. Clements ("שׁחט," 14:563–66) observes that although the HB uses the verb (שׁחט) to specify actions unrelated to sacrifice (e.g., Gen 37:31), "in the overwhelming number of passages ... [it] refers to the slaughtering of animals in connection with cultic acts" (564). The requirement that the "whole assembly of the congregation of Israel" (Exod 12:6) perform the action establishes its use in a cultic context for the observance of Passover.

106. Although 23:18 does not explicitly specify Passover, Alexander ("Passover," 9) points out that it stands in parallel relationship with 34:25. Both verses occur in the context of instructions about the pilgrimage feasts (23:17; 34:23) and have very similar content including: the phrase "blood of my sacrifice," the prohibitions against remnants of the sacrifice remaining until morning, the only occurrences of the verb לין in Exodus, and the only occurrences of the phrase "on leaven" (על־חמץ) in the HB.

107. See 36nn100-101. The requirement that the blood of sacrifices be poured out on or around the altar expresses the profound importance attributed to the blood; it even applied to holocausts (Lev 1:5) which were to be wholly consumed by fire.

slaughter was a sacrifice (*Ant.* 2.311-14; 3.248; 17.213).¹⁰⁸ The most significant NT reference (outside of John's Gospel) to Passover as a sacrifice occurs in 1 Cor 5:7 where Paul tells the Corinthians to "cleanse out the old leaven... as you are unleavened. For Christ our Passover [lamb] has been sacrificed (ἐτύθη)."¹⁰⁹ In the context of Paul's metaphorical use of "leaven" and "unleavened" to contrast the Corinthians' former condition with their having been redeemed in Christ, he implicitly establishes that the slaughter of the Passover lamb was *readily* recognized as a sacrifice (since he makes no attempt to explain his statement).

There is substantial evidence, beginning with the narrative of the feast's origin in Exodus 12 through the testimony of first-century AD witnesses, that the Passover ritual was considered a sacrifice. Furthermore, it has the unique qualitative designation of being called "*my* sacrifice" by Yhwh (23:18; 34:25).¹¹⁰ The sheer number of sacrifices offered through the ritual slaughter affords the Passover ritual quantitative distinctiveness. Thus, the biblical and extra-biblical evidence suggests not only that the OT and first-century AD Judaism considered the slaughter of the Passover lamb *a* sacrifice, but that the religion of Israel and, subsequently, Judaism arguably understood it to be the preeminent sacrifice.

---

108. Josephus also indicates that the first-century understanding of the slaughter as a sacrifice was consistent with, and based upon, the biblical origin of the feast. He observes that: God instructed the people to have a sacrifice ready (2.311), the Israelites sacrificed in Egypt (2.312), and the people still sacrifice in Josephus's time according to the established custom (2.313).

109. BDAG (463) indicates that "*sacrifice*" is "the primary meaning [of θύω; used in the aorist passive in 1 Cor 5:7] and the one most commonly found."

110. Although the phrase "my sacrifice" (זבחי) occurs in three other places in the HB (1 Sam 2:29; Ezek 39:17; 39:19) in which the Passover sacrifice is not the referent, those occurrences convey distinctly different meanings. In 1 Sam 2:29, Yhwh refers to any given sacrifice brought to the temple in Shiloh from which Eli's sons were indiscriminately taking the choice portions for themselves. The RSV reflects this sense in translating the phrase as "my sacrifices." In Ezekiel 39, Yhwh refers to a metaphorical "sacrifice" that he will provide for the birds and for the beasts of the field in the deceased horses and warriors (39:20) of "Gog, the chief prince of Meshech and Tubal" (39:1). Thus, the Passover sacrifice holds the distinctive designation of "my sacrifice" among all of the sacrifices specified in the HB.

JOHN'S PRESUMED CONTEXT OF WORSHIP IN FIRST-CENTURY JUDAISM

SUMMARY

The essential aspects of worship in first-century Judaism addressed in this chapter play a fundamental role in providing the context for the Gospel of John. The temple was Yhwh's dwelling place among his people and the pre-eminent place for liturgical worship. The integral relationship between liturgical and ethical worship, reflected in a prominent way with the Sabbath observance, was a distinctive feature of Judaism. Similarly, the observance of the annual feasts summarized here was inseparable from the temple and, together with the temple, sanctified and integrated the lives of first-century Jews in connecting their current covenantal relationship with Yhwh with past events and future expectations.

The combined feast of Passover, which was the preeminent feast, celebrated the exodus from slavery in Egypt (Exod 12:1—13:16) allowing Yhwh's people to freely worship him (3:12). Tabernacles recalled Israel's time in the wilderness after the exodus (Lev 23:42–43) and was associated with the future expectation of the temple becoming the source of continual light (Zech 14:7), living water (14:8), and the locus of worship for all the families of the earth (14:16–21). The Dedication, closely associated with Tabernacles, celebrated a purified temple consecrated for authentic worship with the dedication of a new altar, and consequently, the temple, through sacrifice. As *the* place of sacrifice the temple was the location for the ritual slaughter of the Passover lamb, which had the distinctive title of "*my* sacrifice" given to it by Yhwh himself (Exod 23:18; 34:25), with its blood being poured out upon its altar for atonement (Lev 17:11).

John presumes knowledge of worship in first-century Judaism on the part of his audience and skillfully utilizes it. He shows that first-century Jewish worship prefigures and points to Jesus and the true worship that he offered and enabled in his hour, as the realization of the worship that the Father seeks (John 4:23–24).[111] The next chapter will demonstrate the overarching theme of worship in the Gospel of John and its use of the context of worship in first-century Judaism (and the OT) to establish that the true worship that it had prefigured has been both fulfilled and made possible by Jesus.

---

111. As mentioned earlier, Jesus' "hour" is a fundamental theme that runs throughout the Gospel of John (2:4—19:27) referring to his "being lifted up" (3:14; 8:28; 12:32, 34) and to his "being glorified" (7:39; 12:16, 23, 28; 13:31, 32; 16:14; 17:1, 5). It is central to the narrative of the Gospel and to its overarching theme of worship.

3

John's Proximate Context of Early Christian Worship

As observed in the previous chapter, John presumes knowledge of first-century Jewish worship and the OT. He draws upon them in establishing the centrality of true worship throughout the Gospel and in demonstrating its culmination in Jesus' hour. In presuming this knowledge, he relies on his audience to make the necessary connections from the various details and allusions he provides. In this way, John facilitates the audience's perception of the true worship offered by Christ in his hour and enabled for those who believe in him, which the OT foretold and temple worship prefigured.[1]

Whereas such knowledge of first-century Judaism is an important aspect of the context for the Gospel, the immediate and, consequently, the most significant aspect is the context of John's audience. There is substantial evidence (both internal and external to the Gospel) that the context of the audience is communal worship. The internal evidence includes the Gospel's overarching theme of worship and its interrelated multidimensional symbolism.[2] The external evidence, which attests the centrality of worship in the

---

1. Through the gift of the Spirit at the culmination of Jesus' hour (19:30), Jesus who is the truth (14:6) makes his dwelling (14:23) in those who believe in him, enabling the audience to worship in Spirit and Truth. The section on worship in the Fourth Gospel in this chapter and, especially, chapter 5 will further address how Jesus enables those who believe in him to participate in the true worship he offered in his hour.

2. The Jewish feasts and institutions (e.g., the Temple) are instrumental in conveying the theme of worship and its multidimensional symbolism through the context that they provide in which the Gospel demonstrates that Jesus (and, subsequently, Christian

life of the early Church, includes the earliest extant witnesses on Christian liturgy, the NT texts in general, and the content and form of the Gospels. Since information provided by these witnesses is beneficial for illuminating aspects of worship in John's Gospel, this chapter will begin by addressing the external evidence prior to taking up the Gospel's theme of worship.

EARLY CHRISTIAN WORSHIP AS THE PROXIMATE CONTEXT FOR JOHN'S GOSPEL

Early Christian Worship in the Earliest Extant Witnesses on the Liturgy

Although the NT implicitly bears witness to the centrality of communal worship from earliest days of the Church (Acts 2:42, 46–47a), it does not provide any extended liturgical descriptions or information on the order of worship. The earliest texts that provide such information are the Didache, Justin Martyr's *First Apology*, and a letter from the Roman governor Pliny the Younger to the emperor Trajan.[3]

Scholars date the Didache from AD 60 to the mid-second century, with the consensus being toward earlier dating.[4] Its first six chapters provide catechetical instructions for leading a moral life (i.e., offering proper ethical worship). Then the text proceeds immediately (with the phrase "having said these things beforehand" [7.1]) to instructions on baptizing (7.1–3).

---

worship) fulfills and transcends them. For example, directly after establishing that Jesus is the New Temple (2:19–22), the Gospel addresses how Christians become members of that temple through the sacramental worship of baptism (3:3–8). The final section of this chapter addresses this topic more fully in tracing the theme of worship through the length of the Gospel.

3. Aune ("Worship," 6:973–89) utilizes these three extra-biblical witnesses for insight into early Christian worship. Bradshaw (*Worship*, 76–100) identifies the Didache as the most ancient church order (76–78) and the *First Apology* as "the earliest substantial description that we have of Christian worship" (98).

4. Aune ("Worship," 6:976) provides a date range of AD 60 to AD 125, but considers ca. AD 100 to be "most satisfactory." Draper ("Didache," 178) states, "a number of recent studies have even argued for a very early date in the mid-first century." In recent studies on the composition of the Didache, Garrow and Pardee, who both assert multiple stages of composition, place the information on baptism and the Eucharist in the earlier stages. Garrow (*Didache*, 150–53) indicates all baptismal and eucharistic information is pre-Matthean. Although Pardee's (*Didache*, 184–91) comments on dating are more limited, they also imply that most of this information (with the exception of 14.1–3) is pre-Matthean.

After directives on fasting and prayer in preparation for baptism (7.4—8.3), the Didache addresses the celebration of the Eucharist (9.1—10.7).[5] This eucharistic section concludes with the expression μαραναθά ἀμήν (10.6).[6] After an intervening section on the treatment of guests (11.1—13.7), it provides instructions for offering a pure eucharistic sacrifice (14.1-3).[7]

Justin Martyr composed the *First Apology* in the middle of the second century.[8] Although the nature of the document is fundamentally different from the Didache (since Justin was writing to pagans to defend Christianity and demonstrate its superiority), they share significant similarities.[9] Similar to the Didache, the *First Apology* spends significant time on the moral teaching of the Church (the basis for acceptable ethical worship) before addressing liturgical worship.[10] It culminates with detailed information on the celebration of baptism and the Eucharist (*1 Apology* 61-67).

Justin indicates that requirements for baptism are belief in the Christian faith and the promise to live in accord with it (*1 Apology* 61). As with the Didache, the sections on baptism leads directly into the celebration of the Eucharist.[11] Justin begins with a brief summary of the eucharistic lit-

---

5. Although the Didache does not include the words of institution, the author uses both the verb (εὐχαριστέω; 9.1, 2, 3; 10.1, 2, 4, 7) and the noun (εὐχαριστία; 9.1, 5) for the Eucharist repeatedly. It also uses the metonyms of "the cup" (9.2) and "the broken [bread]" (9.3, 4) in parallel with one another. Sandt ("Didache," 1-20) observes that the Didache clearly describes the celebration of the Eucharist (rather than an ordinary meal) based on the holiness attributed to the elements consumed (9.5) and the sacrificial language used (14.1-3).

6. BDAG translates the expression, "Lord, come. Amen!" (616). It effectively concludes the eucharistic section since the final verse (10.7) provides an exceptional comment regarding prophets. The next section of this chapter will address the expression's significance.

7. The Didache implicitly conveys the importance of integrating proper liturgical and ethical worship by interweaving liturgical (9.1—10.7; 14.1, 3) and ethical instructions (11.1—13.7; 14.2).

8. He indicates that he wrote it 150 years after the birth of Christ (*1 Apol.* 46.1).

9. Justin addressed the *First Apology* to the Roman emperor, the emperor's sons, the senate, and the whole population of Rome (1.1).

10. Falls (*Justin Martyr*, 24-25) observes that Justin Martyr provides the principles of his discourse in the first 20 chapters and then proceeds to demonstrate the superiority of Christianity in the areas of both faith and morals over pagan religions (chs. 21-60).

11. Justin interweaves teaching on the sacramentology of baptism with christological explanations of certain OT passages in an intervening apologetic section (*1 Apology* 62-64). Shortly after he resumes his liturgical narrative (65.1) he introduces the eucharistic liturgy (65.3).

urgy (*1 Apology* 65) and consequently provides the words of institution in the context of explaining aspects of the sacramentology of the Eucharist (*1 Apology* 66). The final chapter on liturgical worship (*1 Apology* 67) presents a general overview of the order of Sunday worship, which bears witness to the reading of the memoirs of the apostles or the writings of the prophets (67.3).[12] The balance of the Liturgy of the Word consists of teaching and exhortation by the presider followed by the communal prayer of those assembled (67.4–5). Justin conveys the importance of ethical worship by including it as an integral part of his summary of Sunday's order of liturgical worship (67.4–6).

The final text is a letter written by Pliny the Younger to the emperor Trajan in the early second-century.[13] Although the information provided on early Christian worship is limited to just one verse (*ep.* 96.7), its value is significant since it corresponds with and complements the Didache and the *First Apology*. The Christians would "assemble on a fixed day and [sing] music, following each other in turn [i.e., antiphonally], to Christ as a god and bind themselves by oath" to neither commit evil nor to break faith (*ep.* 96.7).[14] The contents of the oath parallel the instructions in the Didache and the commitments in the *First Apology* for those who would be baptized. Pliny also indicates that the Christians would meet later to take food which was "nevertheless common and harmless" (*ep.* 96.7). His statement most likely addresses false rumors of cannibalism associated with Christians' consumption of the Eucharist.[15] In the one verse Pliny's letter affirms the importance of the integration of liturgical and ethical worship as well as the fundamental roles of baptism and the Eucharist in early Christian worship.

---

12. Justin had earlier identified the memoirs of the apostles as the Gospels (66.3). McGowan (*Worship*, 84) observes that the *First Apology* provides the earliest reference to the liturgical reading of the Gospels.

13. It is Letter 96 from Book X of Pliny's Letters. Pliny was the Roman governor of Bithynia-Pontus for a period of less than two years within the time range of AD 109–113. He wrote to the emperor Trajan for guidance on the treatment of Christians under his jurisdiction. See Williams, *Pliny*, 13.

14. The word translated as "oath" is the Latin word *sacramentum*. Christians subsequently employed it as a term for baptism, the Eucharist, and the other Christian sacraments.

15. McGowan, *Worship*, 41; Falls, *Justin Martyr*, 63n6.

Features of Early Christian Worship Reflected in NT Texts

The similarity and complementarity of the witnesses considered in the previous section, which date from the mid-first century through the mid-second century AD, suggests that they hand on information from traditions in existence for some time. Their combined testimony bears witness to the importance of integrating ethical and liturgical worship, the foundational role of baptism, the centrality of the Eucharist, the reading of Scripture (OT and NT), and homilies within the context of worship. These witnesses also provide insight on the order of the liturgies and three general categories of worship: didactic, sacramental and ethical worship.[16] In the liturgy of the early Church, didactic worship preceded sacramental worship.[17] And the sacramental worship of baptism preceded the Eucharist (Did. 7:1–4; 9:1—10:7; *1 Apology* 61; 66) following an expression of faith by the participants.[18] This section will provide corroborating evidence from NT passages that reflect and affirm these fundamental features of early Christian worship.

Since Jesus did not come to abolish the law but to fulfill it (Matt 5:17), proper ethical worship requires the conformity of the heart of the worshiper to the will of God rather than mere external obedience (5:18–48).[19] Such conformity of the heart corresponds with the perfection to which Christians are called (1 Pet 1:16; 2 Cor 7:1; Col 1:18; cf. Lev 19:2) by doing the

---

16. Didactic worship and sacramental worship are different types of liturgical worship. The term didactic worship draws upon insights from Gordley ("Didactic Hymn Traditions," 782) about didactic hymnody in ancient times which "instructs the audience even as it praises the divine." Didactic worship consists of verbal expressions and physical gestures that instruct the audience as they worship God. Forms of didactic worship include hymns, doxologies, professions of faith, homilies, catechetical instruction, and the reading of sacred Scripture. Sacramental worship consists of verbal expressions and ritual actions.

17. In the Didache and the *First Apology* catechetical instruction (Didache 1–6; *1 Apology* 61) precedes baptism (Did. 7:1–3; *1 Apology* 61) and the subsequent celebration of the Eucharist. Additionally, *1 Apology* 67 establishes that readings and a homily precede sacramental worship in the eucharistic liturgy.

18. Since the primary expression of faith occurs prior to baptism, it precedes the sacramental actions of baptism and the Eucharist; only the baptized can partake of the Eucharist (Did. 9.5; *1 Apol.* 66.1). Aside from responses of faith within the liturgy (*1 Apology* 65; 67), the Didache and the *First Apology* affirm the necessity to respond with the whole of one's life (i.e., ethical worship). See Did. 1.1—6.3; 12.1—13.7; 14.4—16.8; *1 Apology* 15; 17; 27; 43; 44; 52–53; 57; 61; 65; 66–67.

19. Philip provides complementary testimony that came Jesus to fulfill the Law when he identifies Jesus as the one about "whom Moses, in the Law, and the Prophets wrote" (John 1:45).

will of the Father (Matt 7:21–23) in accord with Jesus' teaching (6:24–28; Luke 6:27–36, 43–49) and his example.[20] The NT texts consistently convey the necessity of ethical worship and its inseparability from liturgical worship (Matt 5:23–24), as well as its potential impact upon it (Jas 1:26—2:7; 1 Cor 6:9–20; 11:17–22), "so that in everything God may be glorified through Jesus Christ" (1 Pet 4:11).

The NT communicates the fundamental importance of baptism as something Jesus commanded (Matt 28:19–20; Mark 16:15–16).[21] Narratives of the earliest days of the Church affirm its purpose and performance (Acts 2:37–41) along with the centrality of the Eucharist (2:42–47). Luke also demonstrates the necessity of the expression of faith by believers prior to baptism and reception of the Holy Spirit (Acts 8:12–17, 26–40; 9:18; 10:44–48; 16:14–15, 33; 19:1–7).[22] Other NT texts affirm the importance of baptism as they stress different aspects of it (e.g., Rom 6:3–11; 1Cor 12:12–27; Gal 3:25—4:7; Col 2:8—4:6; 1 Pet 3:18–22). Such aspects include its recognition as a participation in the death and resurrection of Christ (Rom 6:3–4; Col 2:12) and incorporation of believers into his body (1 Cor 12:13) making them a dwelling place of God (1 Cor 3:16–17; 6:19; 2 Cor 6:16; Eph 2:21–22; 1 Pet 2:5).[23]

The NT conveys the centrality of the Eucharist in the life and worship of the early Church in various ways.[24] In First Corinthians, Paul frequently refers to the eucharistic liturgy as the community's "coming together" (11:17, 18, 20, 33–34; 14:23, 26) and instructs them on how to properly do this (11:23–34; 14:1–40). He also refers to its celebration by the day on which it occurred (16:2; cf. Rev 1:10). Peter and Paul both employ the

---

20. Following Christ requires conversion of life (Rom 6:18; 7:4–6; Col 2:2; 3:3) by denying oneself and taking up one's cross (Matt 10:38–39; 16:24–25; Mark 8:34–35; Luke 9:23–24), laying down one's life (John 13:34–35; 15:12–17; 1 John 3:16) and enduring suffering in union with Christ (1 Pet 2:20–25; Rom 6:1–11).

21. Bradshaw (*Worship*, 60) observes that baptism was the usual custom for initiating new members from early times.

22. Although every account does not explicitly mention every element (e.g., the reception of the Spirit is not recounted in 8:26–40; 16:14–15, 33) and the reception of the Spirit is distinct from the baptism with water in some cases (10:44–48; 19:1–7), the accounts collectively corroborate baptism's fundamental role and the shape of the baptismal liturgy.

23. God dwells in the individual believer (1 Cor 6:19) as well as in the whole community (2 Cor 6:16; Eph 2:21–22; 1 Pet 2:5).

24. Henrici ("The Sacrifice of Christ," 153) states, "*Paul* presupposes the celebration of the Eucharist in the communities as something self-evident (1Cor. 10:16–22; 11:20–32)."

expression "holy kiss" (1 Pet 5:14; Rom 16:16; 1 Cor 16:20; 2 Cor 13:12; 1 Thess 5:26) which most likely alludes to a ritual action in the liturgy.[25] "The breaking of the bread" (Luke 24:35; Acts 2:42–46; 20:7–12) is arguably one of the earliest metonyms for celebrating the Eucharist.[26] The institution narratives (Matt 26:26–29; Mark 14:22–25; Luke 22:19–20; 1 Cor 11:23–25) establish the fourfold shape of Jesus' actions during the Last Supper as a way for referring to the Eucharist: Jesus *took* the bread, *gave thanks* (or *blessed* the bread), *broke* it and *gave* it.[27] Luke recounts Jesus performing the same actions in his post-resurrection encounter in Emmaus (Luke 24:30). This encounter also exhibits the same overall form for the eucharistic liturgy that Justin relates a century later, with didactic worship (i.e., the Liturgy of the Word; 24:27) preceding sacramental worship (i.e., the Liturgy of the Eucharist; 24:30). Acts 20:7–12 manifests the same structure for a eucharistic liturgy in Troas.

A number of NT texts manifest didactic worship (in particular, the liturgical reading of texts and homilies within the context of worship) as part of the early liturgy.[28] Two NT texts (1 Thess 5:27; Col 4:16) provide specific instructions for their public proclamation.[29] Revelation refers to "the one

---

25. Justin Martyr locates this ritual act (*1 Apology* 65) between baptism and the celebration of the Eucharist. McGowan (*Worship*, 55–59) addresses kissing as a distinctive action in early Christian worship.

26. Cullmann (*Worship*, 29) asserts that no gathering of the community occurred without it. McGowan (*Worship*, 34) argues, "while Christians continued to literally break bread ... this term did not continue as a prominent name for that event." The position of contemporary scholars varies on whether or not this metonym refers to the celebration of the Eucharist. Whereas Barrett (*Acts*, 33–34) contends that it only conveys the action that initiated a normal Jewish meal, Johnson (*Acts*, 58) observes that it "refers to more than ordinary meals" as it emphasizes Jesus' presence in connection with the meal (i.e., the Eucharist).

27. McGowan (*Worship*, 26–27) indicates that the prominence of the metonym still manifests the shape with one of the actions modified (e.g., in Acts 27:34–36 the final action is *eating* rather than *giving*). That all of the accounts of Jesus' multiplication miracles (Matt 14:13–21; 15:32–38; Mark 6:32–44; 8:1–10; Luke 9:10–17; John 6:1–13) effectively manifest this fourfold shape provide further evidence of its prominence and the eucharistic character of those narratives (addressed below).

28. The Letter to the Hebrews provides an example of the existence and interplay of these practices in the early Church. Scholars have characterized it as a sermon or homily in the form of a letter with its frequent recourse to OT texts (as well as to liturgical practices under the Old Covenant) from which it draws insights and provides interpretations. See Cockerill, *Hebrews*, 1, 76; O'Brien, *Hebrews*, 22.

29. Although the texts do not specify that the reading take place within worship, they do specify reading to "all the brothers" (1 Thess 5:27) and "in the church of the

who reads" and to "those who listen" (1:3), with no explanation, suggesting that such public reading was a normal practice.[30] Paul explicitly instructs Timothy "to attend to the reading, the exhortation, and the teaching" (1 Tim 4:13). Other texts (1 Cor 14:26–31; 2 Tim 4:13) indirectly testify to didactic worship in Christian liturgies.[31] Paul establishes that the OT's purpose was to instruct Christians (1 Cor 10:1–11; Rom 15:4) and other NT texts affirm this assertion (Luke 16:29–31; 17:27–31; 24:25–27; John 1:45; 5:39, 46; Acts 10:43; 13:26–44; 18:28).

Recognizing the centrality of the Eucharist in Christian communities and that didactic worship (e.g., scriptural readings and homilies) was the first part of the early Christian liturgy illuminates a unique expression found in the NT and the Didache. In the conclusion of First Corinthians Paul uses the Aramaic expression μαράνα θά (1 Cor 16:22), which means "Lord, come," without any explanation.[32] This suggests that his audience was familiar with the expression and his use of it. The same expression occurs in the Did. 10.6 within the eucharistic liturgy.[33] Similar to First Corinthians the Aramaic expression occurs in the Greek Didache without any explanation.[34] Revelation employs a similar Greek expression in

---

Laodiceans" (Col 4:16). The centrality of the Eucharist in gathering believers together (cf. Acts 2:42; 20:7–11; 1 Cor 11:17–33) and in the life of the early Church (see 51n47) makes worship a likely context for such reading.

30. This verse and the two cited in the preceding sentence utilize the verb ἀναγινώσκω. It is rather common in the NT and does not necessarily imply public reading (e.g., Matt 12:3, 5; Mark 12:10). Its cognate noun (ἀνάγνωσις), however, only occurs three times in the NT (Acts 13:15; 2 Cor 3:14; 1 Tim 4:13). The respective contexts indicate that it refers to public reading in each instance (*BDAG*, 61). Although such public reading of itself does not necessarily denote that it took place in worship, other elements in Revelation (addressed in the following paragraph) establish worship as the context. Justin Martyr uses the verb to refer to reading in the eucharistic liturgy (*1 Apol.* 67:3).

31. Although Rouwhorst ("Christlicher Gottesdienst," 491–572) indicates that there is no clear indication of scriptural readings in Corinth, he observes that Paul presumes his readers possess thorough knowledge of the OT and notes that the Pastorals attest to OT readings. Evidence from the Pastorals includes Paul's reference to the "parchments" in 2 Tim 4:13 about which Rouwhorst observes, "womit doch nur Bücher gemeint sein konnen, die den Bibeltext—also den Text des Alten Testaments oder Teile davon" (549). That the "contributions" referred to in 1 Cor 14:26–31 were likely spoken rather than read does not affect their status as didactic worship. See McGowan's (*Worship*, 73–75) comments on the content of NT writings.

32. *BDAG*, 616.

33. The only differences is that it occurs with "Amen" in Did. 10.6 (see 42n6).

34. *BDAG* (616) states that μαράνα θά is "an Aramaic formula which D 10:6 associates with what appears to be the early Christian liturgy of the Lord's Supper." Whereas

its conclusion (22:20).³⁵ That Revelation uses the imperative rather than the indicative mood establishes that it is a prayer (rather than an objective statement). Thus, Revelation which begins on the Lord's day (1:10) and identifies Jesus as the one who is coming (1:7) concludes by praying that he come (22:20).³⁶ Thus, the content and location of 1 Cor 16:22 and Rev 22:20 implicitly affirm the overall shape of the early Christian liturgy explicitly expressed by Justin (*1 Apology* 67) in the middle of the next century. Along with the other NT witnesses cited in this section, they corroborate Justin's testimony about the liturgical proclamation of Scripture as a fundamental part of early Christian worship.³⁷

The Case for the Liturgical Provenance and Purpose of the Gospels

Justin's description of the liturgy and the subject of the present study merit further comment on the relationship between the liturgy and the Gospels. Whereas NT texts attest to their use in Christian worship, the Gospels

---

its position in Did. 10.6 is at the conclusion of prayers of thanksgiving at the end of the sacramental liturgy, 1 Cor 16:22 seems to be directly before it (assuming the normal pattern of didactic worship preceding sacramental worship). Nevertheless, they serve similar purposes in expressing a desire for Jesus' presence (i.e., for his eschatological coming in the Didache and his sacramental presence in 1 Cor 16:22).

35. Similar to Did. 10.6, Rev 22:20 includes the liturgical term *Amen*: "Amen. Come Lord Jesus!" (Ἀμήν, ἔρχου κύριε Ἰησοῦ). As in Did. 10.6 and 1 Cor 16:22, the Greek equivalent for μαράνα θά ("Lord, Come") lies at the heart of the expression.

36. Scholars have recognized 22:20 to be part of a liturgical dialogue (22:16-21) which forms an inclusio with the opening greeting of the letter (1:4-9) and prays for the Lord's coming in the context of the eucharistic liturgy. Boxall (*Revelation*, 319-20) states, "this urgent emphasis upon the Lord's return links his final coming to that coming which is about to take place in the eucharistic assembly" (320). Similarly, Heil (*Revelation*, 329-33) indicates that 22:20 prays "not only for future judgment and salvation at the end of time but also for their present and ongoing liturgical gatherings to celebrate the Eucharist" (332).

37. Although Bradshaw (*Worship*, 16-98) personally concludes that NT evidence on worship requires one to remain agnostic about the roots of worship practices explicitly present in later witnesses, he provides insights that are particularly valuable here. Bradshaw observes, "we cannot assume that just because something is not mentioned it was not being practiced" because "directions do not generally deal with accepted and customary things, but only with new, uncertain, or controverted points: everything else will tend either to be passed over in silence or to receive the briefest of allusions" (16). This observation provides an explanation for Justin Martyr supplying "the earliest substantial description that we have of Christian worship" (98) precisely because he (in contrast to NT authors) was writing to an audience that was unfamiliar with it.

offer evidence that both their purpose and provenance was the liturgy. The content and structure of the Gospels not only suggests they were to be proclaimed in the liturgy (like other NT texts), but also that early Christian worship influenced their form and content. Although they unjustifiably discredited the Gospels' historical character, Martin Dibelius and Rudolf Bultmann, pioneers of form criticism (*Formgeschichte*) of the Synoptics, deemed early Christian worship as fundamental to the Gospels' composition.[38] Although work by more recent scholars similarly affirms the liturgical provenance of the Gospels (including John), it maintains their integrity as authentic witnesses to Jesus.[39] This latter view concurs with the texts, which present themselves as witnesses (cf. Luke 1:1-4; John 20:30-31; 21:24-25). A complementary relationship exists between the Gospels and the liturgy that manifests their liturgical provenance and purpose. The Gospels contain liturgical content and features, and early Christian worship (when recognized as their proximate context) illuminates them.[40]

The Gospels recall episodes from Jesus' earthly life, making him present to the congregation through the proclamation of memorable words, deeds, and events that help the audience to know him better as they honor him as Lord (cf. 1 Cor 2:2; 2 Cor 4:5). The Gospels also provide the foundation for (and instruction about) the sacramental worship that comprises the second part of the liturgy. Each addresses baptism near the beginning (Matt 3:13-17; Mark 1:9-11; Luke 3:21-22; John 1:31-34) and the Eucharist in their culmination (Matt 26:26-29; Mark 14:22-25; Luke 22:17-19; John

---

38. Bultmann (*Synoptic Tradition*, 373) identifies Christian worship as the origin of the Gospels, and Dibelius (*Tradition to Gospel*, 287-89) indicates they were composed for worship (specifically for teaching or didactic worship) and evangelization. Regarding the Gospels in general, see also Collins, *New Testament*, 173; Eve, *Oral Tradition*, 133-34; McGowan, *Worship*, 86-87.

39. Farkasfalvy (*Inspiration*, 79-86) observes, "contrary to what Bultmann and Dibelius habitually presuppose, the liturgical roots of the narratives [of the Gospels] do not imply that they were created (and manipulated) according to the changing needs of the community" (72). Rather the transmission of the oral tradition involved "an organic process of recalling and retelling the memories of Jesus' ministry ... in a Eucharistic cradle provided by early Christian worship" (72). Eve (*Oral Tradition*, 179) states, "if eyewitnesses did continue to be active in the primitive Christian community for some time ... they are likely to have helped stabilize the tradition."

40. Eve (*Oral Tradition*, 15-185) observes, "oral tradition rarely preserves the past for its own sake ... for purely historical or antiquarian purposes" but rather "its interest in the past is nearly always for its practical application in the present." This complementary relationship between early Christian worship and the Gospels reveals the practical application for which the tradition preserved the past (i.e., liturgical worship).

19:34–35).⁴¹ Although John does not explicitly narrate Jesus' baptism, he implies it with the Baptist's observation about the Spirit descending upon him (1:31–34). He also addresses the sacramentology of baptism in the most extended fashion (3:3–21; cf. Mark 10:38–39; Luke 12:50). Regarding the Eucharist, whereas the institution narratives in the Synoptics summarize and interpret the Passion narratives as they instruct the faithful on the sacrament, the Bread of Life Discourse (esp. 6:51–58) and the eyewitness testimony (19:34–35) perform these functions in John.⁴²

The Synoptics structurally suggest their liturgical provenance in the way they introduce, narrate, and connect pericopes.⁴³ Two features typically introduce an episode; Jesus *comes* and people approach him to petition or question him.⁴⁴ In the liturgy, the community has assembled to encounter Jesus who comes in word and sacrament. They approach him in worship and petition him in prayer (cf. *1 Apol.* 65.1–2; 67.5).⁴⁵ That the Synoptics

---

41. Although John does not have an institution narrative, he provides an account of the source of the Eucharist (as well as baptism) with his eyewitness testimony of the blood and water flowing from the side of Jesus (19:34–35). Kereszty (*Wedding Feast of the Lamb*, 52–54) summarizes various theories offered on the absence of an institution narrative in John before observing, "the way that they [the sacraments] derive from and unite us to his sacrificed and risen body" are more important to John than their institution. The use of an image instead of words to convey this reality is consistent with Hays' (*Echoes*, 284, 336) observation about John's preference for using images rather than verbal links to evoke OT passages and figures.

42. Hays' (*Echoes*, 439n349) comments on John's use of the OT apply to the eucharistic instruction and imagery referred to here. Hays observes that John urges us (as his audience) to imagine ourselves "as though we were among Jesus' early followers, discovering with surprise *after* his death and resurrection how our memories of him awaken unexpected echoes of Israel's Scripture" or, in this case, echoes of the sacramental worship for which the audience has come together.

43. See Farkasfalvy (*Inspiration*, 65–79) for a more comprehensive treatment of this topic and his compelling argument for the eucharistic provenance of the Gospels based on features of the texts.

44. Farkasfalvy (*Inspiration*, 73–74) states that these "two features regularly complement each other." He also observes, "the consistent portrayal of Jesus as the one *coming and being encountered* originates in the way memories about him were recalled, told, and retold in the presence of cultic (Eucharistic) congregations, gatherings held for the purpose of reliving the past encounters . . . and [it] reveals the Eucharistic mold in which the gospel tradition was cast in its primitive oral phase" (74; emphasis original). This corresponds with Eve's (*Oral Tradition*, 6) observation about the oral tradition characteristically preserving the past for practical application (see 49n40).

45. Given the limited space that Justin allots for providing detailed information about the overall liturgy, restricting it to just two of his sixty-nine chapters (*1 Apology* 65 and 67), that he identifies communal petitionary prayer as a constituent of the liturgy

generally do not convey historically identifiable journeys with these loosely connected episodes coheres with such recollections about Jesus being initially introduced and retold orally as discrete events prior to their compilation in the written Gospels.[46] New Testament evidence regarding the centrality of the celebration of the Eucharist in the early Church and its association with community gatherings (Acts 2:42; 20:7; 1 Cor 11:17–33) make it the likely context for such recollection and transmission of stories about Jesus.[47] That both the *Didache* and NT witnesses (1 Cor 16:22; Rev 22:20) utilize an established expression which beseeches the Lord "to *come*" is consistent with a liturgical provenance for introducing Gospel episodes with Jesus *coming*.[48] Their proclamation (*1 Apol.* 67.3) shortly before the community rose together to entreat the Lord (67.5) also makes the structure and content of such episodes particularly fitting for communal worship. Gospel passages (whether narrative or discourse) provided content for didactic worship and prepared the audience to encounter Jesus in their sacramental worship (as well as for his eschatological coming). Such didactic

---

in both places attests to its essential and integral role in early Christian worship. Recall that Justin provides the earliest substantial description of Christian worship (see 41n3).

46. Farkasfalvy (*Inspiration*, 68–86) observes that the Synoptics "describe Jesus' deeds in a chain of more or less loosely connected episodes" that pay "little or no attention to chronological or topographical links between the individual episodes" (69) as would be expected for travel reports of historically identifiable journeys in a "biographical reconstruction of a great man's memory" (86). Although the terms used to connect the stories would also have been appropriate for the evangelists when they committed the Gospels to writing (and they may have introduced them in some cases), the general pattern of loosely connected episodes provides compelling evidence of discrete recollection and proclamation prior to their compilation.

47. Drawing upon Acts 2:42 and 20:7-11, Cullmann (*Worship*, 29) concludes, "the situation is quite clear. We have found a convincing argument for the view that as a rule there was no gathering of the community without the breaking of bread." Although such a sweeping conclusion might initially seem unwarranted, the preponderance of implicit evidence of Christian worship in the NT (see above), especially in light of Bradshaw's (*Worship*, 16) insight that "accepted and customary things ... tend to be passed over in silence or to receive the briefest of allusions," provides considerable support for Cullmann's assertion.

48. See 47–48nn32–36. The slight variations in the expression correspond with its being part of the oral tradition. The paucity of detailed information on the early Christian liturgy makes the thematic correspondence between the introductions of the episodes and the liturgical expressions most relevant here (i.e., the liturgical basis to which one could refer to search for precise terminological connections is extremely limited).

content proleptically addressed the second reason that people approached Jesus (i.e., to question him) in the loosely connected narrative episodes.

Whereas John's Gospel does not exhibit the same pattern as the Synoptics, with Jesus frequently coming and going, it identifies him as the one who comes in more prominent ways (1:15, 27; 3:31; 6:14; 11:27). John's Gospel concludes with Jesus "coming" to his gathered disciples in his three post-resurrection appearances (20:19–23, 24–29; 21:1–14) that are generally liturgical and arguably eucharistic in character.[49] In the first two instances Jesus comes into the midst of the disciples gathered together and greets them with the same words: "Peace be with you" (20:19; 26). Jesus confers the Holy Spirit and the authority to forgive sins in his first appearance (20:22–23). The second encounter emphasizes his tangible presence in the midst of his gathered disciples and leads to confessional worship (20:27–29).[50] In his final appearance "Jesus *comes* and *takes* and *gives* bread" to his disciples (21:13) who only recognized him after they had responded in faith to his instructions (21:6–7).

The Gospels also manifest their liturgical provenance and purpose by their content. The most obvious example (occurring in all of them) is the miracle of the multiplication of the loaves. The evangelists collectively provide six accounts (Matt 14:13–21; 15:32–38; Mark 6:32–44; 8:1–10; Luke 9:10–17; John 6:1–13) of Jesus miraculously feeding a vast crowd from an insignificant quantity of loaves and fish. All of the narratives display significant similarity; at the same time, there are also distinctive features and content. The common feature they share is their eucharistic character. They all essentially manifest the fourfold action, characteristic of the institution narratives, mentioned above. Jesus *takes* the bread, he *gives* thanks (Matt 15:36; Mark 8:6; John 6:11) or *blesses* it (Matt 14:19; Mark 6:41; Luke 9:16), he *breaks* it, and he *gives* it.[51]

---

49. Farkasfalvy (*Inspiration*, 78) argues that these encounters "take on an explicitly Eucharistic meaning."

50. See Heil (*John*, 1–2) for other examples of confessional worship. He observes that Thomas's confession in 20:28 "climaxes this type of worship in John" (2).

51. Such variation between giving thanks (Luke 22:19) and blessing (Matt 26:26; Mark 14:22) also occurs in the institution narratives. In the multiplication of loaves accounts Luke uses "bless" and Matthew and Mark, who narrate two accounts, use both terms (in Mark's first account, Jesus *gives thanks* for the bread [8:6] and subsequently *blesses* [8:7] the fish). The oral tradition transmitted by the worshiping communities is a probable explanation for such variation. Based on studies of oral tradition in the Middle East, Dunn (*Jesus Remembered*, 249) indicates that the content of oral tradition exhibits

John expresses the fourfold action in his narration with just three terms: Jesus took, gave thanks, and distributed (διέδωκεν). The unique term employed, which means "to apportion among various parties," effectively combines the actions of breaking and giving.[52] John's use of other terms affirms the eucharistic character of this account.[53] He uses εὐχαριστέω ("give thanks") for the first action. Although John has no need of the verb *break* (κλάω) since διέδωκεν combines the actions of breaking and giving, he uses the cognate noun (κλάσμα. "fragment") twice (6:12, 13) to refer to the fragments gathered. The other evangelists utilize the same term (Matt 14:20; 15:37; Mark 6:4; 8:8; Luke 9:17) and the multiplication pericopes account for every NT occurrence of κλάσμα.[54] The multiplication pericopes and passages that narrate (Matt 26:26; Mark 14:22; Luke 22:19) or allude to (Luke 24:30; Acts 2:46; 20:7, 11; 27:35; 1 Cor 10:16) the celebration of the Eucharist comprise all NT occurrences of the cognate verb (κλάω).[55] The exclusive use of these unique cognate terms provide compelling evidence of the eucharistic provenance and purpose of these passages. Their use across independent traditions also demonstrate their efficacy in alluding to the Eucharist.

---

the complementary properties of stability (conveying the essence of the content that is transmitted) and flexibility (with nonessential elements).

52. BDAG, 227.

53. Although John omits an institution narrative, he uses an uncommon term (ἀνάκειμαι) associated with Synoptic institution narratives (Matt 26:20; Mark 14:18). It occurs fourteen times in the NT. Outside of the Farewell Discourse (13:23, 28) John only uses it to refer to Lazarus (12:2) identified earlier as someone Jesus loved (11:3, 35). Whereas in the Synoptics Jesus gives the broken bread to the disciples to distribute, in John's Gospel he gives it to those who were reclining (ἀνακειμένοις). Thus, John's account effectively engages the audience who have come together to recline at the Eucharist by identifying them with those present in the multiplication passage (6:11) and those loved by Jesus (12:2; 13:23).

54. Although Mark 8:19, 20 do not occur within a multiplication account, they refer to each of the preceding accounts.

55. Esposito (*Jesus' Meals*) provides evidence from other meals that manifest the liturgical setting in which memories of Jesus' ministry were recalled and retold. He analyzes three meals scenes in Luke (7:36–50; 11:37–54; 14:1–24) and demonstrates that their eucharistic *Sitz im Leben* best explains certain features and also illumines the accounts. Whereas other scholars have argued for the symposium genre for these Lucan pericopes, Esposito observes, "by itself, the claim that Luke employs the symposium genre does not increase our comprehension of the content which Luke presents within that framework, nor does it aid our attempt to better understand why Luke narrates selected scenes around a table" (201). Recognition of their eucharistic *Sitz im Leben*, however, addresses both of these deficiencies.

The preceding observations on elements of both the structure and the content of the Gospels collectively provide evidence that demonstrates their fittingness for use in the liturgy. In light of the evidence of Christian worship identified in the previous sections of this chapter from the earliest witnesses on the liturgy and reflected in various ways throughout the NT, features of the structure and the content of the Gospels, in particular, arguably manifest their liturgical provenance and purpose. In other words, the Gospels implicitly attest to the "eucharistic mold" into which elements of the oral tradition were cast, and their use in the liturgy as a primary reason for the evangelists eventually committing them to writing. The theme of worship in John (addressed in the next section) presumes the audience's knowledge of first-century Judaism (both its worship and the OT) and their proximate context of early Christian worship for which they have come together.

WORSHIP AS AN OVERARCHING THEME IN THE FOURTH GOSPEL

John's Gospel manifests worship from the very beginning with its hymnic prologue (1:1–18).[56] Hymns are characteristic of worship in the ancient world, including early Christian worship.[57] The prologue offers worship as it provides important information for understanding the balance of the Gospel. It presents Jesus as worthy of worship as God (1:1) and as the "place" to offer worship (1:14). The statement, "we saw his glory [δόξαν; 1:14]" affirms Jesus' divinity; that he manifested it when he dwelt (ἐσκήνωσεν) among them (1:14) implicitly identifies him as the true temple, prefigured by the tabernacle and the temple in Jerusalem. The combination of glory (δόξα) and the cognate noun dwelling (σκηνή) evoke images of God's glory displayed at the completion of the tabernacle (Exod 40:34–35), where both terms occur in the LXX, and the inauguration of worship in the temple (1

---

56. This section will show that worship is a prominent theme throughout the length of the Gospel, providing relevant examples from each of its major sections. See Heil (*John*, 1–171) for a comprehensive treatment of worship in John's Gospel in which he demonstrates the pervasiveness of worship throughout its length based on a comprehensive textually-based analysis of the Gospel.

57. See Gordley ("Didactic Hymn Traditions," 782–86) regarding the use of didactic hymnody in worship in the ancient world. A hymn began the worship recounted by Pliny in his letter to Trajan (*ep.* 96.7).

Kgs 8:10–12).⁵⁸ The prologue also establishes that Jesus enables worship by empowering those who believe in him "to become children of God" (John 1:12) and in making God known (1:18). Worshiping Jesus and God the Father, made known by him, realizes and expresses belief in his name.⁵⁹ Thus, the prologue initiates worship and prepares for what will follow.⁶⁰

Didactic worship continues with John the Baptist seeing Jesus *coming* and acknowledging him as "the Lamb of God (ὁ ἀμνὸς τοῦ θεοῦ), who takes away the sin of the world" (1:29).⁶¹ The Baptist's statement concisely identifies Jesus as the true Passover lamb and Suffering Servant.⁶² This identification draws upon the contexts of the Gospel, early Christian worship, and first-century Judaism. The Gospel will affirm Jesus' identity as the true Passover lamb at its climax for the worshipping community (19:14, 36). That ἀμνός occurs in parallel with the LXX's term for the Passover victim (πρόβατον) in Isa 53:7 supports the recognition of the Baptist's dual identification of Jesus as the Passover lamb *and* God's servant, the righteous one, who will justify many by taking away their sins (52:13—53:12). The Baptist, in going on to state that he saw the Spirit descend and remain upon Jesus (1:32–33), definitively establishes that he is "the Chosen One of God" (1:34).⁶³ This testimony, that Jesus is God's chosen Servant who possesses

---

58. Brown (*John*, 1:33) observes that "the radicals *skn* which underlie the Greek verb 'to tent' resemble the Hebrew root *škn* which also means 'to dwell.'" Although the verb "dwell" (σκηνόω) does not occur in the LXX accounts, the Hebrew equivalent (שׁכן) appears in the inaugurations of the tabernacle (Exod 40:35) and the temple (1 Kgs 8:12).

59. This applies to ethical (e.g., 14:15—15:17) and sacramental worship (e.g., 6:51–58). Heil (*John*, 10) observes, "believing in the name of the Word who not only was with God in the beginning, but was God (1:1-2) . . . implicitly is expressed and demonstrated by worshiping God."

60. Scholars have characterized the prologue as an overture since it introduces prominent topics of the Gospel narrative. See Brown, *John*, 1:1; Byrne, *Life Abounding*, 21. Gordley ("Didactic Hymn Traditions," 781–802) demonstrates that the prologue of John's Gospel is a didactic hymn.

61. This sixth occurrence of the verb "come" (ἔρχομαι), with Jesus as the subject in the previous four instances (1:9, 11, 15, 27), announces Jesus' "physically" coming into the narrative and, through it, his liturgical coming to the audience gathered to worship the "coming one" (see 50n44).

62. Köstenberger, *John*, 66–68; Heil (*John*, 18–19); Bauckham (*Gospel of Glory*, 154); Porter (*John*, 208–9) are among current scholars who recognize allusions to the Passover lamb and the Suffering Servant by John the Baptist. Bultmann (*John*, 96n3) observes, "for the Evangelist the τοῦ θεοῦ has the same meaning as elsewhere ἀληθινός 1.9; 6.32; 15.1."

63. Although NA28 chose the reading "the Son of God," Quek ("John 1.34," 22–34) maintains that the variant ὁ ἐκλεκτὸς τοῦ θεοῦ (i.e., "the Chosen One of God") is the

the Spirit, anticipates the true worship he will introduce (4:23–24). It also associates the origins of such worship with his redemptive death (1:29; Isa 53:4–12) and bestowal of the Spirit (John 1:33; 19:30).

Soon afterward (2:4) the Gospel introduces the theme of Jesus' hour with the first manifestation of his glory (2:5–11).[64] The dialogue (2:3–5, 10) and events (2:6–11) associate Jesus' hour with the provision of extraordinary wine. The reference to Jesus' glory (δόξαν; 2:11) recalls its previous occurrence (1:14) and implicitly affirms that he is worthy of worship and identifies him as the true temple. The narrative then brings Passover and the temple into the foreground (2:13). Jesus enters the temple precincts and drives out the merchants who were making it a house of trade (οἶκον ἐμπορίου; 2:16), fulfilling Zechariah's prophecy about the absence of traders (14:21) in the temple when people from all nations will come to worship Yhwh (14:16).[65] The disciples' recognition of the *future* fulfillment of the scripture in association with Jesus' actions in the context of Passover, that "zeal for your house *will* consume me" (2:17), affirms Jesus' identity as the true Passover lamb (1:29, 36).[66] Jesus' response to the Jewish authorities' request for a sign to justify his actions (2:18) explicitly establishes his body as the new temple: "Destroy this temple and in three days I will raise it" (2:19). John underscores the importance of the statement with his narrative

---

original reading and "probably an allusion to the opening lines of the First Servant Song [Isa 42:1]" (30). Heil (*John*, 20n12) provides an important corroborating insight that, "if 'the Son of God' were the original reading, it would detract from the dramatic rhetorical progression in 1:19–51 in which 'the Son of God' title is a climactic confession (1:49)."

64. As mentioned in the previous chapter, Jesus' hour corresponds to his "being lifted up" (3:14; 8:28; 12:32, 34) and "being glorified" (7:39; 12:16, 23, 28; 13:31, 32; 16:14; 17:1, 5). The interconnections between Jesus' hour, his "being lifted up," and "being glorified" demonstrate John's use of multidimensional symbolism to advance and illuminate the theme of worship.

65. The LXX employs Χαναναῖος in Zech 14:21 as a literal rendering of the Hebrew (כנעני). Although the MT primarily uses כנעני as a collective Gentilic to refer to the people of Canaan, *HALOT* (486) lists "tradesman" as a secondary meaning (Zech 14:21; Prov 31:24). Smith (*Micah-Malachi*, 292), commenting on Zech 14:21a, states, "the term 'canaanite' was used often by the prophets to refer to 'traders' in Israel (cf. Hos 12:8 . . . Zeph 1:11; Zech 11:7, 11)." Brown (*John*, 1:119, 121) considers John 2:16 to be "an implicit allusion to Zech xiv 21."

66. Heil (*John*, 33n13) observes, "the scriptural word of God predicted that Jesus' zeal to make the house of his Father a house of true worship will lead to his sacrificial death as the Passover Lamb. It will totally 'consume,' 'devour,' or 'eat up' Jesus, just as the Passover lambs will be eaten in their entirety (LXX Exod 12:9)." The proximate context of the audience, who would soon consume Jesus in the Eucharist, affirms and illuminates the fulfillment in a different sense.

intervention about the disciples' realization of its meaning after the resurrection (2:21–22).[67]

After establishing Jesus as the New Temple, the Gospel addresses how those who believe in him were to become part of that temple (through the sacramental worship of baptism). Jesus' dialogue with Nicodemus on the necessity of being "born from above . . . of water and the Spirit" to enter the kingdom of God (3:3–5) establishes the foundational role of baptism for the believer and the Church's worship. The balance of the passage addresses the essential features associated with this new birth, providing sacramentology on baptism (3:6–21). Following the dialogue on the invisible realities associated with baptism, the narrative shifts to provide references to the visible action of baptizing with water (3:22–26; 4:1–2).

The focus changes to the culmination of true worship in Jesus' discussion with the Samaritan woman (4:7–26).[68] His request for a drink (4:7) and subsequent reference to the *living water* that he possesses (4:10–15) leads to the woman's inquiry about proper worship (4:19–20).[69] Jesus' response associates true worship with his hour, the gift of the Spirit, and his self-identification as the Messiah (4:21–25). Their dialogue implicitly establishes that the Spirit would make it possible to worship the Father "in Spirit and Truth" (4:23–24) in Jesus' hour. The woman departs from the encounter and bears witness in Johannine fashion. She engages her

67. Hays (*Echoes*, 312) indicates that 2:13–22 provides "a hermeneutical key for John's symbolism throughout the narrative. *Jesus now takes over the temple's function as a place of mediation between God and human beings*" (emphasis original). The passage casts new light on earlier statements (1:14; 1:51) and provides the key for understanding future ones (4:21; 14:6–7).

68. Dorothy A. Lee ("In the Spirit of Truth," 277–97) states, "the dialogue between Jesus and the Samaritan woman (Jn 4:1–42) . . . [is], at its centre, a conversation about worship" (278). Lee also observes that the conversation is the most explicit discussion on worship in the Gospel containing nine of the eleven occurrences of προσκυνέω and the only occurrence of its cognate noun (προσκυνητής).

69. The intervening dialogue (4:16–19) only makes sense in light of the contemporary understanding that Samaritans had worshipped five deities (cf. *Ant.* 9.288) following the settlement of foreigners in the land by the Assyrians. The foreigners imported their own gods (2 Kings 17:24–31) which fostered syncretistic worship of Yhwh in Samaria that had apparently persisted until Jesus' time (John 4:18, 22). Whereas the Gospel indicates that the details also apply to the woman's personal life (4:29), failure to recognize the underlying reference to improper worship results in two problematic *non sequitur* statements (4:16, 20). That the OT repeatedly equates idolatrous worship with adultery (Judges 2:17; 8:27, 33; Jer 3:1–10, 20; Ezek 20:23:1–49; Hos 2:1–23; 4:12; Ps 106:36–39) supports such an allusion. Although Brown (*John*, 1:171) only characterizes "such an allegorical intent" as possible, he provides a valuable summary for its basis.

contemporaries and the audience by sharing her experience (4:28-30) and invites them to encounter Jesus and decide for themselves, resulting in many who believe in him and become his witnesses (4:39-42).[70] Jesus' intervening dialogue with his disciples (4:31-38) associates his hour and true worship (4:21-25) with doing the will of the Father and completing his work (4:34). He associates all of them with his sustenance in his response (4:34) to the disciples' attempt to feed him (4:27, 30-33) that immediately followed his discourse with the Samaritan woman (4:7-26). That this was all that took place between his disciples' departure (4:7) and arrival (4:27) equates true worship with the will and the work of the Father.[71]

The temple feasts, which Jesus fulfills and transcends, are prominent in the next section of the Gospel (5:1—10:42) and assist in advancing the theme of worship. This section begins (5:1-47) with an unnamed feast (5:1) associated with a Sabbath (5:9-18), followed by Passover (6:1-71), Tabernacles (7:1—10:21), and the Dedication (10:22-42).[72] The Jews erroneously perceive Jesus' healing of a paralyzed man (5:1-9) as a violation of the Sabbath observance and persecute him (5:15-16). Since proper ethical worship, however, imitates God (as established in chapter 2), the healing was appropriate for the Sabbath because Jesus, as the Son, was not only imitating the Father (5:19) but performing his works (5:20-38). These works bear witness that Jesus, as Son, is worthy of worship. His subsequent interaction with the healed man demonstrates this assertion.

Jesus finds the man in the temple and tells him to "sin no longer" (μηκέτι ἁμάρτανε; 5:14), since he was "missing the mark" by continuing to worship in the old temple (which prefigured Jesus) rather than believing in

---

70. The narrative conveys didactic worship by instructing the audience about Jesus as it praises him (see 44n16). Heil (*John*, 41) observes, "they publicly proclaim that they know Jesus to be a worthy object of worship for all in the audience: 'this is truly the savior of the world (4:42)."

71. Gruber ("Der Quelle," 314-30) identifies 4:34 as a critical intertextual connection for understanding Jesus' thirst, the fulfillment of the Father's will, the completion of his work, and the gift of the Spirit in 19:28-30 (326).

72. John does not explicitly indicate the timing of 9:1—10:21. Brown (*John*, 1:376-90) considers 10:1-21 to be a bridge that accommodates the three months between Tabernacles and the Dedication. Moloney (*John*, 290-300) indicates that Jesus' healing of the blind man (9:1-41) occurred during Tabernacles since there is "no indication of a change of time" in 8:59—9:1 (290). He also observes that 9:1—10:21 is a literary unit (i.e., the context for 9:1—10:21 is Tabernacles) since "no break occurs between 9:41—10:1" (300). Menken ("Jewish Feasts," 187-207) similarly identifies Tabernacles as the context for 7:2—10:21 (198) and believes that "all the events of 7:37—10:21 [are] on one day" (189).

Jesus and worshiping him.⁷³ The man affirms his inadequate belief by his subsequent actions. Rather than worshiping Jesus (cf. 9:38) and bearing witness to him so that others might believe and be saved (5:33–34) he simply reports Jesus (5:15) to the Jewish authorities who persecute him (5:16).

As established in the previous chapter, the combined feasts of Passover and Unleavened Bread celebrate God's deliverance of the people of Israel from bondage in Egypt. The multiplication of the loaves (6:1–15) and the Bread of Life discourse (6:22–71) occur in the context of these feasts.⁷⁴ As demonstrated above, the multiplication of the loaves exhibits distinctive eucharistic features, which correspond to the liturgical provenance and purpose of the Gospel(s). Recognition of the historical context of the Jewish feasts and the liturgical content of the multiplication account illuminates the discourse that follows it.

The liberation that the combined feasts commemorate led to Israel's time in the wilderness and God's provision of manna, the bread from heaven, by which he sustained his chosen people. The manna is the exemplary sign to which the people refer (6:30–31) when Jesus challenges them to believe in him. In response to their request he identifies himself as "the bread of *life*" (6:35) and "the *living* bread having come down from heaven" (6:51) who gives eternal life. Therefore, Jesus reveals that he transcends the manna which simply sustained the *temporal* lives of the people in the wilderness whereas he, the living bread come down from heaven, provides *eternal* life within those who believe in him and consume his flesh and blood (6:35–58).

John uses the verb εὐχαριστέω to establish the Eucharist as the theme for his account of the multiplication of the loaves (6:11) and in recalling it (6:23) when he establishes the context and theme for the "Bread of Life" discourse (6:22–71).⁷⁵ Other terms and features affirm its eucharistic

---

73. The general sense of the verb ἁμαρτάνω is to "miss the mark" (*BDAG*, 49). Elsewhere, Jesus uses the cognate noun (ἁμαρτία) to refer to failures to believe in him after encountering him, his words, and his works (9:41; 15:22–24). Heil (*John*, 58) observes that "Jesus told the man he healed on the Sabbath to no longer sin (5:14), implicitly by worshiping in the Jerusalem temple, since in that 'temple' (2:14) Jesus revealed that his body, which he will raise from the dead after it is destroyed (2:19), is the new temple for the true worship of God (2:15–22)."

74. Although John only mentions Passover (6:4), chapter 2 established that the OT and first-century witnesses (including the NT) sometimes refer to the combined feasts with the name of one of them.

75. Brown (*John*, 1:257–303) identifies the Bread of Life discourse "proper" as running from 6:35–59, but considers 6:35–50 to be primarily sapiential with Eucharistic

theme. The unique term for "eating" (τρώγων), which occurs repeatedly in its climax (6:54, 56, 57, 58) and only as a present participle, indicates the "ongoing or continual eating" associated with celebrations of the Eucharist.[76] The verbs "thirst" (6:35) and "drink" (6:53–56) associate the living bread (6:35, 48), comprised of Jesus' flesh and blood (6:51–58), with the living water (4:13–15) of the Spirit which he will provide with his glorification (7:37–39). Jesus makes the Spirit's role more explicit in his response to a comment about the difficulty imposed by his teaching when he states, "the Spirit is the one giving life, the flesh profits nothing" (6:63a).[77] Thus, the Spirit, given by Jesus to those who believe in him (7:39), grants eternal life by birth from above (3:3–6) through baptism and sustains it through the consumption of the Eucharist.[78]

Peter's profession that Jesus is "the Holy One of God" (6:69) recalls John's testimony that Jesus is the "Chosen One of God" (1:34) "who baptizes with the Holy Spirit" (1:33). Recollecting John the Baptist's testimony, which had occurred between identifications of Jesus as "the Lamb of God" (1:29, 36), in the current context of Passover (6:4) affirms the earlier association of Jesus as God's Chosen One *and* the true Passover Lamb who takes

---

undertones. Moloney (*John*, 205–32) sees the theme of the Eucharist running throughout even if it is not the focus of the earlier part of the discourse. He also observes that the singular noun for "the bread" (τὸν ἄρτον) used in conjunction with "the Lord" (τοῦ κυρίου) and the participle (εὐχαριστήσαντος) in 6:23 serve as "Eucharistic hints" (206). The range designated here for the discourse (6:22–71) simply provides a basis for the following discussion since, as Brown (*John*, 1:263) indicates, "almost every commentator has his own division."

76. Heil, *John*, 55n16. Heil observes that whoever "continually 'feeds on' his flesh and continually 'drinks' his blood in eucharistic worship has divine life eternal (6:54)" (55). Moloney (*John*, 381) observes, "the eucharistic contexts [here and in 13:18] influence the choice of the more physical verb for eating."

77. Moloney (*John*, 231) observes that John uses the term "flesh" (σάρξ) in two different ways. Whereas the flesh of Jesus "is essential for life," the flesh "of human beings is confined to the human sphere or that which is 'below.'" Recognizing Jesus' statement in 6:63 as a response to the concern raised about the difficulty of accepting his teaching (6:60) indicates that this second part of his statement clarifies the use of "flesh" here. The NET translation reflects the essence of Moloney's insight: "The Spirit is the one who gives life; human nature is of no help!" (6:63).

78. To understand Jesus' statement as opposing the Spirit and the flesh ignores the balance of it: "the words that I have spoken to you are spirit and life" (6:63b). The words Jesus just spoke emphatically established the necessity of consuming his flesh. The first part of his statement simply affirms the Spirit's essential role in providing Jesus' risen and glorified flesh in the Eucharist to those who believe in him for eternal life. Beasley-Murray (*John*, 96) states that "the accent in the saying falls on the life-giving Spirit."

away sin (1:29).⁷⁹ It also supplements the Baptist's witness by connecting these identities with Jesus' provision of his flesh and blood for eternal life (6:53–58) through the gift of Spirit (6:63). The worship associated with the combined feasts celebrated Israel's liberation from physical slavery and the sustenance of their *natural* lives. In this context, the Bread of Life discourse establishes that Jesus, as the Lamb and Holy One of God, fulfills the worship prefigured by the feasts and transcends it in providing *eternal* life to those who believe in him and consume his flesh and blood in the Eucharist.

In the context of Tabernacles (7:1—10:21) the Gospel demonstrates that Jesus, as the new temple (2:19–22), fulfills and transcends what was foretold about the eschatological temple and prefigured in the observance of this feast. As established in the previous chapter, the OT associates the eschatological temple with Yhwh's ongoing provision of life-giving water (Zech 14:8; Ezek 47:1–12; Joel 4:18), continuous day (Zech 14:7), and the worship by all peoples on the feast of Tabernacles (14:16; cf. Isa 2:2–5). In this context Jesus explicitly identifies himself as the source of living water (John 7:37–39) and incomparable light (8:12), and he implicitly affirms that he is the "place" for true worship (9:24–41).

It is "on the last, the great, day of the feast" (7:37) that Jesus identifies himself as the source of living water (7:37–38) and John's narrative comment indicates the Spirit is the living water Jesus will provide with his glorification (7:39). The living water of the Spirit will fulfill the OT promise of continual life-giving water (Zech 14:8; Ezek 47:1–12; Joel 4:18) for those who believe in Jesus (John 7:38–39) and transcend it by enabling them to be born from above (3:3–6) and offer the true worship that the Father desires (4:23–24).⁸⁰ Jesus also indicates that as the true temple he is the source of continuous light (8:12; cf. Zech 14:7). Whereas the ritual worship

---

79. The designations "Holy One of God" (6:69) and "Chosen One of God" (1:34) (see 55–56n63) function synonymously and correspond with Jesus' identity as "the Son, the unique one" (3:16). Heil (*John*, 57) observes that the narrative references to Judas who would "'give him over' (παραδιδόναι) to a sacrificial death (6:71; 6:64) . . . accords with the declaration that God so loved the world that he 'gave' (ἔδωκεν) the Son, the unique one (3:16), with the connotation that he gave him over to a sacrificial death as the Passover Lamb of God."

80. The ambiguity associated with the referent of the pronoun αὐτοῦ in 7:38 (i.e., whether it is the believer or Jesus) has received much attention. See, for example, Menken, "John 7:38," 159–74; Kerr, *The Temple*, 231–40. Heil (*John*, 60–61), however, in demonstrating that the pronoun refers to the believer *and* to Jesus, establishes that efforts to limit the referent to Jesus *or* the believer are unnecessary and counterproductive (i.e., rather than illuminating the meaning of the text they unduly confine it).

of Tabernacles sought to attribute this quality to the temple complex by illuminating all of Jerusalem with candelabras lit in the Court of Women each night (m. Sukkah 5:1–5), Jesus will illuminate the world for those who follow him (8:12).[81]

The subsequent account of Jesus' healing of the man born blind (9:1–41) demonstrates the effect of the spiritual light he provides (9:5) to those who believe in him. After receiving his physical vision (9:6–12), the man progressively gains spiritual sight with repeated professions and concurrent growth in his faith in Jesus (9:13–34) in stark contrast to the response of the cured paralytic (5:14–16). The man born blind progresses from stating that Jesus is a prophet (9:17) to attesting that Jesus is a worshiper who does God's will (9:31) and, ultimately, to worshiping him (9:38).[82] Jesus subsequently affirms the man's observation (9:31) when he identifies himself as the Good Shepherd, who will freely lay down his life for his sheep in accord with the will of the Father (10:17–18).[83]

In the context of the Dedication (10:22–40) Jesus identifies himself as the one "whom the Father consecrated and sent into the world" (10:36). His statement reasserts his identity as the true temple (2:19–21) and the progression from worship in Jerusalem's temple (4:21–22) to true worship (4:23–24). The Dedication celebrated the restoration of proper worship in the temple (2 Macc 10:1–8) which Antiochus IV had desecrated through idolatry (1 Macc 1:41–60). The Maccabees restored proper worship when they built a new altar (1 Macc 4:54, 59; 5:1) and *consecrated* (ἡγίασαν; 4:48) the courts of the temple to worship God whom they knew (John 4:22) through Moses and the prophets (1:45; 5:45–46) rather than idols (1 Macc 1:43, 51).[84] Two aspects manifest the progression from worship in the

---

81. Brown (*John*, 1:344) states, "in the Gospel scene Jesus stands in this same Court of Women and proclaims that he is the light, not only of Jerusalem but of the whole world."

82. Heil (*John*, 67) observes that the man's testimony (9:31) "indicates that Jesus, who does the will of God (4:34; 5:30; 6:38), is not only the temple for true worship (2:21) and an object of true worship (1:14, 49; 4:42; 6:69), but also himself a true worshiper of God (cf. 4:23–24)." In contrast, the healed paralytic continued to "miss the mark" (ἁμάρτανε) by failing to recognize Jesus as the true temple and as worthy of worship. Similarly, the Pharisees "miss the mark" (εἴχετε ἁμαρτίαν; 9:41) by failing to benefit from the miraculous sign, the man's testimony, and his example of faith in Jesus (9:35–41).

83. Heil (*John*, 70) observes that Jesus is "a true worshiper of God through his self-sacrificial act of worship as the good shepherd who lays down his life for his sheep."

84. They restored *true* worship at that time in the sense that they rededicated the temple to worship the one *true* God. Such worship was only provisional, however, prefiguring the worship the Father seeks (4:23). The Mishnah (m. Meg. 3:6) indicates that

temple in Jerusalem to the true worship offered in Jesus' hour. Whereas the Maccabees consecrated the temple courts, the Father consecrated Jesus as the true temple (10:36). Secondly, that Jesus is one with the Father (10:31) affirms his incomparable knowledge of the Father (1:17-18) and provides the basis for knowing the worship that he desires (4:23-24).

The subsequent raising of Lazarus attests that Jesus is a true worshiper providing testimony (11:22) as well as evidence that God listens to him (11:41-44; cf. 9:31) and that his actions give glory to God (11:4). That the event concurrently glorifies the Son (11:4) corroborates that Jesus is worthy of worship and reflects his unity with the Father (10:30).[85] Caiaphas's subsequent prophecy that Jesus should die for the nation and to gather the scattered children of God (11:50-52) affirms the self-sacrificial character of the worship he will offer in laying down his life for his sheep (10:14-18).[86] It also implicitly affirms earlier identifications of Jesus as the Lamb of God (1:29, 36) and his Chosen One (1:34; Isa 42:1) as it consolidates them by drawing upon OT imagery and the context of the Gospel.[87]

---

they read "the princes" for the Dedication. Neusner (*Mishnah*, 321) identifies the passage as "Num 7:1ff." In Num 7:1 Moses *anoints* and *consecrates* the completed tabernacle and everything in it as well as the altar. Menken ("Jewish Feasts," 203) observes that the scene begins with "'the Jews' asking Jesus if he is the '*anointed* one' (ὁ χριστός)."

85. The Jewish authorities who had claimed that Jesus was "making himself God" in the context of the Dedication sought to discredit him by identifying him with Antiochus IV Epiphanes who considered himself a god (see *Ant.* 12.258). Jesus' response, appealing to his works as proof of his unity with the Father (John 10:37-38), however, unequivocally differentiates him from Antiochus IV who refuted his self-proclaimed divinity (2 Macc 9:12) when God bore witness against him, striking him down for his arrogance (9:4-28).

86. Heil (*John*, 82) observes, "Jesus will die so that he might 'gather' (συναγάγῃ) into one believing and worshiping community the dispersed children of God, both Jews and Gentiles (11:52)." See also Brown, *John*, 1:440-41. That 1:12 is the only other occurrence of "children of God" recalls that belief in Jesus is the response required to become a child of God. Jesus, the one shepherd, will gather the scattered sheep (10:12) into one flock (10:16). The OT foretells such a gathering of the children of Israel who remain scattered in the diaspora (Deut 30:4-5; Isa 43:5-7; Jer 31:8-11) as well as Gentiles (Isa 2:2-5; 66:18-21; Jer 3:17-18; Pss 22:28; 86:9).

87. Hays (*John*, 284, 336) indicates that John uses visual imagery (preferentially), verbal echoes, and explicit verbal links. That Jesus should die (ἀποθάνῃ) for the people (τοῦ λαοῦ) evokes the Suffering Servant led to death (θάνατον; Isa 53:8) for the transgressions of the people (τοῦ λαοῦ; 53:8). That he should die so that the Roman's will not take away (ἀροῦσιν) the place and the nation (John 11:48) recalls that God's Servant will be taken away (αἴρεται) for his people (Isa 53:8). The context of the imminent observance of Passover (John 11:55) fosters the recollection that Jesus, as the Lamb (ἀμνός) of God, is the one who takes away (ὁ αἴρων) the sins of the world (John 1:29).

The Gospel narrative moves to the onset of Jesus' hour with a precise reference to the arrival of Passover (12:1) soon followed by his declaration that "the hour has come" (12:23).[88] The acknowledgement occurs with Jesus' response to a request by Greeks who had come to Jerusalem to worship and had requested to see him (12:20–22). After Jesus responds (12:23–26), he offers a prayer (12:27–28a) and immediately receives an answer from the Father (12:28b) speaking of the past and future glorification of his name. Here the previously distinct themes of Jesus' hour, his "being lifted up," and his "being glorified" converge (12:27–32). Jesus' association of his hour with the term "glorify" (δοξάζω; 12:27–28) equates it with worship.[89] The request (12:20) of the Greeks, who had come for worship and wished to see Jesus (12:21), prompted Jesus' recognition of the onset of his hour (12:22–23) and his statement about drawing all people to himself when he is lifted up (12:31–33). Thus, Jesus identifies his hour with the fulfillment of the prophecy of universal worship foretold in Zech 14:16–17 (cf. Isa 2:2–5; 66:23). The narrative conveys the major transition associated with the coming of his hour with the first of two sets of double OT fulfillment references (12:38–40) and a different verb to introduce them.[90] After identifying Isaiah as the source of the quotes, John contrasts the prophet who "saw his glory and spoke about him" (12:41) with those who did not believe in Jesus (12:37, 39) or who believed but did not profess their faith due to fear (12:42) and the desire for human praise (12:43).[91] To see and profess Jesus'

---

88. Heil (*John*, 83) observes, "after three notices that the Passover was vaguely 'near' (2:13; 6:4; 11:55) it was now precisely very near." The perfect tense of ἔρχομαι in 12:23 similarly establishes the definitive arrival of Jesus' hour, especially in contrast with John's negation of its pluperfect form in two prior references (7:30; 8:20), which indicated that his hour had not yet come.

89. In the Gospel, δοξάζω either acknowledges or reveals God's (i.e., the Father's) or Jesus' divinity and, consequently, connotes worship. Nielsen ("Glory and Glorification," 343–66) observes that the object of δοξάζω is always God (the Father) (13:31, 32; 14:13; 15:8; 21:19), Jesus (7:39; 8:54; 12:16, 23, 28; 13:32; 16:14; 17:1, 5, 10) or both of them (11:4; 13:31). The subjects of δοξάζω are either God (the Father) (7:39; 8:54; 12:16, 23, 28; 13:32; 17:1, 5), Jesus (13:31, 32; 14:13), or a third party (11:4; 13:31; 15:8; 16:14; 17:10; 21:19). Nielsen also indicates that the perception of Jesus' glory denotes the recognition of his divine status.

90. The other set of double OT fulfillment references occurs at the end of the Passion narrative (19:36–37) with John's final references to the OT. The term γεγραμμένον ("it is written") introduces OT references through 12:16. John shifts to πληρωθῇ ("might be fulfilled") in 12:38. See Moloney, "Scripture," 454–68; Porter, *John*, 200–204.

91. Whereas 12:38 is a citation of LXX Isa 53:1, John 12:40 appears to be a paraphrase of Isa 6:10. Hays (*Echoes*, 332–35) observes that John has performed a "complex textual

glory is to worship him, whereas the failure to do so is to "miss the mark" (i.e., sin; cf. 5:14; 9:41).[92]

Worship remains prominent throughout the Farewell Discourse (13:1–17:26), which occurs within the context of Jesus' hour (13:1; 17:1). The narrative explicitly associates his hour with Passover and implicitly with his self-sacrificial worship offered in accord with the will of the Father (10:18) by laying down his life (10:17) for "his own" (ἴδιος; 10:3, 4, 12; 13:1).[93] Whereas "his own" draws attention back to Jesus' earlier references to the worship he will offer and enable, that "he loved them to the end [τέλος]" (13:1) points forward to its fulfillment at the culmination of his hour.[94]

The discourse begins with the footwashing and its associated dialogue (13:3–35). In performing this action Jesus implicitly anticipates the humiliation associated with his death by crucifixion (13:6–9), affirms his willing acceptance of it (13:2–5), and establishes that such humble service offers ethical worship in response to his example (13:12–15) and command (13:34–35; 15:12–14).[95] Concurrently, it addresses aspects of the sacra-

---

overlay" with 3:13–15 and 12:37–41 (which explicitly cites Isa 53:1) by which he interprets "the story of Jesus' crucifixion as an event that is *simultaneously* a glorious exaltation to power (Dan 7) and a painful vicarious suffering for the sin of others (Num 21:4–9 + Isa 52:13—53:12)" (335). Hays indicates that 12:31–33 supports this interpretation and concludes, "it would appear that John has performed an astonishing intertextual fusion of Dan 7:13–14, Numbers 21 and Isaiah 52:13" (335).

92. See 59-62nn73-82 on sinning, or "missing the mark," by failing to worship Jesus. Heil (*John*, 90) states, "those who believed but did not worship Jesus loved the 'glory of human beings,' which amounts to false worship, rather than the 'glory of God' (12:43)."

93. Moloney (*John*, 373) states that "the two 'times' running through the story, the feasts of 'the Jews' (2:13, 23; 4:45; 5:1, 9; 6:4; 7:2; 10:22; 11:55–57; 12:1) and the 'hour' of Jesus, are determined by the design of God (2:4; 4:21, 23; 7:30; 8:20; 12:23, 27)." And that "they now join, as there is a feast of 'the Jews' that is also the hour of Jesus (13:1a)." See also Köstenberger, *John*, 402. Heil (*John*, 95) observes that 'his own' (13:1) "reminds the audience that, as the good shepherd, Jesus will lay down his life in love for 'his own' sheep (10:3–4, 11–12, 15), an act of self-sacrificial worship that will establish him as *the* Passover Lamb of God (1:29, 36)" (emphasis original).

94. Moloney ("Scripture," 459–60) states that John uses τέλος (its only occurrence in the Gospel) to convey that Jesus' death "not only fulfills the promises of Scripture, but it brings them to their τέλος . . . [with the understanding that] the OT not only continues to be narrated in the Gospel of John; it comes to its completion, its fulfillment, its τέλος." The combination of the cognate verbs τελέω (19:28, 30) and τελειόω (19:28) at the culmination of Jesus' hour will underscore that it is indeed the τέλος.

95. Whereas John 10:17–18 establishes that Jesus will freely lay down his life, the footwashing conveys his readiness to submit to a shameful death (cf. 1 Cor 1:23; Phil 2:8; Heb 12:2) and it provides a model for his disciples (13:12–15). Byrne (*Life Abounding*,

mental worship of baptism and the Eucharist. The use of water (13:5), the reference to having been washed (λελουμένος) and made clean (13:10), and the necessity of being washed with water to "have a part" with Jesus (13:8) address aspects of baptism and its essential role in uniting his disciples with him.[96] Jesus' reference to his betrayer as "the one eating my bread" (13:18) provides linguistic and thematic connections with the Bread of Life Discourse and, consequently, to the sacramental worship of the Eucharist. Linguistically, the same unique term for eating occurs in 13:18 and in the Bread of Life Discourse (τρώγω; 6:54, 56–58) along with the term for bread (6:51, 58).[97] Jesus' references to his betrayer in 13:18 and 6:64 thematically link the passages.

Worship remains prominent for the balance of the discourse. Jesus employs temple imagery as he explicates the role of the Spirit in enabling his disciples to offer true worship. He introduces temple imagery by referring to his Father's house (οἰκία) and its many dwellings (μοναί; 14:2) and goes on to establish that his disciples will constitute the new temple as the dwelling (μονή) of the Father and of Jesus (14:23).[98] The two occurrences of the unique term μονή form an inclusio around a corresponding verb (μένω) which provides insight into the new temple and the role of the Spirit

---

229–31) states that "there is no parallel in extant literature for a person of superior status voluntarily washing the feet of someone of inferior status" (229) and "that Jewish, as distinct from Gentile, slaves could not be required to wash their master's feet" (230n7). Byrne goes on to observe that the footwashing "will equip them to understand the 'service' of Jesus on the cross" (231).

96. Moloney (*John*, 375–78) asserts that the necessity of the footwashing in order "to have part" with Jesus (13:8) is "a veiled reference ... to baptism" (375) and that "the passage presupposes the ritual within the life and practice of the Johannine community (cf. 3:3, 5; 19:34)" (376).

97. The verb used for eating (τρώγω) in 13:18 only occurs one other time in the Bible (Matt 24:38) outside of this passage and the Bread of Life Discourse (John 6:54, 56–58). The verb in the passage cited (Ps 41[LXX 40]:10) is the more common term for eating (ἐσθίω). The LXX also employs the plural of bread (i.e., "loaves;" ἄρτους) in the psalm whereas John 13:18 uses the singular, which corresponds with the form used repeatedly throughout the Bread of Life discourse (6:31–58).

98. Coloe ("Johannine Temple," 47–58) observes that οἰκία (14:2) and μονή (14:2, 23) convey temple imagery and identify the disciples with it. She also indicates that the use of the term οἰκία (versus its cognate οἶκος; cf. 2:16–17) reinforces the meaning of house as a household and the "series of interpersonal relationships between the Father, Jesus, Paraclete and believers" (50). See also Michel's ("οἶκος, οἰκία," 5:119–34) observation on John's unique use of οἰκία in 14:2 (vs. οἶκος) to refer to the house of God (121).

in establishing it.⁹⁹ As the Father is remaining (μένων) *in* Jesus (14:10), so the Spirit remains (μένει) with the disciples and will be *in* them (14:17). The indwelling of the Spirit of truth (14:16), as the other advocate whom the Father (14:16) and Jesus will send (16:7), enables Jesus both to go away and remain with his disciples (14:3, 27) as he and the Father dwell in them (14:23).¹⁰⁰

The Spirit of truth will lead them on the way "into the whole truth" (16:13) and so enable them to offer the worship the Father seeks in Spirit and Truth (4:23-24). That the Spirit will lead them on *the way* into *the truth* corresponds with his glorifying Jesus (16:14-15) who is *the way, the truth* and the life (14:6). This includes bringing to remembrance all that Jesus said to them including his commandment to follow him in the way (14:5-6) of self-sacrificial love (13:34-35; 15:12-17). Jesus had previously established the Spirit as the one who gives *life* (ζωοποιοῦν) in the context with the Bread of Life discourse (6:63).¹⁰¹ Thus, the Spirit makes Jesus present to his disciples in the Bread of Life (6:63) and through the life-giving water (3:5-6; 4:10-14; 7:37-39) for the sacramental worship that will build the new temple and produce the fruit (καρπόν) of new believers to glorify Jesus and the Father (15:2-8, 16).¹⁰² The Spirit will also enable liturgical worship in glorifying Jesus by taking from him all that he received from the Father (16:12-15) to teach (διδάσκω) and remind the disciples (14:26).¹⁰³

---

99. F. Hauck ("μονή," 4:579-80) observes, "in the NT μονή occurs only twice in John's Gospel (14:2, 23)" and that "the two statements correspond" (580). Jesus had established earlier that true worship would not take place in a specific location (4:20, 4:23-24). Now he indicates that he will prepare a "place" (τόπος) by means of the disciples. Coloe ("Johannine Temple," 51-54) provides evidence of expectations in Judaism that the Messiah would build a new temple and demonstrates how subsequent references to Jesus "the Nazarene" (18:5, 7; 19:19) might allude to him as this messianic builder.

100. With God dwelling in the disciples, they would possess the essential characteristic for serving as the New Temple (cf. Ezek 43:7, 1 Kgs 8:12-50; 2 Chr 6:1-39).

101. That the Father and Jesus are the only other subjects of this verb (5:21) reflects that the Spirit will continue the life-giving work that Jesus received from the Father (6:32-33).

102. Jesus first used the term καρπόν (4:36) when he spoke of the harvest (4:35-38) in the context of the many Samaritans who came to believe (4:39). He also established that his self-sacrificial worship was the ultimate source of such fruit (12:24). These insights would resonate with John's audience gathered for sacramental worship.

103. This constitutes didactic worship. That Jesus is the subject of διδάσκω in seven of its nine other occurrences in the Gospel concurs with the Spirit's role of teaching and reminding the disciples (14:26) of Jesus (16:13-15) and proclaiming coming things to them (16:13). The Father and the man born blind are the only others who taught. The

As the other advocate (14:16), whom Jesus will send after he departs (16:7), the Spirit will empower the disciples to offer ethical worship by bearing witness to Jesus (15:26-27). He will lead them in Jesus' way (14:4-6), of self-sacrificial love (13:34-35; 15:12-17), even to the point of laying down their lives (15:12-16; 16:2-4). In and through such ethical worship Jesus will be present to them (14:21-23) and they will be his witnesses (13:35; 15:27) glorifying the Father (15:12) by bearing much fruit (15:16). The Spirit will empower them to continue the work of Jesus (4:34; 5:36; 6:38; 10:37-38) through their liturgical and ethical worship by dwelling in them (14:17) and enabling them to abide in Jesus, the true vine, as he abides in them (15:1-11).[104] That Jesus' only other reference to such mutual abiding with his disciples occurred in the Bread of Life discourse for those who eat his flesh and drink his blood (6:56) conveys the centrality of the Eucharist in fostering this mutual immanence.[105]

Jesus concludes the discourse by praying for the disciples. His prayer confirms that they are to continue Jesus' work, which includes constituting the new temple. Just as the Father consecrated (ἡγίασεν) and sent (ἀπέστειλεν) Jesus into the world as the new temple (10:36), so also Jesus sent (ἀπέστειλα) his disciples and he asks the Father to consecrate (ἁγίασον) them in the truth (17:17, 19).[106] Through their unity with the Father and

---

Father taught Jesus (8:28) who has everything that the Father has (16:15). The man born blind also taught about Jesus and the Pharisees cast him out for doing so (9:34).

104. Jesus establishes that they will continue his work by bearing the fruit (15:2, 4, 5, 8, 16) that he made possible through his self-sacrificial death (12:24). He indicates that they will bear "much fruit" (καρπὸν πολύν; 15:8), as Jesus does through his death (πολὺν καρπόν; 12:24), by becoming his disciples and abiding in him as the way to the Father through self-sacrificial love. Gruber ("Der Quelle," 322) observes, "Jesus 'sucht' Menschen, die von seinem Wasser trinken (Joh 4,1–15) und in der Kraft des dadurch empfangenen Geistes mit ihm die 'Frucht' glaubender Menschen sammeln (Joh 4,35–42)."

105. Feuillet (Études Johanniques, 83) observes, "l'immanence réciproque du Christ et des disciples, traduite par le verbe μένω, est in VI,56 le fruit de la réception de l'Eucharistie; or cette idée d'immanence réciproque, toujours avec le verbe μένω, est reprise constamment dans la péricope de Jn XV, 1–11 (vv. 4, 5, 6, 7, 9, 10) et ne se retrouve nulle part ailleurs dans le quatrième évangile." That the Didache refers to Jesus as the holy vine (9.2) in the prayer over the cup affirms the association of Jesus as the vine (15:1, 4, 5) with the Eucharist.

106. Jesus, who is the truth (14:6), in asking the Father to consecrate his disciples in the truth (17:17) and consecrating himself for them (17:19), establishes that their status as the true temple subsists in their union with him (17:21). That the only references to consecrated persons are Jesus (10:36) and his disciples (17:17, 19) strengthens this connection.

the Son (17:21-23) Jesus' disciples are to continue his work of making the Father known (1:18) by revealing Jesus to the world as the Son sent by the Father (17:2-5) so that those who believe may have life through him (6:40). Jesus establishes that their work fundamentally consists of offering true worship (4:23-24) by the many occurrences of glorify (17:1, 4, 5, 10) and glory (17:5, 22, 24) in his concluding prayer (17:1-26).

The theme of worship continues with Jesus' response to those who came to arrest him when he reasserts his divinity by using the divine name, "I am" (18:6). Their reaction, with the soldiers falling to the ground, implicitly acknowledges his divinity.[107] Jesus' subsequent responses (18:7-11) reaffirm that he is the Good Shepherd who will lay down his life for his sheep in self-sacrificial worship (18:7-9; cf. 10:14-16) in accord with the Father's will (10:17-18) and associate his willingness to do this with drinking the cup the Father has given to him (18:11; cf. 10:18).[108]

During his interrogation, Pilate questions Jesus about whether he is a king (18:33). Jesus acknowledges his royal identity by referring to his kingdom (βασιλεία; 18:36). That the only other occurrences of βασιλεία were Jesus' parallel references to the Kingdom of God in his conversation with Nicodemus (3:3, 5) implies that Jesus' reply to Pilate identifies his kingdom as the kingdom of God. His subsequent qualification that his kingdom is not "from here" (ἐντεῦθεν), used in parallel with "this world" (18:36), calls to mind his corresponding use of the contrasting term "from above" (ἄνωθεν) to refer to the heavenly origins of baptism (3:3) and its necessity to see or enter the Kingdom of God (3:5). These multiple points of contact

---

107. Falling to the ground is the basic meaning of the verb προσκυνέω (BDAG, 882) which conveys worship when its object is God (4:20-24; Exod 4:31; 33:10). John distinguishes their action from intentional worship by not using προσκυνέω here, but rather the neutral expression ἔπεσαν χαμαί ("they fell to the ground"). The response of hundreds of armed men (Brown, *John*, 2:807-9) falling to the ground in response to a verbal reply is clearly extraordinary. Although some scholars deny its historical character (e.g., Brown, *John*, 2:811), others defend it (e.g., Köstenberger, *John*, 507-8; Beasley-Murray, *John*, 322-23).

108. Heil (*John*, 119) observes that "Jesus' willingness to 'drink the cup' the Father has given him resonates with his being the good shepherd/high priest who freely sacrifices his own life for the sheep and people of God (10:11-15; 11:50-52)." That Jesus associates his desire to freely lay down his life with *his desire to drink* (i.e., his thirst) has great significance for the culmination of his hour (19:28-30).

affirm Jesus' kingship (1:49; 6:15; 12:13, 15) and, in establishing that his kingdom is the Kingdom of God, that he is worthy of worship.[109]

Whereas Pilate's interrogation affirms that Jesus is a king and implicitly establishes that his dominion is the kingdom of God, his presentation of Jesus to the Jews assembled at Gabbatha (19:13) affirms his identity as *the* Lamb of God. That Pilate presents Jesus to those assembled by stating: "Behold [ἴδε], your king" (19:14), recalls John the Baptist's presentation of Jesus when he first appeared in the Gospel: "Behold [ἴδε] the Lamb of God, who takes away the sin of the world" (1:29)! Furthermore, that Pilate's statement occurs in the context of "the day of preparation of the Passover" establishes that Jesus' freely laying down his life in his forthcoming crucifixion (10:14-18; 18:11), by which he would offer true worship as *the* Passover Lamb of God, would transcend the worship of Passover (cf. 13:1) which prefigured it.[110] That Pilate hands Jesus over in the "sixth hour" (4:6) affirms the association of his hour with offering true worship by evoking Jesus' dialogue with the Samaritan woman about such worship in the "coming hour" (4:23).[111]

The subsequent narrative explicitly affirms Jesus' kingly status (19:19-22). Pilate placed an inscription on the cross that identified Jesus as "the King of the Jews," which was written (γεγραμμένον) in Hebrew, Latin, and Greek (19:19-20). There are repeated references to its written character, with various forms of the verb (γράφω) occurring six times in four verses (19:19-22). That the verb only occurs elsewhere to refer or allude to the OT (e.g., 1:45; 2:17; 5:46), an action of Jesus (8:8), or the content of the Gospel (20:30-31; 21:24-25) implies that the inscription is authoritative and

---

109. Beasley-Murray (*John*, 330) states that "despite the fact that the expression βασιλεία τοῦ θεοῦ, 'kingdom of God,' occurs only in John 3:3 and 5, the whole Gospel is concerned with the kingship of God in Jesus. And that is what Jesus was referring to in his utterance to Pilate."

110. Heil (*John*, 126) indicates that Pilate's statement in 19:14 recalls and complements John's declarations (1:29, 36) "alluding to Jesus as the sacrificial Passover Lamb."

111. That there are not only numerous other linguistic and thematic connections between the Samaritan and Passion narratives, but also that, as Gruber ("Der Quelle," 327) observes, if "der intratextualität" between 4:1-42, 7:37-39, and 19:28-35 is not recognized, "bliebe das Verständnis der Samaritererzählung unvollständig," affirms the intended reference here. The other connections include the "thirst" (4:13-15; 7:37; 19:28), "water" (4:10-11, 13-15; 7:38; 19:34), "Spirit" (4:23-24; 7:39; 19:30) and "believe" (4:39, 41-42; 7:39; 19:35) which are present in each of the passages and integral parts of the same trajectory. The passages collectively and progressively establish that "*Jesus dürstet nach dem Glauben und ist selber die Quelle des Geistes, der diesen Glauben ermöglicht, der sienen Durst stillt*" (emphasis original). See also Heil, *John*, 126.

indirectly affirms Jesus' divine dominion (cf. 18:36) by identifying him as "King of the Jews."[112] Jesus' testimony had established that his kingdom was the kingdom of God and the Jews anticipated that their promised Messiah (i.e., the King of the Jews) would bring about this kingdom as foretold by Daniel. That the inscription was in Hebrew, Latin, and Greek conveys the universality of Christ's divine kingship.[113]

The soldiers who crucified Jesus along with the associated narrative attest to his identity as the true high priest.[114] Although the soldiers divide Jesus' garments into four portions, they decide to cast lots for his tunic rather than tear it (19:23-24). The narrative indicates that the soldiers did not tear the tunic because it was without seam, woven from the top (ἄνωθεν) as a whole (δι' ὅλου; 19:23). Its woven construction corresponds with the vestments of the high priest (Exod 28:6, 32; LXX 36:10, 12, 15, 29, 34).[115] That it was woven as a whole (δι' ὅλου; John 19:23) corresponds with the high priest's robe, in particular; being woven "as a whole" (ὑφαντὸν ὅλον) of blue (LXX Exod 36:29). The observation that Jesus' tunic was woven ἄνωθεν ("from the top"), especially in light of its earlier occurrences in John's Gospel (3:3, 7, 31; 19:23), attest to the divine "origin" of its construction. This corresponds with the fabrication of the original high priestly vestments in accord with divine commands (Exod 39:7, 21, 36, 39, 31). The Lord had also instructed Moses to weave the high priest's robe in such a way "that it may not be torn" (Exod 28:32; MT 39:23).[116] The narrative associated with the soldiers' decision to refrain from tearing Jesus' tunic establishes that it

112. That two of the occurrences are in the passive (19:19-20) enhances this effect. Heil (*John*, 127) recognizes these occurrences as divine passives indicating, "it was decisively 'written,' ultimately by God."

113. Moloney (*John*, 502) observes, "Pilate, who insisted on Jesus' royal status during the trial (cf., 18:33, 37, 39; 19:14, 15), continues this ironic proclamation of the truth in Hebrew, Latin, and Greek (v. 20b), the languages of the cultured world of the Roman empire. The kingship of Jesus is proclaimed universally and can be read by all who pass by (20a)."

114. John Paul Heil ("High Priest," 729-45) demonstrates how John's Gospel conveys that Jesus is the unique high priest who offers himself in sacrifice. Heil provides evidence from textual analyses of Caiaphas's advice to the Sanhedrin (11:45-53), Jesus' arrest and trial (18:1-27), and the soldier's treatment of his tunic (19:23-24), that establishes that Jesus' priesthood supersedes and surpasses the Jewish institutions.

115. Heil ("High Priest," 742), observes that the various vestments were woven works and states, "this was true of the ephod (Exod 28:6; 36:10, 12), the breastpiece (Exod 36:15), the robe (Exod 28:32; 36:29) and the tunic (Exod 36:34)."

116. Whereas the LXX only includes this clause in 28:32, the MT has it in 28:32 and 39:23.

possessed this characteristic and implicitly bears witness to him as high priest (John 19:23-24). Their actions fulfilled the Scripture (Ps 22 [LXX 21]:19]) as they attested to the unity that Jesus would effect as the true high priest (John 10:15-16; 11:50-52).[117] His identity as the true high priest affirms that he offers himself, as *the* Lamb of God, in self-sacrificial worship (10:18).

The reemergence of Jesus' mother in 19:25 (cf. 2:1-12) introduces the culmination of his hour and reaffirms the earlier observations (12:23; 13:1; 16:32; 17:1) that his hour had come (cf. 2:4). In seeing his mother with the beloved disciple, Jesus addresses them with performative statements that, with their cooperation, effect a new reality (19:26-27a).[118] By addressing his mother as "woman" (19:27) in the context of the hour, Jesus identifies her with the woman in labor whose hour has come (16:21).[119] The narration conveys the reality of the "birth" of her new child by progressively referring to Jesus' mother as "his mother" (19:25), "the mother" (19:26), and finally "your mother" with respect to the beloved disciple (19:27). In taking Jesus' mother the disciple openly manifests his assent to Jesus' command and his mother (in "being taken") implicitly conveys her consent (19:27b). Their response collectively demonstrates their faith in Jesus and their love for him (14:21; 15:10). In taking Jesus' mother for "his own" (τὰ ἴδια), the beloved disciple receives her on behalf of all who hear Jesus' voice (10:3-4, 27)

---

117. Stones on the high priestly vestments symbolized the unity of the twelve tribes of Israel (Exod 28:9-12, 21; 36:13-14, 21). Heil ("High Priest," 743) indicates that the stones "symbolized the whole people of Israel, presented in remembrance before the Lord when the high priest wore the breastpiece in the sanctuary (28:29)." He also observes, "the Roman soldiers' desire not to divide the dying Jesus' seamless tunic woven from above as a whole (δι' ὅλου), a symbol of unity, corresponds to the high priest Caiaphas' advice to preserve the unity of the whole (ὅλον) Jewish nation by putting the one man Jesus to death (11:50). Indeed, as the unique high priest who surpasses the Jewish high priest, Jesus dies not just for the unity of the nation but to gather the scattered children of God into unity (11:52)."

118. Culpepper ("John 19:16b-30," 21-37) observes that the language used in 19:25-27 is both revelatory and performative since it "effects the new relationship that it declares" constituting "a new family, mother and son" (30). Dauer ("Das Wort des Gekreuzigten," 80-93) maintains that Jesus' statements are "nicht nur eine Empfehlung an beide, sondern eine offizielle Verfügung in der Art einer doppelgliedrigen Adoptionsformel" (81).

119. In addressing his mother as "woman" (19:26; cf. 2:4, 16:21), Jesus associates her (along with her current suffering) with his disciples (16:21-22). This title anticipates the new role she assumes in becoming the mother of the beloved disciple (19:26-27) and, thus, the Mother of the Church (see 75n131). The ensuing narrative establishes and elucidates this reality.

and believe in him (1:12; cf. 1:11; 10:26).¹²⁰ John associates the formation of this new family (or community) of Jesus' own with the last occurrence of the term "hour" (19:27) and subsequently affirms its culmination.¹²¹

With the new community now formed Jesus recognizes "that everything had now been accomplished" (19:28) and initiates the action that will allow him to manifest that he is freely laying down his life (10:17–18b), out love for his Father (10:18c; 14:31) and his own (10:15; 13:1, 15:13–15).¹²² John had earlier indicated that Jesus, knowing that his hour had come to depart from the world to the Father, loved "his own" to the "end" (τέλος; 13:1). Now he indicates that the end had come (τετέλεσται; 19:28), including the completion (τελειωθῇ) of Scripture.¹²³ Jesus had earlier expressed his desire to do the Father's will by rhetorically asking whether he should not "drink" the cup that the Father had *given* him (18:11) near the beginning of the passion narrative. He communicates this desire once again at the culmination of his hour by saying, "I thirst."¹²⁴ They respond with a

---

120. The expression τὰ ἴδια occurs multiple times (10:3, 4, 12) in the Good Shepherd Discourse (10:1–21) where it refers to the shepherd's *own* sheep. The Gospel identifies receiving (1:12; cf. 1:11) and following Jesus (10:3–4, 27; cf. 10:26) as distinctive characteristics of "his own," whom Jesus would love to the end (13:1). The audience would readily identify themselves with being "his own" through birth from above (3:3–6).

121. Heil (*John*, 131) observes, "the mutual acceptance of the mother of Jesus and the beloved disciple to form a new family thus serves as a model for the audience as believers to become a familial household of worship by loving one another for divine life eternal."

122. That John begins 19:28 by referring to what had just taken place (19:25–27) with the introductory phrase "after this" (μετὰ τοῦτο) indicates the significance of the mutual responses of Jesus' mother and the disciple to his performative statements. With their manifestation of faith in Jesus, "*everything* had now been accomplished" (19:28).

123. The evangelist recalls his observation in 13:1 by referring once again to Jesus' "hour," "his own," (19:27) and the end (19:28–30) in quick succession. He conveys that the end has come with the first (19:28) of two occurrences of the cognate verb of τέλος (τελέω), which had occurred as a hapax in 13:1. Another cognate and synonymous verb (τελειόω), which has "the Scripture" as its subject, complements τελέω as it draws upon the contexts of its previous occurrences (4:34; 5:36; 17:4, 23). Moloney ("Scripture," 459), who maintains that John understood himself to be producing Scripture, observes that his use of τελέω with τελειόω in 19:28 conveys that Jesus' death "not only fulfills the promises of Scripture, but it brings them to their τέλος."

124. There is an intrinsic complementarity between the verbs in 19:28 (διψάω) and 18:11 (πίνω), since the former expresses a fundamental desire and the latter conveys the means for its satisfaction. John's Gospel associates thirst and drinking with worship (4:7–26) and Jesus' glorification (7:37–39). Charbonneau ("Jésus en croix," 5–23, 161–80) observes, "on ne peut pas séparer la soif de Jésus du contexte de l'arrestation: «La coupe que m'a donnée le Père ne la boirai-je pas?» (Jn 18,11). En croix, Jésus se veut totalement l'expression de la volonté du Père" (166).

sponge full of "sour wine" (ὄξος) placed on hyssop (19:29). In receiving the sour wine, Jesus completes the Scripture as he manifests his love for his own (to the end) in laying down his life for them in perfect self-sacrificial worship to the Father.

Although John states that Jesus expressed his thirst "in order that the scripture might be completed [τελειωθῇ]," he provides no words from a particular OT verse (cf. 12:38; 13:18; 15:25; 19:24, 36, 37). The subsequent narration, however, indicates that LXX Ps 68:22 is the primary referent with the soldiers providing "sour wine" (ὄξους) in response to Jesus' proclamation, "I thirst [διψῶ]."[125] His reception of the sour wine (John 19:30) does not simply fulfill the psalm, but perfects it.[126] The words of LXX Psalm 68 are those of a righteous sufferer in the midst of persecution (68:2-13; 20-22) who prays that God deliver him (68:14-19, 30) and punish his enemies (68:23-29).[127] Jesus "perfects" the psalm by manifesting his desire to freely lay down his life in his zeal to accomplish the work(s) of his Father (John 4:34; 5:36; 17:4, 23).[128] In perfecting the psalm and accomplishing his Father's work, Jesus completes Scripture with the worship the Father desires (4:22-23), prefigured in the OT and the Jewish feasts, by his complete

125. Although scholars have posited other OT passages (LXX Pss 21:16; 41:3; 62:2), none compare to 68:22 in terms of linguistic connections. It contains the cognate noun (δίψος) of the verb that Jesus uses to express his thirst (διψάω) in conjunction with the use of the term for the sour wine (ὄξος) which occurs three times in John 19:29-30. The term ὄξος only appears three other times in the OT (Num 6:3; Ruth 2:14; Prov 25:20).

126. John's use of the verb τελειόω in 19:28, which differs from the verb employed (πληρόω) for fulfillment passages (12:38; 13:18; 15:25; 19:24, 36, 37), distinctively conveys a sense of completion or perfection. See Moloney, "Scripture," 459; Obermann, *Erfüllung*, 363.

127. Obermann (*Erfüllung*, 130-31) observes that the audience would have been familiar with the entire psalm from which an NT author cited a passage. Consequently, John would have had to consider the original context for psalm texts as well as his literary context. John's multiple references/allusions to Psalm 68 (John 2:17; 15:25; 19:28) imply particular familiarity with this psalm within his community.

128. John's unique use of τελειόω in 19:28, which refers to Jesus accomplishing the work of the Father in its previous occurrences (4:34; 17:4, 36; "works" in 5:36), effectively incorporates the work(s) of the Father in the perfection he acknowledges. Its first use in 4:34 explicitly associates this work with accomplishing the will of the Father, and implicitly with Jesus' thirst, the living water (i.e., the Spirit) he will give, and the culmination of true worship in his hour. Gruber ("Der Quelle," 327) observes that Jesus "hungert (und dürstet) danach, den Willen des Vaters zu erfüllen (4,34), der sich in seinem Tod und seiner Verherrlichung vollendet (19,28). Damit der Spender des lebendigen Wassers in den Menschen die Quelle zum Sprudeln bringen kann (4,14; 7,38), muss er selber zum Dürstenden werden (4,7; 19,28)."

self-sacrifice offered in obedience to his Father (10:18) out of love for him (14:31) and his friends (15:13). Having manifested his final assent to the work of the Father, Jesus pronounces its accomplishment in the culmination of his hour and "gives over" (παρέδωκεν) the Spirit (19:30).[129] John's narration of Jesus' final action is no mere euphemism for his death, but an expression created by the evangelist for a deliberate purpose.[130] He hands over the Spirit to the Church in the persons of his mother and the beloved disciple who demonstrated their belief in him by assenting to his commands.[131]

The narration of the events that immediately follow Jesus' death (19:31–35) and the testimony from the OT (19:36–37) elucidate the account that precedes them and establish its relevance for the audience in the proximate context of liturgical worship. The central event is the blood and water that flowed from Jesus' side (19:34) to which the Gospel bears emphatic witness (19:35).[132] John utilizes the collective testimony (of what transpired following Jesus' death, the attestation from the OT, and the eyewitness account) to affirm his understanding of what took place in Jesus' hour and through it provides valuable insight into his distinctive passion

---

129. Jesus pronounces the accomplishment of the Father's work by stating, "It is accomplished" (τετέλεσται; 19:30). John's earlier use of the same verb in the identical form (19:28) creates an inclusio that includes the formation of the new community since it was "after *this*" that Jesus recognized that "everything was accomplished" (πάντα τετέλεσται; 19:28). Brown (*Messiah*, 2:1077) observes, "since 'I thirst' comes under the rubric of 'all being finished' [19:28], we might think of it and 'It is finished' as functionally constituting one saying."

130. De la Potterie (*The Hour of Jesus*, 163) indicates, "it is a fact that 'to hand over the spirit' in the sense of dying is never found in antiquity . . . there is not a single instance. For there are other expressions." He goes on to observe, "when an author, for such a simple fact as the death of a man, invents a new expression, it must be for a deliberate purpose." Swetnam ("Bestowal of the Spirit," 556–76) states, "the reason for the unique language is the wish of the author to make a theological claim . . . that the death of Jesus is accompanied by his bestowal of the Spirit" (566).

131. Swetnam ("Bestowal of the Spirit," 571–72) indicates, "in the act of dying, Jesus 'hands over' the Spirit to his mother, who thereby is transformed from Daughter of Sion, i.e., Jerusalem as symbol of all faithful Hebrews, to Mother of the Church" (571). He also observes that the two persons in 19:30 upon whom Jesus bestows the Spirit "symbolize the entire people of God" (572).

132. Moloney (*John*, 505) observes, "the narrator unexpectedly launches into a personal comment that has no parallel in the rest of the Gospel." This emphatic intervention indicates that "the blood and water must mean something to the readers of the Gospel, and the narrator is anxious that the readers have no doubt about the fact that blood and water flowed from the crucified Jesus."

narrative. Namely, that Jesus offered and enabled (19:28–30), for the newly formed community of "his own" (19:25–27), the true worship foretold and prefigured in the OT and the Jewish feasts and institutions.[133] Chapter 5 will address this portion of John's passion narrative in depth.

SUMMARY

This chapter addressed the theme of worship in John's Gospel. After acknowledging the importance of the OT and worship in first-century Judaism for understanding the Gospel, it identified early Christian worship as its proximate context. The chapter began by focusing on this proximate context in considering evidence provided by extra-biblical witnesses on early Christian worship, the NT texts in general, and the Gospels in particular. The remainder of the chapter demonstrated the theme of worship that runs throughout John's Gospel in light of its presumption of knowledge of the OT and worship in first-century Judaism along with its proximate context of early Christian worship.

An analysis of the earliest extant witnesses on liturgical worship identified several notable features associated with early Christian worship. These included the importance of integrating ethical and liturgical worship, the foundational role of baptism, the centrality of the Eucharist, the reading of Scripture (OT and NT), and homilies. The analysis identified the three general categories of didactic, sacramental, and ethical worship, and it established that didactic worship preceded sacramental worship in the liturgy. The NT texts implicitly corroborated the abovementioned features of early Christian worship and the insights from the liturgical witnesses illuminated passages from the biblical texts. The analysis of the NT texts also attested their liturgical purpose. The final section of the first part of this chapter made the case for the liturgical provenance of the Gospels based on their content and structure.

The balance of the chapter traced the theme of worship in John's Gospel from the prologue to the culmination of Jesus' hour. It gave particular

---

133. That the events narrated in 19:31–34 transpired in the context of Passover demonstrates Jesus' definitive fulfillment of Passover as *the* Lamb of God (1:29, 36). In definitively fulfilling Passover, as the preeminent feast of Judaism, Jesus fulfills all of the Jewish feasts and institutions and enables true worship for those who believe in him. Gruber ("Der Quelle," 327) observes that those who, finding Jesus, drink of the Spirit become the source for others and "so ist das die Anbetung des Vaters in Geist und Wahrheit (Joh 4,23f)."

attention to his hour due to its significance in conveying and advancing the theme of worship from its narrative introduction near the beginning of Jesus' public ministry (2:4) to its final occurrence (19:27) in its consummation (19:28–30). It demonstrated how John utilizes the theme to convey that Jesus completes Scripture (19:28) by offering the true worship that the Father desired (4:23–24) and enabling it for those who believe in him (19:30, 34). In this way, Jesus does the will of the Father and completes his work (4:34) as he perfects the Scripture (19:28). John's final fulfilment citations (19:36–37) affirm the realities conveyed by the words and events in the narrative that precedes them. The next chapter will address particular practices of OT exegesis and allusions utilized around the turn of the era that are relevant to the current study. Chapter 5 will use this information in examining 19:36–37 and the OT passages to which they allude.

4

Ancient Exegetical Methods Relevant to John 19:36–37

As established in the previous chapters, John presumes the contexts of first-century Judaism and early Christian worship. The primary aspects of Judaism presupposed are knowledge of first-century worship and the OT. Chapter 2 addressed essential features of first-century Jewish worship prior to the destruction of the temple; namely, the temple, the feasts, and sacrificial worship. Chapter 3, in demonstrating John's theme of worship and its proximate context of the audience gathered for worship, related various ways the evangelist utilizes the presumed features of first-century Jewish worship to illuminate the true worship Christ offers and enables in his hour. The previous chapter also identified numerous citations and allusions that presumed knowledge of the OT.

Beyond general and particular knowledge of the content of the OT, John presupposes familiarity with contemporary methods of scriptural exegesis. The absence of explanations (cf. 1:38, 41; 5:2; 19:13; 20:16) for apparent adjustments made to various OT texts manifests such an assumption.[1] That other NT texts and various other Second Temple witnesses exhibit similar practices attest to the customary use of such methods and the

---

1. Menken (*Old Testament Quotations*, 206–7) indicates, "the evangelist modified his quotations in various ways and for various reasons" (206). Menken observes that John, "changed the tense of the verb . . . (2:17; 7:18) . . . [and] added, omitted, or changed elements on the basis of analogous OT passages to adapt a quotation to his general ideas or to the specific context of the quotation in the gospel, or to make it more comprehensible (6:31; 7:38; 12:15, 40; 13:18; 19:36)" (207).

reasonability of the evangelist's presumption of his audience's familiarity with them. This chapter will first identify general characteristics associated with biblical interpretation in late Second Temple Judaism based on various textual witnesses from that period. Subsequent sections will describe particular exegetical methods relevant to John's use of the OT in 19:36–37, provide examples of their application in the Second Temple era, and offer evidence that suggests the use of such methods in the subject passage.

BIBLICAL INTERPRETATION IN THE NEW TESTAMENT AND LATE SECOND TEMPLE JUDAISM

New Testament authors often utilize the OT to demonstrate how it prefigures Jesus, in and through whom it realizes its fulfillment.[2] Textual witnesses from Second Temple Judaism also make recourse to the authority of Scripture. Such witnesses, including the Dead Sea Scrolls, Philo, and other intertestamental texts (e.g., *Jubilees, Letter of Aristeas*), extend from the final centuries before the turn of the era through the first century AD. In the process of utilizing the OT in their works, the ancient authors concurrently interpreted it (whether explicitly or implicitly). That the translations of the HB into Greek and Aramaic occurred in this time period likely contributed to such utilization and interpretation of Scripture by ancient authors.[3] The translations themselves not only provided greater access to the sacred texts for those who were not proficient in biblical Hebrew, but were themselves interpretations of the OT.[4] In this regard, the practice of nonbiblical and

---

2. The number of OT references observed in the Gospels and Paul provides a sense of how frequently NT authors refer to it. Hays (*Echoes*, 284) tabulates more than 300 OT references in the Synoptics alone, providing the following totals for the Gospels (including allusions): "Matthew 124; Mark 70; Luke 109; John 27." Stanley (*Paul and Scripture*, 65) states, "modern studies of Paul's use of Scripture have been unanimous in finding just under a hundred quotations in the various letters that make up the Pauline corpus."

3. Emmanuel Tov (*Textual Criticism*, 131–50) indicates that the Greek translation of the Torah took place in the third century BC and that the translation of remaining texts began in the early second century BC (131). With revisions taking place from the first century BC until the beginning of the second century AD (131–32), the origins of the major versions of the Greek OT transverse this entire period. Similarly, textual witnesses of some Targums date from the second century BC (148).

4. Grobel ("Interpretation," 2:718–24) observes, "every translator 'carries over' into the new language only what he understands the original language to be saying; in other words, between the translator's reading of the original and his transmutation of it there lies a fundamental act of interpretation" (2:719). Cook and Wise ("Aramaic Translation of

NT authors interpreting OT passages in their works is part of a trajectory established by the translators. In some cases, ancient Jewish authors interpreted the OT in continuous or thematic commentaries (called pesharim) on particular biblical texts (e.g., Genesis, Isaiah) and, in many others, they interpreted the OT by incorporating passages (whether by citation or allusion) into their works.[5] John's use of the OT corresponds with the latter practice.

In utilizing OT passages in their works, the authors implicitly interpreted them by the new contexts into which they placed (or alluded to) them. Although such intertextual interpretation already took place within the HB (e.g., 1 Chr 5:1; 2 Chr 35:13), it became more prevalent in texts from the third century BC through the first century AD (and beyond).[6] Witnesses within both Palestine and the diaspora indicate that ancient Jewish and Christian authors employed various methods to incorporate and interpret the OT in their works during the Second Temple period. That there were generally no attempts to explain or justify such exegetical practices corroborates the recognition and acceptance of them by ancient audiences as implied in John's Gospel.[7]

Job," 577–88) provide insight into such interplay based on a Qumran targum of Job: "For the most part, the translation of Job presented by this targum is literal and straightforward... Still, the translator not infrequently *understood* the identical Hebrew text that we see differently than modern scholars... offering new ways of seeing the problems in the book" (577; emphasis original). Nehemiah 8:8 provides a possible biblical basis for such interpretation (*HALOT* 3:976).

5. Dimant ("Pesharim," 1050–56) indicates, "there are fifteen compositions among the Qumran corpus that are recognized as 'continuous pesharim'" (1050), and she identifies five related works "that have been designated 'thematic pesharim'" (1051). This study follows Hays's (*Echoes*, 10) understanding that "an 'allusion' usually embeds several words from the precursor text, or it at least in some way explicitly mentions notable characters or events that signal the reader to make the intertextual connection." He also adds, "the meaning of a text in which an allusion occurs would be opaque or severely diminished if the reader failed to recognize the implied reference to the earlier text."

6. First Chronicles 5:1 explains why Joseph was given the birthright instead of Jacob's firstborn son Reuben (Gen 29:32; 49:3; Exod 6:14; Num 1:20) and 2 Chr 35:13 clarifies a potential inconsistency in instructions for the preparation of the Passover lamb between Deut 16:7 (possibly indicating boiling) and Exod 12:9 (which prohibits boiling). Kugel ("Biblical Interpretation," 121–41) observes, "this was the golden age of biblical interpretation, the period in which various groups of (largely anonymous) interpreters put their stamp on the Hebrew Bible and determined the basic way in which the Bible would be interpreted for the next 2,000 years" (130).

7. See 78n1 for evidence of such practices displayed in John.

ANCIENT EXEGETICAL METHODS RELEVANT TO JOHN 19:36-37

Though there is considerable breadth in the methods employed, scholars have identified common underlying tenets for them.[8] These beliefs included the understanding that all of Scripture was of divine origin and, based on this common origin, that every passage was part of a harmonious whole which collectively conveyed the truth of God's revelation to humanity.[9] The aforementioned characteristics enabled Scripture to interpret itself (i.e., the exegete could use one passage to interpret another).[10] That the ancient authors implicitly or explicitly interpreted the passages they cited (or to which they alluded) presumed that the sacred texts conveyed meaning beyond what was apparent and that the authors had privileged insight into them.[11] The ancient authors' utilization of Scripture also implied its current relevance to their audiences.

The rabbinic literature catalogs exegetical methods that proceeded from these underlying tenets and attributes them to particular individuals.[12] It attributes the earliest list of rules to a Pharisee named Hillel (t. Sanh. 7:11) who lived in the first century BC.[13] The Pharisees, like the rabbis, recognized the authority of the fathers (i.e., the oral tradition) in addition to that of Scripture, whereas other important groups in Second Temple Judaism (e.g., the Sadducees) refused to acknowledge the oral tradition as authoritative. Hillel's list formally recognizes particular exegetical methods as appropriate for properly understanding and safeguarding Torah

---

8. The following tenets are a combination of those identified by Kugel ("Biblical Interpretation," 131–32) and Longenecker (*Exegesis*, 6–7) who provide similar and complementary lists.

9. This understanding applied to the texts that particular authors and their communities considered inspired. Avemarie ("Interpreting Scripture," 83–102) observes that although the canons may have differed for Paul and "the Qumran exegetes, their very approach was a 'canonical' one" (102).

10. Wise ("Last Days," 254) indicates that the author of 4Q174 (4QFlorilegium) provides an extended example of the utilization of this principle.

11. Wise ("Last Days," 254) observes that the author of 4Q174 understood statements by Moses (as author of Genesis), David (as author of the Psalms), or one the prophets in the future tense as "prophecy, and fair game for the interpretive methods that could crack open a verse and reveal its hidden meaning." Philo (*Cherubim* 27) considered himself inspired at times in interpreting Scripture.

12. Instone-Brewer (*Techniques and Assumptions*, 4) indicates that there are three lists of exegetical rules (or *middôt*) in early rabbinic literature and asserts that their origin is the scribal tradition practiced in the Second Temple period.

13. Instone-Brewer (*Techniques and Assumptions*, 4) states the earliest list contains "the 7 rules attributed to Hillel (1st C. BCE)." Daube ("Rabbinic Methods," 239–64) indicates that Hillel was "the great Pharisee who flourished about 30 B.C." (240).

observance in accord with the tradition he received (i.e., the oral law), and which he considered to be included in Scripture.[14] Textual witnesses indicate that ancient Jewish authors had been employing practices reflected in Hillel's list (e.g., CD-B XX, 21–22a; 11Q 13, II, 2–3; Let. Aris. §155), as well as various other exegetical methods (e.g., CD-A VIII, 14–15; 4Q 174 I, 2–3; *Alleg. Interp.* 3.4), in the final centuries of the Second Temple.[15] The particular practices he enumerated (which subsequent rabbinic lists expanded upon) served to fortify and further develop the "fence" erected around the Torah by means of the oral law (established to safeguard its observance), to ensure its relevance for his contemporaries, and to demonstrate that the oral law proceeded from (and concurred with) the biblical precepts.[16]

Since the primary purpose of rabbinic exegesis was Torah observance, it focused on that portion of the OT and, specifically, on content related to guiding ethical conduct.[17] Due to this objective, rabbis often applied the exegetical methods differently than observed in many earlier Jewish (i.e., first-century AD and the centuries immediately preceding it) and NT texts which interpret the OT from a broader perspective.[18] Nevertheless, even though the objectives and results of rabbinic exegeses differed from those of earlier Jewish and NT texts, the correspondence between the methods

14. Daube ("Rabbinic Methods," 244–45) states, "Hillel declared that Scripture itself included the tradition of the fathers . . . if read as, on the most up-to-date teaching of philosophical schools, a code of laws ought to be read."

15. An example of an acceptable exegetical method not included in the list is thematic association (or *heqesh*), which, as Instone-Brewer (*Techniques and Assumptions*, 18) observes, Hillel "assumed to illustrate the list although it was not named in it." Brooke (*Exegesis*, 13) indicates that Hillel's list was delimiting in that it enumerated methods "from already existing exegeses." He observes that even in combination with the later lists (of 13 and 32 rules) the methods specified "are far from representative of all the principles at work even in early rabbinic literature."

16. The Mishnah ('Abot 1:1) attributes the image of the fence to the "Great Synagogue" in the fifth century BC (cf. Ezra 3:1; Neh 8:1–12).

17. Such exegesis concentrated on *halakah*, which addressed "behavior and the regulation of conduct" (Longenecker, *Exegesis*, 10). Michael Fishbane (*Biblical Interpretation*, 281–82) characterizes halakhic exegesis as being "concerned with developing and expounding the law" (281) and "with making pre-existent laws applicable and viable in new contexts" (282).

18. This latter exegesis addressed *haggadah*, a corresponding and complementary term to *halakah*. Longenecker (*Exegesis*, 10) observes that *haggadah* "concerns the illustration of biblical texts and edification." Fishbane (*Biblical Interpretation*, 282) indicates that haggadic exegesis "is primarily concerned with utilizing the full range of the *traditum* [i.e., the content of a biblical tradition] for the sake of new theological insights, attitudes, and speculations."

employed is considerable. Similarly, although the fundamental presumptions and results of exegeses in Second Temple Jewish texts often diverge from those of the NT in significant ways, both corpora employ comparable (or identical) methods.[19]

Textual witnesses from the broader Hellenistic culture manifest interpretative methods present in ancient Jewish and NT texts, and address the underlying principles from which they proceed. Although the object of the interpretation for Jewish and NT authors is distinctive (i.e., the OT), many of the methods utilized were apparently of Greco-Roman origin. Hillel's list and the underlying principles manifested by exegeses attributed to him (performed in the contexts of teaching and debates) in the rabbinic literature attest to such origins. The evidence includes the basis for employing interpretative techniques to authoritative texts, the methods utilized, and their ordering.[20] The incorporation of Greco-Roman terminology and expressions into Hebrew also suggests such influence.[21] On the other hand, there is evidence that Jewish scholars sometimes incorporated distinctive

---

19. Regarding OT use in the NT, Manns ("Zacharie 12,10," 301-10) observes, "le Christ est le canon ultime d'interprétation des Ecritures" (302). Although Manns makes the observation specifically about John's use of the OT, it applies to other NT authors (cf. Luke 24:27; 2 Cor 3:12-16; 1 Pet 4:10-12; Heb 1:1-2). Brooke ("Biblical Interpretation," 60-73) speaks of the similarity in "the methods in the handling of scripture" among DSS and NT authors as well as the distinctive differences between them regarding "the purpose and resultant character of the scriptural interpretation" (72).

20. Daube ("Rabbinic Methods," 246-64) argues convincingly for the Hellenistic influence on Hillel and his exegetical methods by providing many examples in the abovementioned categories (and numerous others) of parallels in Greco-Roman texts. Examples include the recognition and juxtaposition of written and unwritten law (e.g., Plato, *Pol.* 295; Cicero, *Inv.* 1.13.17) and the authority of the latter, as well as particular rhetorical (or exegetical) methods and their ordering (e.g., Aristotle, *Rhet.* 2.23.4-5; Cicero, *Top.* 4.23).

21. Schürer (*History of the Jewish People*, 29-77) provides extensive evidence of the Hellenistic influence in both the non-Jewish (29-52) and Jewish (52-80) regions of Palestine. The evidence includes many Greek and Latin loan words in the Mishnah (53-77) and Greek loan words in "Aramaic papyri from Murabba'at and Naḥal Ḥever" (78) and the Hebrew Copper Scroll (3Q15) found at Qumran. The presence of Greek in various other papyri and inscriptions found in Palestine has "persuaded some scholars [to conclude] that bilingualism was widespread in Jewish Palestine in the first century A.D." (79). In his analysis of the use of Homer by four first-century Greco-Roman authors, Stanley (*Paul and Scripture*, 267-91) found significant methodological similarities with Paul's use of the OT.

features with their adoption of the methods.²² That the authors from the broader Greco-Roman culture utilized such interpretive methods establishes that the Gentile audiences of various NT authors would have been familiar with them. That Judaism "customized" features associated with the methods attests to their adaptability in application.

The presence of the type of exegetical methods enumerated in rabbinic literature in texts from the Second Temple era, which incorporate and (implicitly or explicitly) interpret OT passages (or other texts considered authoritative), attests to the acceptance of such practices in first-century Judaism and the broader Hellenistic culture. The next section will address particular exegetical methods either identified or utilized in rabbinic literature that are arguably operative in John 19:36–37.

EXEGETICAL METHODS RELEVANT TO JOHN 19:36-37

This section describes seven exegetical methods attested in Second Temple Jewish texts that are relevant to the current study of John 19:36–37. The first three serve as principles for associating (i.e., lexematic, thematic, lesser and greater) distinct OT texts.²³ They act as bases from which exegetical operations proceed.²⁴ The second three methods are operations performed on the OT texts (i.e., combining, conflating, and adjusting). The final method described, which does not fit neatly into either of the abovementioned categories, is the presumption of the original contexts of OT texts (by authors who cite them) to supply meaning to their new contexts.

As mentioned above, although these methods are among the exegetical principles and operations manifested in Second Temple and NT texts, the earliest extant classifications of (or references to) them occur in the

---

22. Daube ("Rabbinic Methods," 258) provides such an example with Hillel's use of "the words '*al pe*" (meaning "by mouth") for "oral Torah," rather than something equivalent to the Greek (ἄγραφοι) or Latin (*non scriptum*) expressions for "unwritten law." He goes on to observe that the Hebrew words in the transformed expression "frequently signify 'by heart,' 'from memory,'" and that "this meaning is certainly relevant" as it evokes numerous OT passages (cf., Exod 17:1; 38:21; Num 3:51; 9:23; Jos 22:9).

23. This section utilizes the term "method" in a general sense and further distinguishes between the methods addressed (identifying three as principles, three as operations, and one as possessing the attributes of both) to recognize their distinctiveness and complementarity.

24. Menken ("John 7:38," 173) uses the term "exegetical operations" to describe *actions* Philo performs on OT texts that he incorporates in particular works based on another one of Hillel's middoth (i.e., one not discussed in this study).

rabbinic literature. Even though application of rabbinic classifications to Second Temple and NT texts is anachronistic, since there is no evidence that such classifications existed for the authors who employed them, the discussion that follows employs them for the utility that they provide for analyzing such texts.[25] There is no evidence of any attempt to classify or delimit exegetical practices employed by authors in the Second Temple era and it is not unusual to find multiple methods concurrently active in a given text. The examples presented in the following section will demonstrate the application of the individual methods as well as the presence (and interaction) of multiple methods in particular texts.

Exegetical Principles for Associating OT Texts

Lexematic Association

Lexematic association links two texts based on common vocabulary (i.e., lexemes). This association implicitly (or explicitly) serves as the basis for using information from one OT text to interpret another or for employing them in a complementary manner to gain insight into meaning of both texts and the reality to which they relate (e.g., an aspect of salvation history foretold or prefigured in the OT and fulfilled in Christ). The rabbinic literature refers to this practice as *gezerah shavah*.[26] A practical translation of the somewhat ambiguous Hebrew expression is "a comparison with the equal."[27] In the strict sense, rabbinic exegesis utilized *gezerah shavah* to clarify or define a term or expression in one OT passage based on its meaning in

---

25. As Instone-Brewer (*Techniques and Assumptions*, 23) observes, "it is unlikely that any of these exegetical modes or techniques were defined or categorized before 70 CE, so the analysis of the exegeses in these terms is anachronistic. However, analysis must always use categorisation and comparison, and in the absence of categories defined by the scribes themselves, categories must be imposed on them."

26. Scholars sometimes use the Hebrew terms *gezerah shavah*, *heqesh*, and *qal vahomer* to denote these first three methods (or principles) for associating texts. For consistency, this study utilizes Instone-Brewer's (*Techniques and Assumptions*, 17–18) transliterations of these terms except where they appear in citations.

27. Lieberman (*Hellenism in Jewish Palestine*, 59) deduces this meaning from the Hebrew in light of a corresponding expression employed in contemporary Greek rhetoric. Although the noun *gezerah* is rabbinic, the semantic range of its verbal root (גזר) includes "decide, decree" (*DCH* 2:341) and the basic meaning of the verb *shavah* is "be equivalent" (8:299).

another passage.²⁸ Such exegesis supported the construction (or the fortification) of the fence around Torah observance (with the oral law) by applying the method to gain insight to guide ethical, cultic, and ritual behavior (i.e., the halakhic exegesis mentioned above). The more general expression of lexematic association used here refers to the same basis of associating OT texts, but with the objective of gaining insight into their meaning (i.e., haggadic exegesis).²⁹ Since this broader objective corresponds with the interest of the present study, the balance of this chapter will address such use and refer to it as lexematic association.³⁰

Thematic Association

Thematic association implicitly (or explicitly) connects OT texts without relying on lexematic overlap. This principle of association, however, is similar to and may occur along with lexematic association in practice. That the distinction employed here for the purpose of analysis may not have been operative for ancient Jewish and NT authors is plausible since the rabbinic exegetical lists do not distinguish between them as they do not even enumerate thematic association (or *heqesh*) as an exegetical method. Although his list does not explicitly mention *heqesh*, the Tosefta, which contains the earliest record of Hillel's list (Sanh. 7:11), attests to its validity as an exegetical method by providing an account of Hillel employing it in arguing that the celebration of Passover overrides Sabbath observance (Pesah.. 4:13).³¹ That textual witnesses from subsequent rabbinic midrashim and

---

28. Bakhos ("Midrash," 944–49) observes that *gezerah shavah* is "an inference from similarity of words or expressions" (945). Lieberman (*Hellenism in Jewish Palestine*, 61) indicates, *gezerah shavah* "applied . . . to identity of words (i.e., verbal congruities in the text)."

29. Avemarie ("Interpreting Scripture," 86–102), who utilizes this expression, states, "lexematic association can serve a variety of purposes" including, "accumulative enhancement of scriptural evidence . . . [and] exploration of implicit meaning by inference from a related biblical verse" (102).

30. Avemarie ("Interpreting Scripture," 86) observes, "the rabbinic use of *gezerah shavah* was essentially limited to halakhic exegesis whereas Qumran and Pauline texts . . . deal, rabbinically speaking, with haggadic matters." His observation on the Qumran and Pauline texts applies to John's Gospel as well.

31. Instone-Brewer (*Techniques and Assumptions*, 18–49) indicates, "when Hillel's list of middoth was made, the rule of Heqesh was assumed to illustrate the list" (18). He also suggests that there was originally no distinction made between the methods and that "it is therefore likely that the rule of Heqesh was originally another name for Gezerah Shavah"

earlier Hellenistic literature define thematic association by contrasting it with lexematic association attest to the recognition of an inherent relationship and complementarity between these methods among ancient authors.[32] Whereas the overlap of vocabulary is the basis for relating distinct OT passages with lexematic association, similarity in subject matter is the primary operating principle for establishing an analogy with thematic association. In light of the recognition of their similarity and complementarity among ancient authors, that both types of association would be operative in a given passage is understandable.

Lesser and Greater Association

This frequently used exegetical principle, referred to as *qal vahomer*, associates lesser or greater matters.[33] It is the first principle in Hillel's list as well as in lists of Greco-Roman rhetoricians beginning with Aristotle (*Rhet.* 2.23.4).[34] The rabbinic expression *qal vahomer* ("light and heavy") only indicates a relationship without specifying the procession from one type of truth to another. Such associations in the Judeo-Christian tradition

---

(18). The greater likelihood of abuse of a method without any textual basis, however, may explain why it does not appear in the rabbinic lists, since they evidently sought to delimit the exegetical practices used in the Second Temple period by enumerating only those considered valid for *halakhic* exegesis. Instone-Brewer observes that even *gezerah shavah*, which establishes a textual basis, "had to be supported by another method or by a received tradition" (49) to guard against its misuse.

32. Lieberman (*Hellenism in Jewish Palestine*, 61) refers to a phrase employed frequently for thematic association (סופנה להקיש ולדון ססנו גזירה שוה)in the midrash of the School of Rabbi Ishmael (mid-first through the mid-second century AD) that speaks of the word being "vacant [for the purpose] of juxtaposing (=παρατιθέναι) it and deducing a *gezarah shawah* (=σύγκρισις) from it" (bracketed and parenthetical text original). Lieberman indicates that the Greek historian Polybius (second century BC) "expresses himself in similar style" (61) by employing cognates of these terms together in comparable fashion (*Histories* 3.32.5; 16.29.5).

33. Bakhos ("Midrash," 945) indicates *qal vahomer* is "one of the most common principles" and Louis Jacobs ("Qal Va-Ḥomer," 226) observes, "its use is not limited to any single phase in Israel's history but, it would appear, was employed in all periods." He provides numerous examples of *qal vahomer* from the HB as well as some from the LXX and NT.

34. With regard to the order of these methods in Hillel's list, Daube ("Rabbinic Methods," 252) states "one could imagine the reverse order. But it is interesting that, right from Aristotle, wherever in rhetorical literature the methods of interpretation are set forth in tabulated form, this is the order we find."

proceed either from matters of lesser to greater importance (e.g., Exod 6:12; Matt 12:10-12) or in the reverse direction (e.g., 1 Kgs 8:27).[35] The argumentation based on this principle of association follows the form, at least implicitly, that "if A is true, then (how much more that) B must also be true."

Exegetical Operations for Associating OT Texts

Combining OT Texts

Ancient Jewish and NT authors sometimes combined two or more OT texts when incorporating them into their works. Similarly, writers in the broader Greco-Roman culture commonly employed this practice. The characteristic utilized in the present study to distinguish this exegetical operation from conflation (below) is that the author divides the citations in some manner.[36] In some cases, the divisions between the OT texts consist of longer, formulaic introductions (e.g., Rom 10:19-21) and in other instances, the ancient writers use simple connectives.[37] Although combined citations often manifest particular exegetical principles for relating discrete texts (e.g., lexematic, lesser or greater association), the basis for connecting the texts is not always readily apparent. In such cases, the ancient writer's act of associating distinct OT passages by combining them in an independent work is an act of interpretation and implies, at a minimum, a common theme between them (i.e., thematic association).

---

35. Bakhos ("Midrash," 945) defines this method as "an argument from the lesser to the greater, or vice versa," while Instone-Brewer (*Techniques and Assumptions*, 226) correspondingly describes it as an "argument from major to minor and vice versa."

36. This definition generally concurs with Instone-Brewer's (*Techniques and Assumptions*, 22-23) description of "chain quotations" in which he indicates, "several texts are cited one after another and they are divided by no more than a simple 'and' . . . but this is sufficient to show that more than one passage is being used." Stanley (*Paul and Scripture*, 258-59) employs a broader definition for combined texts. He includes verses melded together in such a way that "an uninformed reader would have no way of knowing that the resulting 'quotation' did not come from a single biblical context" (259) as long as "the individual verses stand on a relatively equal footing and retain a measure of their original independence" (259n27). The definition employed in this study eliminates the subjectivity inherent with Stanley's definition.

37. Stanley (*Paul and Scripture*, 273) indicates that both Paul and the Greco-Roman authors that he examined employ "more or less formulaic expressions" and that "linking back-to-back citations by καί ['and'], καὶ πάλιν ['and again'], or some similar connective short phrase is also a common practice."

Conflating OT Texts

Conflation is another operation used by the ancient authors to incorporate OT texts into their works. Whereas the exegetical operation of combining texts involves demarcating a division between distinct OT passages, this study distinguishes the complementary process of conflating texts by the absence of any explicit indication of the presence of multiple passages.[38] There are two basic ways that ancient authors employed this method. Simple conflation abuts one OT passage with another without any apparent modification of the source texts (e.g., Rom 3:13).[39] A second type of conflation modifies the OT texts in the process of adjoining them (e.g., 11:8).[40] This latter type incorporates the additional exegetical operation of adjusting OT source texts (described below). Similar to combining citations, since conflation is an act of interpretation performed on the OT passages utilized, it implies a common theme between the conflated texts (i.e., thematic association) unless it manifests another basis for associating them.

---

38. Instone-Brewer (*Techniques and Assumptions*, 22) uses the term amalgamation for this exegetical operation. He describes it as "the construction of a 'text' by joining two texts, without any indication that more than one text has been used." Stanley (*Paul and Scripture*, 258–59) defines conflation in a more restrictive manner. He characterizes melded texts as a conflation if "one verse [from the OT] is clearly dominant and the other subordinate" (259n27). Otherwise he classifies such a merging of texts as a combination.

39. Stanley (*Paul and Scripture*, 252–53n2) classifies Rom 3:10–18 as a combined (versus a conflated) citation that "contains six distinct biblical verses." The conjunction καί appears three times in the passage, but it is not clear that any of these instances connect distinct OT verses. Therefore, the entire passage is a conflation based on the guidelines employed in this study. Although Paul adjusts most of the OT texts that he incorporates in this passage, he simply abuts two of them (LXX Pss 5:10, 139:4) in Rom 3:13 without adjusting either text.

40. The characterization of such modifications is speculative since variation can also be due to other factors (e.g., variants from textual transmission or memory variants introduced by an author's recollection) in the absence of additional evidence. Paul's conflation of a phrase from Isa 29:10 in the midst of content taken from Deut 29:3 in Rom 11:8 provides such evidence. The apparent adjustment made to Deut 29:3 in the conflation attributes a more active role to God (by inducing a stupor, rather than simply not granting understanding) in Israel's failure to comprehend his actions. That the modification lends stronger OT support to Paul's argument that the current failure of many in Israel to believe in the Gospel (9:1–11:36) is in accord with God's plan of salvation attests to the likelihood that it was intentional.

Adjusting OT Texts

This method refers to the intentional alteration of OT texts by ancient authors when they incorporate them into their works. Textual witnesses indicate that this was a fairly common and accepted practice.[41] Examples of adjustments include altering the grammar of terms present in the source texts as well as substituting words or phrases into the OT passages.[42] The previous section recognized that ancient authors sometimes made modifications in the process of conflating OT texts when incorporating them into their works. That such modification involved adjusting texts reflects that this operation overlaps with conflation and is often operative along with it and other exegetical operations.[43] The new context and perceptible authorial intent often provide reasonable explanations for textual adjustments. Such explanations include eliminating or replacing content in the OT texts that is problematic or irrelevant for the current context, modifying the word order of original texts for clarity or emphasis, and modifying the grammar of the source texts to agree with their new context.[44]

---

41. In his comprehensive study of Paul's use of the OT, Stanley (*Paul and Scripture*, 259–64) employed "clear and relatively strict criteria for determining the origins of each reading," and identified "112 different readings (in fifty separate verses) where it can be affirmed with reasonable confidence that Paul has indeed adapted the wording of the biblical text" (259). He insightfully observes, "Paul takes no pains to conceal from his audience the fact that he has incorporated interpretive elements into the wording of his quotations," and that "had such a practice been unique to Paul, or even to the early Christian community, one would expect to see more circumspection in the use of the technique" (264).

42. Stanley (*Paul and Scripture*, 260–343) identifies distinct categories of Pauline adaptations, for example, that he broadly classifies as grammatical. These include adjustments made to the word order, changes in grammar (e.g., person, number, case . . .), omissions, additions, substitutions, and limited selection. He identifies numerous examples of Pauline texts for each of these categories (260–61). Stanley also indicates, "adjusting the grammar of the source text (person, number, case, tense, mood, etc.) to suit the new context is another technique that appears widely throughout the [early Jewish and Greco-Roman] literature" (343).

43. Stanley (*Paul and Scripture*, 260–61) treats "the inevitable substitutions that characterize so-called 'conflated texts'" (261n37) separately from substitutions not associated with that exegetical method. See 89n40 for an example of textual adjustment occurring with conflation.

44. In Stanley's (*Paul and Scripture*, 267–360) comparative studies of writings in early Judaism (292–337) and Greco-Roman literature (267–91) he generally found practices comparable to those employed by Paul for adjusting source texts. He observes, for example, "the most common technique for virtually every author is simply to omit words, phrases, or even whole clauses deemed irrelevant to the author's purpose in adducing

ANCIENT EXEGETICAL METHODS RELEVANT TO JOHN 19:36–37

Presumption of the Original Context as an Exegetical Method

The final exegetical method specified in Hillel's list is an ancient author's implicit use of an OT text's original context to supply meaning to its new context.⁴⁵ Whereas the previous methods enumerated in this section fell under the general classifications of principles or operations, the current exegetical method manifests characteristics of both categories. It is similar to a principle in that it serves as a basis from which exegetical operations can proceed and a resource from which author-exegetes can implicitly draw. It is like an exegetical operation in supplying meaning to the reader when the author presumes upon the audience to draw from the original OT context of a passage for relevant information not explicitly provided with its incorporation into its new context.⁴⁶ In this sense, this method is somewhat unique with the ancient authors manifesting its presence (i.e., their presumption of the original context) by choosing to refrain from providing elements of the context of a cited OT text(s) that are valuable (or even necessary) for advancing their argument or improving its cogency by filling in apparent gaps.⁴⁷ Conversely, texts that explicitly supply the meaning for a cited OT passage (i.e., when authors leave no "gaps" for their audience to fill) imply that this method is *not* operative.⁴⁸

---

the citation" (343). He also indicates, "by far the most common motive for adapting the wording of a quotation is to insure that it communicates the precise point that the author wanted to make in adducing the text" (347).

45. Instone-Brewer (*Techniques and Assumptions*, 226) translates the final method as "meaning is learned from the context" (דבר הלד מעניינו) and indicates, "the meaning may be deduced from nearby texts."

46. Dodd (*According to the Scriptures*, 126) observes that NT authors sometimes quoted particular OT passages "as pointers to the whole context ... [and that] in the fundamental passages it is the *total context* that is in view, and is the basis of the argument" (emphasis original). The authors fostered the active engagement of their audiences by employing this method.

47. Paul provides an extended example of this in Galatians (3:6—4:31) in which he incorporates numerous OT texts from much of the biblical narrative about Abraham (spanning Gen 12:7—21:10) and draws upon the context of the OT narrative without providing it. The qualification of this characteristic as *somewhat* unique recognizes that authors also imply thematic association as the primary basis for connecting distinct OT passages in their work by *not* supplying other bases (e.g., lexematic or lesser and greater association) for relating the texts. In other words, they manifest both of these methods by what they do *not* provide.

48. That Paul explicitly indicates the meaning he intends the audience to perceive for each of the two OT texts cited in Rom 10:6, 8 (directly after each citation) implies that he does not presume upon his audience to utilize the original context.

EXAMPLES OF APPLICATIONS OF THE METHODS RELEVANT TO JOHN 19:36-37

This section will provide examples from ancient texts to illustrate the exegetical methods described above.[49] Each of the following subsections will also demonstrate how multiple methods interact within a text.

Combining OT Texts, Thematic Association, Presumption of Original Context

The DSS text 4QFlorilegium (4Q174) combines and interprets multiple OT passages in foretelling the future for the author's community, referred to as the House of Judah. The author combines 2 Sam 7:10-11a and Exod 15:17-18 based on the common theme of God building a temple for his people. That the passages cited contain different terms for temple ("sanctuary" in Exod 15:17-18 and "house" in 2 Sam 7:11) indicate that the author combined the texts based on thematic association.[50] That the portion of 2 Sam 7:11 initially cited does not contain the text in which Yhwh states that he will build a house for David suggests that the DSS author presumes that the audience is familiar with its original context.[51] In particular, the text relies on the audience to recall Yhwh's response to David's desire to build a physical temple to honor him (7:1-7) by promising to build an eternal kingdom (i.e., an eschatological temple) through David's offspring

---

49. Each subsection will provide a detailed example of the application of the particular methods listed in the respective headings from a DSS text along with a reference to a similar use in an ancient Jewish or NT text. Jassen (*Scripture and Law*, 18) provides insight into the value of utilizing DSS texts to illustrate these methods that became more prevalent in the Second Temple period when he observes, "the Dead Sea Scrolls are the most significant body of texts available to scholars to illuminate the transition from the sacred writings of ancient Israel to the emergence of new forms of Judaism deeply indebted to these ancient and authoritative writings."

50. Lexematic association may also be operative based on the word "plant" (נטע) found in both (biblical) passages.

51. The author subsequently quotes the portion of 7:11 (4Q174 I, 10) in which the term for house appears. Nevertheless, the evidence suggests the presumption of the original context at the point of the combination as well as with the active interplay between the establishment of the physical house (i.e., the temple; Exod 15:17-18) and the kingdom (2 Sam 7:11) that is central to both 2 Samuel 7 and the DSS author's use of the OT texts employed.

(7:11b–17). The DSS author connects the OT citations with an interpretive comment about the "house" to be established (4Q174 I, 2b–3a):

> ..."[I appointed judges] over my people Israel" [2 Sam 7:11]. This is the house which [he shall establish] for [him] in the last days as it is written in the book of [Moses]: "[The sanctuary] Yhwh, your hands established. Yhwh shall reign forever and ever" [Exod 15:17–18] ... (4Q174 I, 2–3)[52]

In *Alleg. Interp.* 3.4, Philo provides a similar example of combining OT texts. He connects Exod 17:6 to Deut 4:39, associated thematically, with an intervening introduction of the second text.

Simple Conflation of OT Texts, Lexematic Association

The Damascus Document provides an example of simple conflation along with lexematic association in CD-B XX, 21–22a. The author connects Exod 20:6b and Deut 7:9 as part of a moral exhortation to persevere in covenant faithfulness. The DSS text of the conflated OT passages is essentially the same as the MT. Lexemes that convey God's covenant faithfulness (חסד) and the appropriate responses from his people (of loving and being devoted to him) associate the two short texts and provide a substantial lexematic basis for connecting them.[53] The author simply abuts the text of Deut 7:9 to Exod 20:6b without providing any conjoining term(s) and does not modify the source texts in placing them into their new context. That the one term missing from the MT version of the OT passages in CD XX, 21 corresponds with a prevailing theme of the overall document suggests that the DSS

---

52. This translation and the other DSS translations in this section utilize the transcribed Hebrew text of Martínez and Tigchelaar, *Dead Sea Scrolls*, unless otherwise noted. Bracketed words or segments, missing (or uncertain) in the textual witnesses, translate terms postulated in the transcriptions. The Hebrew texts of the citations in 4Q174 I, 2–3 are substantially the same as the MT. Furthermore, the differences that exist between them provide no indication that the author employed the exegetical method of adjusting the OT texts to fit them into their new context or to serve a particular purpose of the author.

53. Both texts also contain the lexemes for "thousand" and "commandment" (not reflected in CD 20:21) so that Exod 20:6b shares five of its six independent terms with Deut 7:9.

author did not intentionally exclude it from the text.[54] The text of CD-B XX, 21–22a states:

> He keeps faithfulness [with thousands] for those who love him and for those who are devoted to him for a thousand generations.[55]

Paul provides an example of a simple conflation in Rom 3:13 when he connects Ps 5:10 and LXX Ps 139:4 (MT 140:4) with no indication of the end of the first text and the beginning of the second. The lexematic association is "their tongues." In both OT passages, the psalmist uses these terms to describe dishonest people.

Conflation of OT Texts, Lexematic Association, Adjusting OT Texts[56]

The Damascus Document also provides an example of the second type of conflation mentioned above, in which the author substantially modifies the OT texts in the process of conflating them. In CD-A VIII, 14–15, the DSS author melds Deut 9:5 with 7:8 to emphasize God's covenant faithfulness to the patriarchs. The verb for swearing an oath provides the lexematic basis for associating the OT texts. The citation merges the passages and leaves behind aspects of each text that the author apparently considers irrelevant or inappropriate for the purpose at hand. The quotation omits the reference to the wickedness of the nations as a cause for Israel's dispossessing them (Deut 9:5) and transforms God's love for the people (7:8) into his love

---

54. Although a term ("thousands") is *potentially* missing from Exod 20:6b, the transcribers postulate that it was originally present in CD-B XX, 21. The term for "commandment" *is* missing from Deut 7:9. Cook's ("Damascus Document (CD)," 49–78) observation that, "obeying the rules of God" is one of the "broad themes" of the *Damascus Document* indicates that the term "commandment(s)" concurs with the author's purpose (i.e., there is no basis to suggest an intentional modification; 49). Additionally, that the pronominal suffix on the participle in the DSS in lieu of the term "commandment" (in the MT tradition) presents a corresponding and complete thought suggests a different reading in the author's source text rather than a variant introduced due to an oversight.

55. The text translated here as "for those who are devoted to him" is more literally "for those who keep him." *HALOT* (1584a) indicates that the verb (שׁמר) also conveys, "to hold on to, devote oneself to" (cf. Hos 4:10; Ps 31:7; Prov 27:18; 1 Chr 12:30).

56. That ancient authors commonly adjusted OT texts when conflating them is not surprising given the practical consideration of harmonizing previously distinct texts now connected in a new context and that such adjustment was apparently an accepted practice in the ancient world (see 90n41).

for their fathers (CD-A VIII, 14–15). It seems that the author changes the phrase "Yhwh loves you" (Deut 7:8) in order to connect God's love with the faithfulness of their forefathers, establishing them as a model, and exhorting the audience to imitate them a short time later (CD-A VIII, 16b–18a). The conflated and adjusted text of VIII, 14–15 reads:

> But as Moses said: "It is not for your righteousness or uprightness of heart that you are going to dispossess these nations, but because he loved your fathers and he has kept his oath."

A passage in the Letter of Aristeas (§155) similarly melds two verses of Deuteronomy (7:18; 10:21) associated thematically by the wonders the Lord worked for Israel and lexematically by the verb employed (with God as the subject in both verses). Aristeas provides enough material to identify each of the source texts while displaying substantial freedom in conflating them and removing irrelevant material.[57]

Lesser and Greater, Thematic Association, Presumption of the Original Context

The author of 11QMelchizedek (11Q13) implicitly utilizes a lesser and greater association to supplement a text that addresses the Jubilee year (Lev 25:13) by juxtaposing it with a corresponding text that pertains to the Sabbatical year (Deut 15:2).[58] The juxtaposition associates the two texts based on the theme of special years occurring at specified intervals.[59] Whereas Leviticus specifies the manumission of Hebrew bonded servants (Lev 25:13, 39–55) and the return of ancestral property (25:13–31) in the Jubilee

---

57. Aristeas transformed the finite verb held in common by both texts into a genitive absolute. That he removes reference "to Pharaoh and all of Egypt" (7:18) unnecessarily avoids distracting his audience from his purpose of defending the Jewish law in this section of the letter. Regarding Aristeas's purpose in this section of his letter, Charles (*Pseudepigrapha*, 2:84–85) indicates, "the vindication of the purpose and function of the Jewish law forms the theme of one of the most important sections . . . (§§ 128–71)."

58. Bartos and Levinson ("Exegesis in 11QMelchizedek," 351–71) indicate, "the author of the Melchizedek scroll most likely used the Jubilee text of Leviticus (25:8–13) as the primary source, which he explicitly interpreted as eschatological, by way of supporting and secondary citations. We suggest that he also used the secondary citation of Deut 15:2 as an implicit legal interpretation" (357).

59. The Jubilee occurs every fifty years (25:8–55) and a Sabbatical year every seventh year (Deut 15:1–18). Although both passages cited contain the term for "years," it is the theme (i.e., of special years designated based on intervals of time) that associates them.

year, Deuteronomy stipulates the remission of *all* debts of fellow Israelites (15:1-3) as well as the release of Hebrew bonded servants (15:12) in the Sabbatical year.[60] The author of 11Q13 effectively "completes" Lev 25:13 (11Q13 II, 2a) by combining it with Deut 15:2 (11Q13 II, 2b-3), which provides the debt remission procedure for the Sabbatical year, and establishes that the remission of *all* debts (שמטה; II, 3) applies to the Jubilee year.[61] He accomplishes this with the implicit lesser and greater association established by the parallelism between the texts and a subsequent authorial interpretation (II, 4-6).[62] That the Jubilee year includes the remission of the *greater* debts incurred by impoverishment (i.e., of becoming a bonded servant due to insuperable debt), the DSS author effectively infers that the remission of all of the *lesser* debts required in the Sabbatical year would (certainly) also apply.[63] That the reader must rely on the contexts of the original texts to understand the argument in 11Q13 II, 2-6 implies their presumption by the author. The section of 11Q13 manifesting the lesser and greater association states:

> [...] And concerning what Scripture says: "In [this] year of jubilee [you shall return, every one of you, to your property" (Lev 25:13) and what is also written, "And this] is the [ma]nner of [the remission:] every creditor shall remit the claim that is held [against

---

60. Leviticus specifies that persons return to their ancestral land (25:13) from which they have separated themselves due to becoming impoverished (cf. 25:25, 35, 39). Whether they sell ownership of the land or themselves, a Jubilee year requires rectification of the situation by restoration of the inherited land to its original owner. The remission of debts occurs at the end of the seventh year (Deut 15:1-3) and the release of bonded servants in the seventh year (15:12). Although Leviticus 25 uses the term "your brother" rather than "Hebrew," both Leviticus 25 and Deuteronomy 15 are referring to the same reality (i.e., Hebrew bonded servants).

61. *HALOT* (4:1558) indicates that the term שמט, used only in Deuteronomy (15:1, 2, 9; 31:10) in the HB in reference to the Sabbatical "remission of debt," corresponds to a more general debt forgiveness than conveyed in Leviticus 25. The semantic range of the corresponding Jewish Aramaic and Akkadian terms encompass "remission of commercial debts, remission of private slaves, freeing security deposits."

62. The DSS author spiritualizes the remission in the Last Days (II, 4) to the forgiveness of *all* their sins by Melchizedek (II, 5-6).

63. Bartos and Levinson ("Exegesis in 11QMelchizedek," 365-69) indicate that two Tannaitic midrash commentaries (*Sipre Deuteronomy* and *Sipra Leviticus*) acknowledge the potential lesser and greater association between Lev 25:13 and Deut 15:2, but reject it by presuming that the texts "refer to two different legal situations" (369). Jacobs and Derovan ("Hermeneutics," 9:25-29) use the term "certainly" in their model for the complex *qal vahomer* method (25-26).

a neighbor, not exacting it of a neighbor who is a member of the community, because God's] remission [has been proclaimed" (Deut 15:2)] (II, 2–3)[64]

The Gospels provide examples of Jesus using lesser and greater associations, explicitly in Matthew (12:10–12) and implicitly in Luke (13:15–16; 14:5–6), to demonstrate the appropriateness of healing on the Sabbath.[65] Requirements in the Pentateuch to assist a neighbor's animal in distress (Exod 23:5; Deut 22:4) serve as the basis. If the Jewish authorities, who took issue with the healings, would assist *their own* distressed *animal* on the Sabbath (Matt 12:10), how much more appropriate that Jesus would assist a distressed *neighbor* on the Sabbath.[66]

POTENTIAL EVIDENCE OF THESE EXEGETICAL METHODS IN JOHN 19:36-37

The content and features of John 19:36–37 suggests that the evangelist employed at least some, and possibly all, of the particular exegetical methods enumerated and illustrated in the two preceding sections of this chapter.[67] The passage occurs after the evangelist recounts the events following Jesus' death in which the soldiers decide to forego their implied orders to break his legs (John 19:31–33) and to pierce his side instead; upon which

---

64. The translation is from Wise ("Coming of Melchizedek," 591–92). Although most of the text of Lev 25:13 is missing (i.e., the bracketed portion) and the extant terms in the manuscript are identical with another passage (27:24), Martínez, Tigchelaar, and Woude, (DJD 23, 230) indicate that the citation of Lev 25:13 "is certain." They base this conclusion on their observations that "not only is Lev 27:24 too long, but the column repeatedly refers to Leviticus 25."

65. Jesus explicitly makes the association in Matt 12:12 (i.e., "how much more...") and implies it in Luke 13:15–16 and 14:5. Jacobs ("Qal Va-Ḥomer," 223) indicates that an implicit lesser and greater association "does not state the *qal va-ḥomer* argument explicitly but invites us to draw the *qal va-ḥomer* from the premise that is stated in the verse."

66. That they would assist their own animals on the Sabbath implies that the obligation to assist a *distressed animal* of a neighbor (Exod 23:5; Deut 22:4) applies to the Sabbath. Therefore, how much more appropriate that Jesus would assist a *distressed neighbor* on the Sabbath. In Luke 13:15–16, Jesus mentions provision of normal care for their animals on the Sabbath and in 14:5–6 he refers to a son or an animal in distress. Jacobs and Derovan ("Hermeneutics," 9:25) would categorize this as a complex *qal vahomer* since "an extraneous element has to be adduced."

67. The following chapter will perform a detailed exegesis of the verses. This section only addresses potential evidence of the presence of particular exegetical methods.

blood and water poured forth (19:34) according to eyewitness testimony (19:35). Immediately after this narrative, the evangelist recognizes the fulfillment of Scripture in stating: "for these things happened in order that the scripture might be fulfilled: '*a bone of him shall not be broken* [ὀστοῦν οὐ συντριβήσεται αὐτοῦ].' And again another scripture says: '*they shall look to whom they pierced* [ὄψονται εἰς ὃν ἐξεκέντησαν]'" (19:36–37).

The content and form of the citation in 19:36 suggests that John conflates as many as four different OT passages (LXX Exod 12:10; Exod 12:46; Num 9:12; Ps 34:21 [LXX 33:21]).[68] Each of these texts contain all of the lexemes present in John 19:36. The passages from the Pentateuch, which pertain to the prohibition against breaking any of the bones of the paschal lamb, correspond with the form of the noun and the order of the terms. LXX Psalm 33:21, referring to Yhwh's protective care of the righteous, matches the form of the verb, which occurs just eleven times in the OT and only once with the term for "bone" (ὀστοῦν).[69] The evidence implies that John conflated the Pentateuchal passages with the psalm and adjusted the texts when conflating them in a way that the contribution of each of the contributing parts of the OT remains discernible.

The conflation indicates that John recognized the ultimate fulfillment of the paschal prohibition, as it pertained to *the* Lamb of God (cf. John 1:29, 36), in the soldiers' decision to refrain from breaking Jesus' legs, as well as the fulfillment of God's promised care for *the* Righteous One. Given that the LXX speaks of "the righteous ones" (Ps 33:20), John's recognition of the fulfillment of 33:21 in Jesus' passion suggests a lesser and greater association. In other words, if God provides such care for all righteous persons, how much more so for *the* Righteous One (John 18:38; 19:4, 6) whom he has chosen (1:34) and sent (10:36; 17:3).[70] That the Gospel earlier alludes to Jesus as the Lamb of God (1:29) and God's Chosen One (1:34) identifies him as the true Passover Lamb and the Suffering Servant (Isa 42:1).[71] The

---

68. Menken ("Jn 19,36," 2102–6) provides a convincing argument for this position. See also Schuchard, *Scripture*, 133–40; Bynum, *John 19:37*, 120–24.

69. The verb form in the LXX Ps 33:21 and John 19:36 is the third-person singular future passive of συντρίβω whereas all of the Pentateuch passages contain plural active forms.

70. In a complementary manner, the MT speaks of "the Righteous One" with a singular adjective used substantively. See 55n63 for the basis of reading 1:34 as "the Chosen One of God."

71. See 55–56nn62–63 and 63n87 regarding the Gospel's recognition of Jesus as the Suffering Servant.

reference to the Suffering Servant as "the Righteous One" in Isaiah (53:11; cf. 53:9) provides vital insight into the source texts of John 19:36, their conflation, and its features. Collectively, they establish that the preceding events confirm and complement the verbal testimony provided by John the Baptist with Jesus' first appearance in the Gospel (1:29) that identified him explicitly as "the Lamb of God" and implicitly as the Suffering Servant.[72] The elucidation provided by the original contexts of the source texts (and the broader context of the OT) attests to John's use of this exegetical method (i.e., presumption of the original context) in 19:36-37.

The passage cited in John 19:37 is Zech 12:10. Although the citation arguably differs from both the MT and the LXX, its content is much closer to the MT.[73] The *Vorlage* of the MT enables John to recognize the fulfillment of the prophecy with the soldier's decision to pierce Jesus' side. John's use of the verb ὁράω ("look"), which he utilizes frequently throughout the Gospel, suggests that he either selected this verb in translating the Hebrew text or intentionally adjusted a Greek source text.[74] Finally, the pointing in the MT, which denotes the first-person pronominal suffix attached to the preposition, indicates that "they will look to *me*, whom they pierced" (Zech 12:10), suggesting that John modified the text by omitting this pronoun. Given that the pointing in the MT is a much later addition and the consonantal text corresponds with a form of the preposition alone in the Book

---

72. As discussed in chapter 3, John's use of ἀμνός in 1:29 (and 1:36) for "lamb" rather than the LXX's term for the Passover victim (πρόβατον) along with the reference to taking away sins implicitly identified Jesus with the Suffering Servant. The two terms for "lamb" occur in parallel in Isa 53:7 in referring to God's servant, the righteous one, who will justify many by taking away their sins (52:13—53:12).

73. Whereas the MT verb corresponds to John 19:37 with the meaning "to pierce," the LXX conveys the meaning "to dance in triumph." A plausible explanation for the significant difference in verbs between the versions is that the pointing of the text in the MT suggests that Yhwh is the object of the piercing. Dines ("Minor Prophets," 438-55) indicates that although it is inconsistent in the prophets, the LXX tends to eliminate anthropomorphisms of Yhwh (447). Whereas Menken ("John 19:37," 494-511) argues that John used "an independent Greek translation of the Hebrew" (504), Bynum (*John 19:37*, 171-73) concludes that he made recourse to both the Greek and Hebrew texts of his time in this and other passages.

74. The verb נבט utilized in the Hifil in Zech 12:10 is rather common in the MT with more than sixty occurrences. Although the LXX translates it with ὁράω in three instances (Num 12:18; Job 6:19; Isa 38:11), it uses ἐπιβλέπω more than twenty times, including Zech 12:10. Menken ("John 19:37," 502) contends that the reason for ὁράω in John 19:37 is "because it was already in use in connection with the *parousia*" (i.e., it was an intentional modification of the source text).

of Job (3:22; 5:26; 15:22; 29:29), however, the OT provides a textual basis for positing an independent translation of the Hebrew text and agreement between the citation and the source text on this issue.[75]

John combines the citations in 19:36 and 19:37 with the commonly used connective phrase "and again" (καὶ πάλιν). The combination conveys thematic correspondence between the respective OT passages. The theme that unites them is Jesus, whom the Gospel identifies as the Lamb of God (1:29; 36), the Suffering Servant (1:29, 32–34), and the Messiah (1:41; 4:25–26). John's presumption of the original context of the OT passages utilized, in light of the overall context of the Gospel, also affirms Jesus' identity as the new Temple and the culmination of true worship.[76]

SUMMARY

This chapter addressed exegetical methods shared by ancient Jewish and NT authors to provide insight into John's use of the OT in 19:36–37. The first section covered the general exegetical methods utilized by Second Temple authors and underlying principles associated with them. The three subsequent sections focused on particular exegetical methods relevant to John 19:36–37.

The first of these sections began by establishing the value of employing the rabbinic lists that enumerate exegetical methods utilized in the Second Temple period for analyzing texts from that era. It went on to identify seven exegetical methods (divided into three different categories) of interest to the present study and provided a brief description of each of them. It also indicated that the methods were both distinct and complementary to one another. The subsequent section illustrated them by providing examples of their application in Second Temple texts. At the same time, in identifying the presence of multiple methods in each example, it demonstrated their complementarity. The final section provided potential evidence of the presence of each of the seven methods in John 19:36–37. The next chapter will utilize this information in light of John's presumed contexts (addressed

---

75. With the occurrences being limited to the Book of Job, *HALOT*'s (1:50) classification of it as a "by-form" of the preposition might be a stretch. Nevertheless, the OT provides a textual basis for John's translation with the repetitive occurrences of this form as the preposition alone extending over a significant portion of the length of Job.

76. The next chapter will address the content of this statement (and of this entire section) in much greater detail.

in the preceding chapters) of the OT, worship in first-century Judaism, early Christian worship, and the overall Gospel to perform an exegesis of 19:36–37.

5

Exegesis of John 19:36–37

THE PREVIOUS CHAPTERS ADDRESSED important contexts presumed by John as well as practices utilized by ancient authors for handling OT citations. Chapter 2 discussed first-century Jewish worship and identified its fundamental features. These included the temple, its feasts, and its sacrificial worship. Chapter 3 showed how John utilized such knowledge along with the OT and the proximate context of early Christian worship in conveying the Gospel's theme of worship. Chapter 4 identified exegetical methods utilized by ancient Jewish and NT authors to incorporate OT passages into their works that are relevant to John's use of Scripture in 19:36–37. This chapter will analyze the text and utilize the results along with important contextual information either presumed or provided by John to gain insight into the fulfillment attested by 19:36–37.

The chapter begins with a textual analysis of the passage that includes a discussion of the scriptural passages to which John refers and their textual traditions as well as his presentation of them. The following section addresses the original contexts of John's OT sources that the evangelist presumes and upon which he draws in utilizing portions of them in 19:36–37. The third section identifies significant contextual elements from the Gospel that provide valuable information for properly understanding its final fulfillment citations in 19:36–37 and the testimony they provide in conjunction with their primary referents (19:33–34). The fourth section addresses the most significant elements of the Gospel's presumed context of first-century Jewish worship. The final section synthesizes the preceding analysis and information in light of the proximate context of early Christian worship to demonstrate the fulfillment attested by 19:36–37.

ANALYSIS OF THE TEXT OF JOHN 19:36–37: ITS PRIMARY REFERENTS AND OT SOURCES

The events that transpire directly after Jesus' death (19:31–34) and John's attestation to the veracity of the eyewitness testimony about them (19:35) immediately precede 19:36–37.[1] John reports that the Jewish authorities had asked Pilate that the legs of Jesus and those crucified with him be broken and their bodies be taken away since it was the "preparation [day]" (παρασκευή; 19:31). John infers Pilate's assent to the request by the conjunction utilized (οὖν; "therefore") and the subsequent narrative of the soldiers breaking the legs of the two men crucified with Jesus (19:32). When the soldiers come to Jesus, however, seeing that he was already dead, they disregard their implied orders by not breaking his legs (19:33).[2] Rather one of the soldiers pricks Jesus' side with a lance which results in the immediate flow of blood and water (19:34).[3] John's dramatic intervention regarding the veracity of the account just provided (19:35) establishes its importance to his audience to evoke or nurture belief.[4]

At this point, John affirms the significance of what has just transpired by recognizing in it the fulfillment of Scripture: "for these things happened in order that the scripture might be fulfilled: '*a bone of him shall not be broken*'. And again another scripture says: '*they shall look to whom they pierced*'" (19:36–37). The introductory phrase ("these things happened") points to the content of the narrative segment that immediately precedes (19:31–35)

---

1. The eyewitness testimony indicates that the reason John recounted these events (19:31–34) and provided the OT witnesses that affirm and illuminate their significance (19:36–37) is "that you also may believe" (19:35).

2. John conveys unanimity in their decision with plural forms of the finite verbs for seeing and breaking.

3. The term "prick" translates νύσσω here to reflect John's decision to employ a related, but distinct term from the one appearing in 19:37 for "pierce." Translations of 19:34 in this section use the term "prick," but subsequent references to the action that took place employ the term "pierce" to concur with 19:37. This is both practical and consistent with the Gospel since it conveys correspondence between the action in 19:34 and the citation in 19:37.

4. Moloney (*John*, 509) characterizes 19:35 as a "remarkable intervention" by the evangelist in the form of a "direct address to the reader."

the scriptures (19:36-37) and the purpose clause ("in order that") indicates that they had taken place in accord with God's will as foretold by the OT. The phrase "these things" (ταῦτα) refers to *at least* two things from the preceding narrative. The correspondence of the citations with the soldiers' two primary "actions" (19:33-34) identifies them as the direct referents for the fulfillment recognized. The scriptures (19:36-37) bear witness to the significance of those actions (19:33-34) and together they illuminate the narrative of Jesus' hour that precedes them (18:1—19:30) by validating Jesus' identity and attesting to the completion of the work the Father has given him (4:34; cf. 5:36; 17:4) in the culmination of his hour (19:25-30) and its significance for John's audience.

The first "action" of the soldiers is their decision to ignore their orders from Pilate and forego breaking Jesus' legs (19:33). The piercing of Jesus' side, in lieu of the bone-breaking, is the second (19:34). Immediately after reporting, "as they saw he [Jesus] was already dead, they did not break his legs" (19:33), John connects the account of the piercing by introducing it with an adversative conjunction, "rather [ἀλλά] one of the soldiers pricked his side with a spear" (19:34a). Correspondingly, he connects the two discrete "scriptures" provided in 19:36-37 to each of these narrative elements with a short conjunctive phrase "and again [καὶ πάλιν] another scripture" (19:37a), which reflects the correspondence between the events narrated and the scriptures they fulfill.[5] In a similar way, John's account of the flow of blood and water communicates its inextricable relationship with the piercing of Jesus' side by introducing the flow with the phrase "and immediately" (19:34ba) directly after the verb (i.e., νύσσω) of the preceding action.[6] Its Gospel context as well as the original context of the citation provided in 19:37 (addressed below) affirm the inherent relationship between the piercing and the consequent flow from Jesus' side as integral to the scriptural fulfillment recognized by John.

---

5. Although "the scripture" in 19:36 is an apparent conflation of two distinct passages, John refers to it as a single "scripture." Hence, the reference to the *two discrete* "scriptures" provided in 19:36-37.

6. Brown (*Messiah*, 2:1185-88) twice refers to a scholarly position (1185, 87) that argues that 19:37 refers only to the piercing of Jesus' side, "but not to the flow of blood and water (v. 34b)." Although he does not provide any examples of scholars who hold such a position, Brown opposes it and asks, "why would 'these things' which introduces the citations in v. 36, not refer to what happened in the immediately preceding verses, especially to the startling flow of blood and water from the side of Jesus?" (1188).

The content, word order, and verb form of 19:36 suggest that John draws upon multiple OT passages and utilizes exegetical techniques employed by first-century Jewish and NT authors, conflating texts from the Pentateuch (Exod 12:46; LXX 12:10; Num 9:12) and Psalms (34:21 [LXX 33:21]) and recognizing their collective fulfillment in what has occurred.[7] The pentateuchal texts express the prohibition against breaking any bones in the Passover lamb. The psalm attests to God's providential care of the Righteous (One).

Whereas the prohibition is essentially the same in each case (since the circumstances for Num 9:12 explain the different verb form in that instance), Exod 12:46 appears to be the primary (or original) source for the pentateuchal contribution to the scripture in John 19:36.[8] The prohibition in LXX Exod 12:10, identical with the one found in 12:46, is an apparent harmonization of the two verses by the translator.[9] Numbers 9:12 is part of the instructions (9:9–12) for the second Passover established in response to a concern raised in the wilderness of Sinai (9:6–8) for those ritually unclean at the first Passover. The multiple appearances of the mysterious requirement in the OT attest to its importance and references to it in extra-biblical literature indicate that it remained an integral part of the ritual observance of Passover through the end of the Second Temple era.[10]

7. Although Menken ("Jn 19,36," 2112) prefers the possibility, "that Ps 34(33),21 is the basic text of the quotation and that the Pentateuchal texts supply the material for the changes," Brown (*Messiah*, 2:1186) thinks "the evidence favors the paschal-lamb image as the primary reference." Whereas the primary reference depends on the perspective taken (addressed further below), both scholars allow for (and Menken specifies) the contributions from both sources.

8. The Greek texts of the respective prohibitions are ὀστοῦν οὐ συντρίψετε ἀπ' αὐτοῦ (Exod 12:46) and ὀστοῦν οὐ συντρίψουσιν ἀπ' αὐτου (Num 9:12). Consequently, the discussion of the Pentateuch's contribution to John 19:36 (below) will utilize Exod 12:46 whenever it provides a single pentateuchal referent.

9. Salvesen ("Exodus," 29–42) observes, "the translator [for Exodus] was both faithful to his Hebrew text and also tried to make sense of it, introducing harmonisations with the book" (35). The MT and the LXX are essentially identical in 12:10 apart from prohibition inserted into middle of instructions for handling any remnants from the Passover lamb. The MT reads, ולא־תותירו ממנו עד־בקר והנתר ממנו עד־בקר באש תשרפו, while the LXX states, οὐκ ἀπολείψετε ἀπ' αὐτοῦ ἕως πρωὶ καὶ ὀστοῦν οὐ συντρίψετε ἀπ' αὐτοῦ τὰ δὲ καταλειπόμενα ἀπ' αὐτοῦ ἕως πρωὶ ἐν πυρὶ κατακαύσετε.

10. Its inclusion in LXX 12:10 attests to its importance during the time of the translation. That Jubilees attempts to provide a basis for the mysterious requirement (49:13–14) and the rabbinic literature refers to it in instructions on Passover (m. Pesaḥ. 7:11–12) and on the validity of a sacrifice (Zebaḥ. 3:6) attest to its continued observance and perceived importance through the Second Temple era.

The scripture provided in John 19:36 consists of four terms. The first two terms (ὀστοῦν οὐ) are identical with the bone-breaking prohibition from the Pentateuch. Whereas the same verb occurs in both passages, its form in 19:36 (singular passive) differs distinctively from the verb form (plural active) in Exod 12:46. The final term in John 19:36 (αὐτοῦ) corresponds with the bone-breaking ban, but the preposition that occurs before the pronoun in the Pentateuch is absent.[11] Thus, the bone-breaking prohibition contains all four terms of the scripture provided in 19:36, in the same order, and three of these four terms are identical in form. Conversely, four of the five terms in the ban in Exod 12:46 are present in John 19:36. The scripture in 19:36 also reflects the prohibition in its compactness, especially in comparison with the other OT source (LXX Ps 33:21 [MT 34:21]) upon which it draws.

The distinctive contribution of LXX Ps 33:21 (MT 34:21) is the verb form.[12] The psalm addresses God's providential care for the righteous. Whereas LXX Ps 33:21 and MT 34:21 correspond with one another in word order, they differ significantly from that of the scripture in John 19:36. Although LXX Ps 33:21 contains all the terms present in the scripture provided, the term for bone and the pronoun are plural in the psalm whereas they are singular in the Gospel. In MT 34:21, the term for bone is also plural, but the personal pronoun is singular. Whereas the Hebrew and the Greek texts both speak of God's care for "the righteous" by using the adjective substantively, the Hebrew text employs the singular ("the Righteous *One*") and the Greek utilizes the plural ("the righteous *ones*"). Nevertheless, John's presentation of the text and the context into which he places it clearly establish a singular referent for his citation (i.e., Jesus as the Righteous One). In both versions, the psalm texts are considerably longer than the scripture in John 19:36.[13] The word order and compactness of the citation in 19:36

---

11. The Greek text for Exod 12:46 is ὀστοῦν οὐ συντρίψετε ἀπ' αὐτοῦ, and the scripture provided by John is ὀστοῦν οὐ συντριβήσεται αὐτου (John 19:36).

12. The text of LXX Ps 33:21 states: κύριος φυλάσσει πάντα τὰ ὀστᾶ αὐτῶν ἓν ἐξ αὐτῶν οὐ συντριβήσεται. Menken ("Jn 19,36," 2112) indicates, "the verbal form [in 19:36], the nucleus of the clause, comes from the psalm."

13. LXX Ps 33:21 has eleven terms and the MT 34:21 effectively contains ten terms compared with only four in John 19:36. Although the overall verse of Exod 12:46 is considerably longer than the citation, the prohibition is an independent clause (introduced by a conjunction) from which only one term is missing in the scripture in John 19:36. In the case of the psalms, however, it is necessary to consider the full length of the verse as a unit to maintain its sense and its use of the terms that appear in the scripture in John 19:36.

manifest the pentateuchal prohibition and its verb form combined with its content point to its psalm source. LXX Ps 33:21 contributes the distinctive third-person singular future passive form of συντρίβω.¹⁴ John's conflation of the discrete texts from the Pentateuch and the Psalms enables his audience to recognize the presence of the passages from both OT sources and their fulfillment in Jesus with the events that just transpired.

Whereas significant textual evidence indicates that John conflated texts from the Pentateuch and the Psalms in the citation in 19:36, the scripture provided in 19:37 has Zech 12:10 as its sole source. Although the OT text provided by John in 19:37 does not agree completely with either the MT or the LXX, it manifests a much greater resemblance to the MT. In fact, *none* of the terms in 19:37 match the LXX for the portion of the verse cited.¹⁵ Therefore, scholars tend to agree on the *Vorlage* of the MT as the source for the citation in 19:37 even though they disagree regarding the means utilized by the evangelist to provide the Greek translation.¹⁶ The fundamental difference is whether John used a Greek source text or translated the passage directly from Hebrew.¹⁷ Since the first extant Greek translation of Zech 12:10 that matches John 19:37 does not appear until the mid-second century AD, all scholars who assert a Greek source text base their arguments on hypothetical translations.¹⁸ In contrast, the *Vorlage* of

---

14. The form appears eleven times in the LXX and this is the only time it occurs with the noun ὀστέον ("bone"). Whereas the MT manifests the Nifal perfect form, the context suggests that it acts as a perfect consecutive (or *WEQATAL*), effectively conveying a future tense. Although a ו is not present (which would formally establish it as a perfect consecutive), the terse, paratactic style of poetry (and possibly meter considerations) can account for its absence.

15. Whereas the citation in 19:37 states, "they shall look to whom they pierced" (ὄψονται εἰς ὃν ἐξεκέντησαν), the LXX for Zech 12:10 states, "they shall look to me because they danced in triumph" (ἐπιβλέψονται πρός με ἀνθ' ὧν κατωρχήσαντο). The LXX employs the verb κατορχέομαι, translated here as to "dance in triumph" (*LSJ*, 930). It is a hapax in the Bible.

16. Menken ("John 19:37," 502); Schuchard (*Scripture*, 149); Bynum (*John 19:37*, 107-9, 147); Cavicchia ("Gv 19.37," 208-19) and Kubiś (*Zechariah in John*, 171-81) all effectively indicate that the MT *Vorlage* is the ultimate source for the scripture in 19:37.

17. Menken ("John 19:37," 504); Schuchard (*Scripture*, 149); and Bynum (*John 19:37*, 153-69) argue on different bases that John used a Greek translation of the MT *Vorlage*. Cavicchia ("Gv 19.37," 208-19) and Kubiś (*Zechariah in John*, 171-81) conclude that the evidence supports direct translation from Hebrew.

18. It is not until Justin Martyr (*1 Apol.* 52.12) that the identical citation appears. Justin's reference to the regular reading of the Gospels (*1 Apol.* 66.3; 67.3) in the liturgy, however, makes John 19:37 the likely source of Justin's citation. Rather than recognizing

the MT arguably provides a consonantal textual basis for the citation in 19:37. Additionally, scholarly analyses of other OT citations in the Gospel have determined them to be independent translations from the Hebrew, indicating that John possessed such capability.[19]

Menken's analysis of the scripture provided by John in 12:40 is valuable for recognizing his citation in 19:37 as a direct translation from the Hebrew. Menken observes that the structure of 12:40, particularly the placement of the pronouns in John's citation of Isa 6:10, differs from the LXX translation of the text with no apparent reason for such a change if the LXX were his source.[20] Through statistical analysis of John's placement of genitives of personal pronouns, Menken demonstrates that his personal style accounts for the difference in the pronoun placement relative to the LXX.[21] Consequently, the influence of John's style in translating the Hebrew text readily explains the difference.[22] Whereas personal style explains the difference in structure, John's conscious choice would account for the source chosen and his use of it. Regarding the latter, Menken offers an important insight that supports the evangelist's translation of the Hebrew text for 19:37 when he observes that John, "operates, however, selectively; he chooses a vocalization of the Hebrew text that suits him."[23] Although

---

this more probable explanation, Menken ("John 19:37," 497) uses its presence in Justin to argue that it is "the standard early Christian version of Zech 12:10" and, based on this presumption, that John used this hypothetical translation for his citation.

19. Plummer (*John*, 152–352) identifies such evidence in 6:45; 12:13, 15; 13:18 and 19:37. In commenting on 19:37, he collectively refers to the "evidence of the Evangelist having independent knowledge of Hebrew, and therefore being a Jew of Palestine" (351–52n37). Humann ("Old Testament Quotations in John," 31–54) performed an in-depth analysis of OT citations in John and concluded that he rendered the citations in 13:18 and 19:37 "directly from the Hebrew using his own vocabulary" (39). Menken (*Old Testament Quotations*, 206) indicates that the citations in 12:40 and 13:18 make "major recourse to the Hebrew" and concludes that John "produced his own translation."

20. Menken, "John 12:40," 99–122.

21. Menken's ("John 12:40," 113) analysis indicates that John "displays a comparatively strong tendency to place genitives of personal pronouns, when used attributively with a substantive (especially of parts of the body) or with a substantivized adjective, before these and the article accompanying them" even though "as a rule, the pronouns have no emphasis in these cases."

22. Based on his analysis, Menken ("John 12:40," 114) concludes, "from these observations concerning lines 1 and 2 of the quotation we may conclude that in these lines the Hebrew text has been translated independently of the LXX."

23. Menken, "John 12:40," 114. Although Menken (120–21) observes that the last three words (in line 5) of the citation come from the LXX, he concludes that most of the

Menken personally attributes the citation in 19:37 to a hypothetical Greek translation, his analyses of citations in 12:40 and 13:18 provide compelling support for recognizing it as a translation from the MT's *Vorlage*.[24]

Menken's analysis of 12:40 and his statistically-based observation that John's positioning of the personal pronouns reflected his personal tendency when translating the citation (or most of it) directly from the Hebrew provides a likely explanation for John's verb choice at the beginning of the citation in 19:37. That he used the more general verb for seeing (ὁράω) to translate the Hebrew verb in Zech 12:10 rather than the more particular verb for looking (ἐπιβλέπω) utilized by the LXX coheres with such an explanation. John uses the former frequently throughout the Gospel, but never employs the latter, which occurs just three times in the NT.[25] Although John was surely aware of the verb in the LXX, his choice might not only reflect his personal preference, but also the rarity of ἐπιβλέπω in his time. Since its translation differs substantially from the HB in the passage cited, there is no benefit for John to employ the unique verb to associate his translation with the one provided by the LXX. Additionally, the relationship between seeing and believing (cf. 1:50-51; 20:8, 20:29) is of great import in the Gospel and the combination "of the one who has *seen* [ὁ ἑωρακώς]" in 19:35 who offers his testimony "in order that you also may *believe*" and the next occurrence of ὁράω (19:37) in the future tense (ὄψονται) effectively *activates* that relationship.[26]

John's proficiency with Hebrew combined with exegetical methodology attested in ancient Jewish and NT texts provides a plausible explanation

---

citation is an independent translation from the Hebrew rather than a correction of the LXX based on the Hebrew text.

24. Whereas elsewhere Menken ("John 19:37," 504) bases his analyses and insights in 12:40 and 13:18 on objective evidence, he rejects the scripture cited in 19:37 as a direct translation based on theological speculation. He contends that had John translated it directly from Hebrew, "he would not have had reason to leave out the 1st pers. sg. (cf. the quotations in John 2:17; 12:38, 40; 13:18; 15:25; 19:24)." Such a presumption, however, fails to recognize John's tendency to engage his audience by enabling them to make the connections about Jesus on their own and, as Hays (*Echoes,* 439n2) observes, to discover "with surprise *after* his death and resurrection how our memories of him awaken unexpected echoes of Israel's Scripture."

25. John uses ὁράω 89 times and it occurs some 700 times in the NT.

26. John's use of ὁράω in the scripture translation (19:37) *activates* the seeing-believing relationship and associates the believing in 19:35 with looking to the pierced one (19:34) and believing in him. Subsequent sections will show how other contextual elements of the Gospel affirm that John intends to encompass 19:37 in the seeing-believing relationship evoked in 19:35.

THAT THE SCRIPTURES MIGHT BE FULFILLED THROUGH PERFECT WORSHIP

for his rendering of what appears to be a suffixed preposition referring to God in the first-person (אלי) in Zech 12:10 as the poetic form of the preposition alone.²⁷ His expertise with Hebrew allowed John to approach the difficult construction of 12:10 and to translate it as he judged best for his audience. As discussed in the previous chapter, two of the common exegetical methods utilized by ancient Jewish and NT authors when they incorporated Scripture passages into their works were lexematic association and adjustment of OT texts. Lexematic association attests to the value associated with having a textual basis for an interpretation and the adjustment of OT texts attests to a certain degree of freedom granted to the ancient author-exegetes. John's apparent translation of the Hebrew effectively utilized both principles. The consonantal Hebrew text of Zech 12:10 gave him a textual basis for his translation and he "adjusted" it by translating what most often conveys the preposition with the first-person singular pronominal suffix (אלי) as the rare form of preposition alone.²⁸ In doing so, he establishes the messianic fulfillment inchoate in the OT with a sense of clarity (identifying Jesus as the one "whom they pierced") that may not have been possible had he included the first-person preposition in his translation ("they shall look to *me* whom they pierced"). At the same time, by concurring with the consonantal *Vorlage* of the MT, John's translation (consistent with his allusive style) engages members of his audience familiar with his source text to *discover* the attestation to Jesus' divinity as well (cf. John 14:7–11).²⁹

John thematically associates the scriptures provided in 19:36 and 19:37 with the commonly used connective phrase "and again" (καὶ πάλιν). With Jesus being the object of both of the "actions" (19:33–34) in which the scriptures provided (19:36–37) find their fulfillment, John implicitly

---

27. Theodotion's revision of the LXX translation reflects such a reading in accord with the vocalization manifested in the MT. Additionally, most occurrences of the form in the HB attest to this meaning for אלי.

28. The consonantal Hebrew text, which is all that existed at the time, provides an objectively verifiable basis for John's translation with the four occurrences of אלי as the poetic form of the preposition alone in Job 3:22; 5:26; 15:22; 29:29.

29. This would apply to members familiar with the MT *Vorlage* and the crux it had posed to translators. Concerning John's tendency to engage his audience in this manner, Hays (*Echoes*, 348) observes, "in light of the unfolding story of Jesus, it is both right and illuminating to *read backwards* and to discover in the Law and the Prophets an unexpected *foreshadowing* of the later story" (emphasis original). John allows knowledgeable and perceptive members to recognize this attestation to Jesus' divinity and the resolution of the interpretive crux while clearly demonstrating the messianic fulfillment for all members. The final section will further address this aspect of the fulfillment of Zech 12:10.

establishes Jesus as the theme that unites them. The conflated citation of Exod 12:46 (cf. LXX 12:10; Num 9:12) and LXX Ps 33:21 (MT 34:21) in John 19:36 identifies Jesus as *the* Passover Lamb and *the* Righteous One. The citation in 19:37 identifies him as "the Pierced One" at the center of the mysterious prophecy contained in Zech 12:10.[30] Whereas the OT testimony presented by John in 19:36–37 establishes the significance of "these things" that happened in 19:32–34, they collectively bear witness to *all* "these things" that took place in the culmination of Jesus' hour. The following sections consider aspects of the contexts presumed by John that provide further insight into the fulfillment attested by 19:36–37.

THE ORIGINAL CONTEXTS OF JOHN'S OT SOURCES

Hillel's list identifies presumption of the original context of OT texts as an exegetical method utilized by ancient authors. The previous chapter provided examples of how ancient Jewish (11Q13 II, 2–6) and NT (Gal 3:6—4:31) texts implicitly manifest this technique by relying on the audience's knowledge of OT passages to supply information presumed in the works that incorporate them. The following subsections provide such information from the original contexts of the OT sources for John 19:36–37.

The Pentateuchal Prohibition
(Exod 12:46; cf. LXX 12:10; Num 9:12)

The worship of Yhwh on Passover is the context for the pentateuchal prohibition. It is an integral part of the instructions given for the ritual observance of the first Passover. The way that Exodus 12 frames the narrative of the tenth plague and the exodus (12:29–42) with instructions for observing the first Passover (Exod 12:1–28, 43–50) and interweaves them with a closing narrative comment on the exodus (12:51) conveys their inherent relationship. This relationship incorporates the subsequent worship in Jerusalem's temple that the exodus enabled into the context evoked by the bone-breaking prohibition. God's instructions in his initial encounter with Moses established worship as the goal for the exodus (Exod 3:12, 18) and,

---

30. The balance of the chapter will utilize the phrase the Pierced One (without quotation marks after this occurrence) as a convenient way of referring to the individual to whom the portion of text utilized by John from Zech 12:10 refers in a manner analogous to Isaiah's "Suffering Servant."

consequently, for Passover (11:1; 12:21-32). The exodus narrative reflects this goal with worship terminology recurring from Moses' call (3:1—4:15) to his return to Egypt and the exodus (4:17—12:50) through the giving of the Law (20:1—23:33) and the ratification of the covenant (24:1-8).[31]

Since the Passover and the exodus led to Sinai, the gift of the Law, and the ratification of the covenant, these are all part of the context evoked by the bone-breaking prohibition. Yhwh set the people free from service (slavery) to Pharaoh and the Egyptians that they might serve (worship) Yhwh. The gift of the Law instructed them on proper liturgical and ethical worship of Yhwh and the Israelites obliged themselves through the covenant.[32] John's audience would also be aware, however, of the grave failure of the people that occurred even before Moses had descended from Mount Sinai with the stone tablets of the Law (32:1-20) and the subsequent incapacity to offer the true worship that the Father desired (John 4:22-23) in the Jerusalem temple and its sacrificial worship (4:21). The bone-breaking prohibition evokes this overall context of Passover along with the ritual slaughter of the lamb as the preeminent sacrifice offered in the observance of the foundational feast of temple worship (i.e., the apex of liturgical worship in first-century Judaism).[33]

God's Care for the Righteous [One] (Ps 34:21 [LXX 33:21])

Psalm 34 (LXX 33) is a song praising Yhwh and inviting the audience to join in (vv. 2-4). The psalmist speaks from experience in the first person

---

31. The verb for offering sacrifice (θύω; 3:18; 5:3, 8, 17; 8:4, 21, 22, 23, 24, 25; 12:21; 24:5) and verbs associated with worship (λατρεύω; 3:12; 4:23; 7:16, 26; 8:16; 9:1, 13; 10:3, 7-8, 11, 24, 26; 12:31; 20:25; 23:24-25, and προσκυνέω; 4:31; 11:8; 12:27; 20:5; 23:4; 24:1) occur repeatedly in these sections of Exodus. Most of the occurrences refer to (or instruct Israel about) proper liturgical or ethical worship.

32. The Law conveys the integral nature of liturgical and ethical worship in the way that it interweaves liturgical (Exod 20:2-6, 23-26; 22:28-29; 23:13-19, 24-26, 32-33) and ethical ordinances (20:7-17; 21:1—22:27; 22:30; 23:1-12, 20-22).

33. Propp (*Exodus*, 451) maintains that the Passover ritual slaughter "is the penultimate prefiguration of the sacrificial cultus" with the sacrifices at Sinai being the ultimate prefiguration. He argues that this is the case because at Sinai Yhwh instructed Israel on "sacrifice, presided over by the priesthood." That Yhwh had instructed the people on the ritual worship of Passover prior to Sinai (Exod 12:1-28, 43-50) and that such worship enabled the people to receive the instruction and to offer the sacrifices at Sinai, however, provide strong bases for recognizing Passover as the *ultimate* "prefiguration of the sacrificial cultus."

(vv. 5-7) then alternates between addressing his audience directly and making objective statements (vv. 8-15) before finishing with a string of such statements (vv. 16-23). The MT and the LXX provide distinct and complementary bases for identifying Jesus as the Righteous One. Whereas the LXX corresponds with the MT in shifts of person and number throughout most of the psalm, the two diverge in the verses of greatest interest to the present study (vv. 20-21).[34] Although the shift to the singular form of the adjective "righteous" used substantively in 34:20 could simply be a stylistic change by the psalmist (i.e., an alternate way of expressing the category of "righteous ones"), it provides a sound textual basis for John's recognition of it as a future prophecy about an individual. That the OT (cf. Zech 9:9; Jer 23:5-6; MT 33:15; Isa 53:11) and subsequent Jewish literature (cf. 4Q252 Frag. 1 V, 3-4; Pss. Sol. 17:32; 1 En. 38:2; 53:6) identify "the Messiah" as "the *Righteous* King/Shoot/One" not only supports the interpretation that 34:20-21 applies to an individual, but to the Messiah.[35]

That Isa 53:11 uses the adjective for righteous (substantively) as the subject of its cognate verb provides significant linguistic evidence to associate Ps 34:20-21 with the messianic Suffering Servant. Aside from their occurrence together in Isa 53:11, there are only four other passages in the OT in which the cognate verb and adjective (used substantively) occur in such proximity (Deut 25:1; 1 Kgs 8:32; 2 Chr 6:23; Isa 5:23) and all of them refer to rendering proper judgment for the righteous. Whereas the context of these other occurrences connote *declaring* one righteous, in the context of Isaiah 53 the verb conveys *making* many righteous (53:11).[36] This unique

---

34. Both the LXX and the MT begin in the first person of the psalmist (vv. 2-7), shift to the third person plural in v. 8, the second person plural in vv. 9-10, the third person singular in vv. 13-15, and back to the third personal plural in vv. 16-19. The MT, however, shifts to the third person singular in vv. 20-21 and back to the plural for vv. 22-23 while the LXX persists in the plural for the remainder of the psalm (vv. 20-23) after the transition in v. 16. Although MT 34:18 does not provide an explicit subject, the presence of the plural verb form for "calling out" implicitly establishes the righteous ones of 34:16 as the subject here also.

35. Jeremiah 23:5-6 refers to the Messiah as "a Righteous Shoot" (23:5) and "the Lord [יהוה] our righteousness" (23:6). Collins (*Apocalyptic Literature*, 220-21) indicates that J. T. Milik's thesis contending that 1 Enoch 37-71 was a third-century composition . . . has attracted considerable attention," but also that "no aspect of his argument has withstood the test of criticism" (220). Collins, Charlesworth ("Parables of Enoch," 37-113), and Nickelsburg and VanderKam (*1 Enoch*, 5-6) are among scholars who date this section of 1 Enoch to before AD 70.

36. Whereas *HALOT* (3:1004) attributes the meaning, "to assist someone towards his rights" to the Hifil form of the Hebrew verb (צדק) used here, such a meaning does not

sense of the verb combined with its cognate adjective provides an additional basis for recognizing the Servant as *the* "Righteous One" par excellence.[37] Although LXX Ps 33:20-21 refers to "the righteous ones," it also supports John's recognition of seeing its fulfillment in Jesus as "the Righteous One" through a lesser to greater association in that if Yhwh provides such protection for "the righteous ones" (the lesser), even more so would he provide it for the Righteous One (the greater). In this sense, the LXX complements the MT. In attesting to his messianic identity as the Righteous One (John 19:36; cf. Ps 34:21 [LXX 33:21]), the soldiers' restraint in John 19:32-33 establishes Jesus' innocence concerning the charges brought against him (19:7) and so implicitly affirm his divinity (cf. 8:28).[38]

Looking to the Pierced One (Zech 12:10)

As established above, the consonantal Hebrew text present in the MT along with the recognition of a unique form of the preposition attested in Job 3:22; 5:26; 15:22; 29:29 collectively provide a textual basis for the Johannine translation of Zech 12:10 directly from Hebrew. John's use of the portion of 12:10 in 19:37 identifies Jesus as the Pierced One that it foretells. Although

---

cohere with the observation that the Servant "shall bear the iniquities of the many," which directly follows it (53:11; cf. 53:5, 10). The meaning that Gottlob Schrenk ("δικαιόω," *TDNT* 2:215-19) associates with Paul's use of the Greek verb (δικαιόω) that translates צדק in Isa 53:11, however, corresponds well with the context of Isa 52:13—53:12. Schrenk indicates that for Paul δικαιόω, "implies the justification of the ungodly who believe, on the basis of the *justifying action* of God" (215; emphasis added). In other words, it conveys a *transformative action* that effects righteousness in others rather than simply assisting "someone towards his rights" as would be the case with exercising judgment (Deut 25:1; 1 Kgs 8:32; 2 Chr 6:23; Isa 5:23). That an NT sense coheres so well with the context of 52:13—53:12 reflects the inherent christological character of the passage and the Servant it foretells.

37. The provision of such care through the soldiers' unanimous decision to disobey their implied orders (John 19:31-33) attests to the Father's intervention in what has transpired (see 12:28).

38. That the Jewish authorities' ultimate charge for seeking capital punishment was that Jesus had "made himself the Son of God" (19:7) recalls their earlier attempts to kill him for "making himself equal to God" (5:18; cf. 10:33). The soldiers' restraint, identifying him to be the Righteous One, attests that Jesus is innocent of any wrongdoing in attesting to his equality with God (5:17-18; 10:30; cf. Isa 53:9; 1 Pet 2:22)). Consequently, their restraint fulfills Jesus' own prophecy to the Jewish authorities that they would (come to) know his divinity when they lifted up the Son of Man (8:28). Subsequent sections of this chapter will address aspects of this topic further.

EXEGESIS OF JOHN 19:36–37

there has been much scholarly debate about the identity of the Pierced One as presented in Zechariah, the fulfillment of 12:10 recognized in John 19:37 is consistent with the information provided by the proximate and broader context of the text cited.[39]

Both the intertextual and intratextual connections in Zechariah are pervasive. The latter supports its recognition as a unified work. Such recognition provides the opportunity to identify a key in 1:1–6 for understanding Zechariah.[40] This introduction explicitly establishes the book's continuity with the revelation provided through the extant texts and traditions at the time of the prophet that would eventually comprise the OT (along with his own work).[41] The rest of Zechariah implicitly manifests such continuity by frequently drawing upon passages from each of the categories that would eventually compose the OT (the Law, the Prophets, and the Writings).[42] The abundance of intertextual and intratextual connections in Zechariah make it necessary to limit the discussion to those of greatest significance for understanding John 19:37.

The connections valuable to the original context of Zech 12:10 as it relates to John 19:37 are those with Isaiah's Suffering Servant passages (42:1–7; 49:1–6; 50:4–9; 52:13—53:12) and the messianic allusions in Zech

---

39. Petterson (*Behold Your King*, 227–31) provides a summary of scholarly opinions before observing, "there is therefore a wide range of suggestions by scholars on the identity of the Pierced One" (231).

40. Boda (*Zechariah*, 39–40) observes, "the opening paragraph of the book of Zechariah (1:1–6) orients the reader . . . to the role that earlier revelations will play in the book as a whole . . . The explicit claims of 1:1–6 concerning the relationship between Zechariah's words and those of the prophets which preceded him establishes a hermeneutical grid which is essential for reading the remainder of the book of Zechariah."

41. Wolters (*Zechariah*, 7) indicates, "the concern for continuity is evident throughout the book of Zechariah. We see this . . . in the way Zechariah presents himself as standing in the same tradition of the 'former prophets,' and in the pervasive intertextuality which marks his own prophecies, which are laced with allusions to earlier Scripture." Similarly, Boda (*Zechariah*, 40) states, "as the book progresses, earlier biblical traditions within the Torah, the Former Prophets, and especially the Latter Prophets can be discerned in the form and language of the various pericopae."

42. Boda (*Zechariah*, 39–910) provides an extensive three-column list of OT references in his Scripture index (820–910). Hays (*Echoes*, 10) utilizes the terms "quotation," "allusion," and "echo" as "approximate indicators on the spectrum of intertextual linkage, moving from the most to the least explicit forms of reference." Zechariah's intertextual connections occur through allusions and echoes.

3:8–10; 6:12–15; 9:9–10; 13:7–9.⁴³ Among these messianic allusions, 9:9–10 is particularly important. First, it explicitly foretells Jerusalem's future king (9:9) who will have universal dominion (9:10). Secondly, John uses part of this passage (and so implicitly alludes to all of it) to provide the reason (John 12:15) for Jesus' use of the young donkey for his entry into Jerusalem (12:14) during which he acknowledges the onset of his hour (12:23, 27). Finally, whereas the astounding effects of the future king in Zech 9:9–10 (e.g., the establishment of peace within Israel as well as among the nations, his universal dominion) allude to the Messiah (e.g., 2 Sam 7:12–17; Isa 9:1–6; Ps 2:2–8; 72:1–17; 89:2–5, 28–38), his personal characteristics (Zech 9:9) associate him with the Suffering Servant (Isa 53:3–11).⁴⁴

The term "Shoot" (צמח) in the earlier passages (Zech 3:8–10; 6:12–15) alludes to the messianic king promised through the prophet Jeremiah (23:5; cf. 33:15).⁴⁵ That the initial reference to "the Shoot" indicates that he is Yhwh's servant affirms his messianic identity.⁴⁶ In Jeremiah, Yhwh refers to the messianic king as a "*Righteous Shoot* for David" (23:5; cf. 33:15), who will make "judgment and righteousness" (23:5) and whose name will be "Yhwh our righteousness" (23:6). That Zech 3:9 indicates, "my servant, the Shoot" (3:8) will remove iniquity from the land corroborates the primary

---

43. Aside from parallels presented in the analysis that follows, Lamarche (*Zacharie*, 139–47) provides substantial evidence regarding the correspondence "entre l'ordre des poèmes du Serviteur et le plan de Zach 9–14." He argues that "le Roi Pasteur quatre passages: 9,9–10; 11,4–14; 12,10–13,1; 13,7–9" (139) correspond with Isa 42:1–4; 49:1–3; 53:5–12, respectively (with each of the final two poems listed for Zechariah corresponding with Isa 53:5–12).

44. Psalm 2:2–8 explicitly combines the term "Messiah" (משיח), which only occurs thirty-eight times in the HB with most instances referring to a contemporary person (e.g., a priest [Lev 4:3, 5, 16; 6:25] or king [1 Sam 16:6, 24:7, 11; 26:9–23]), with a future universal dominion. Whereas Psalm 89 uses "messiah" (89:39; 52) to refer to a defeated Davidic king, it also recalls promises made to David of an eternal dynasty (89:2–5, 28–38; cf. 2 Sam 7:12–17) and so implicitly alludes to the future Davidic Messiah. Lamarche (*Zacharie*, 43–44) sees the observation of "righteous and saving" being characteristic of the king in Zech 9:10 as a way of "nous préparant ainsi aux chapitres suivants qui décriront le rejet et l'oppression du Pasteur de Yahweh" and as an allusion "au Serviteur de Yahweh opprimé et sauvé" (44).

45. The noun צמח occurs twelve times in the OT and only in Jer 23:5; 33:15; Zech 3:8; 6:12 does it clearly refer to a person. Isaiah 4:2 is more ambiguous and seems to refer to circumstances rather than to a person.

46. Block ("Servant," 17–56) indicates, "the evidence for David [as Yhwh's messianic servant] is overwhelming." This evidence includes the frequency of such references, with some forty of them manifesting "David" and '*ebed* ("servant") "in appositional relationship" (47).

allusion to Jer 23:5 and manifests striking parallels with "the Righteous One, my servant" in Isaiah, who will "make many righteous and bear their iniquities" (53:11). That Yhwh will raise up this Shoot to tend to the flock scattered by the pre-exilic kings of Judah (Jer 22:1-30) identifies him as Yhwh's shepherd and the Messiah.[47] This identification associates the Shoot with the Servant whose sacrificial suffering would attend to the scattered flock by bearing their guilt (Isa 53:6, 11). The final verse of Zech 3:8-10 affirms the Davidic character of the Shoot with an allusion to the height of glory of the Davidic kingdom (in the early days of Solomon's reign) by indicating that everyone will invite their friends "under a vine and under a fig tree" (Zech 3:10; cf. 1 Kgs 5:5; LXX 2:46).

The second reference to the Shoot in Zech 6:12-15 establishes that "he shall sprout in his place and build the temple of Yhwh" (6:12). The MT implicitly identifies him as both a priest and king by indicating, "he shall sit and reign upon his throne *and* there shall be a priest *upon* his throne and a counsel of peace [i.e., harmony] between the two of them" (6:13).[48] That people will come from a distance to build the temple (6:15) implies that the Shoot will gather people from afar for worship. That he will build the temple identifies him as a descendant of David (2 Sam 7:13). Yhwh foretold that he would establish the throne of such a Davidic temple-builder forever (7:13). Whereas Solomon had built the original temple, his reign ended with his death and his throne remained vacant from the time of the exile.[49] Hence, the unending reign promised to the David temple-builder awaited fulfillment.

---

47. The OT identifies both David (2 Sam 5:2; 7:7; 24:17) and the Messiah (Ezek 34:23-31; 37:21-28) as shepherd-kings.

48. The LXX addresses the implausibility of two men sitting on the same throne, as the MT seems to indicate, by specifying "and there shall be a priest to his right." That John's Gospel attests to Jesus as both king (1:49; 19:14-15, 19-22) and priest (11:45-53; 19:23-24) indicates that "the two of them" in the MT refers to the *two offices* of king and priest and the harmony that will exist with Yhwh's Messiah fulfilling both.

49. Zechariah also connects these three messianic references (3:8-10; 6:12-15; 9:9-10) with the phrase "on that day" (3:10; 6:10; 9:16). Its first occurrence (2:15) is also messianic in that it speaks of an eschatological situation of many nations joining themselves to Yhwh (2:14; cf. 8:20-23; 14:16-21) with a call for "Daughter Zion" to rejoice (2:14) as when receiving her messianic king (9:9). Its fifth occurrence prepares for a fundamental change with the breaking of Yhwh's covenant (11:11). It subsequently resonates throughout Zech 12:3—14:20 with seventeen of its twenty-three occurrences. Jesus uses this phrase three times in his Farewell Discourse (John 14:20; 16:23, 26).

The abovementioned messianic passages in Zech 3:8–10; 6:12–15; 9:9–10; 13:7–9 collectively correspond with Isa 40:1–55:13, which encompasses the four Suffering Servant passages (Isa 42:1–7; 49:1–6; 50:4–9; 52:13—53:12), in their content and order. This section of Isaiah foretells the salvation Yhwh will accomplish through his servant. In both cases, the initial passages focus on the outcomes (Zech 3:8–10; 6:10–15; Isa 42:1–7; 49:1–6) and the latter provide insight into the means (suffering) of their accomplishment (Zech 12:10—13:1; 13:7–9; Isa 50:4–9; 52:13—53:12). Zechariah 9:9–10 plays a pivotal role in subtly making the transition. Whereas it focuses primarily on results (salvation, peace, and universal dominion), the description of the king (literally, "poor" or "afflicted") reflects the means.[50]

Recognizing the unity of the book of Zechariah enables interpreters to benefit from the recurring and complementary messianic prophecies in the earlier chapters that provide information for understanding later ones (cf. 12:10—13:1; 13:7–9), particularly the reference to the Pierced One in 12:10.[51] There are also intratextual and intertextual allusions in the proximate context of 12:10, which bring the Suffering Servant to the foreground by introducing the oracle that includes the Pierced One with language from the first Suffering Servant passage. Zechariah 12:1 introduces the oracle with a clause referring to Yhwh, as the one who stretched out the heavens, established the earth, and gave breath (or spirit) to man. That Zech 12:1 corresponds with Isa 42:5 in the first Suffering Servant passage (42:1–7) implicitly associates the Servant with the oracle that Zech 12:1 introduces through the linguistic links and thematic parallels between them.[52] The immediate context of 12:10 also contains numerous messianic allusions

---

50. Although *HALOT* (2:856) indicates that in 9:9 עָנִי means, "humble," it adds that this definition is "often difficult to distinguish" from its more common sense which conveys, "in a general sense poor, wretched, in a needy condition, with consequent reference to God" (emphasis original). That the Servant in Isa 52:13—53:12 willingly places himself in such a condition illuminates the meaning conveyed for the coming messianic king in Zech 9:9 when one recognizes that both passages refer to the same person.

51. Petterson (*Zechariah*, 263–64) indicates, "if this passage is read in isolation, it is not clear who is meant and a myriad of suggestions have been made" (263). Then he goes on to observe, "yet if this passage is read in light of the unfolding themes of the book, not just chs. 9–14 . . . then the interplay of the themes of the coming Shoot, king and shepherd strongly suggests that the one who is pierced is to be associated with the coming Davidic king" (264).

52. Since 12:1 is an allusion rather than a citation of Isa 42:5 (characteristic of Zechariah) the linguistic links (e.g., stretch, heaven, earth, breath) are limited. These links in combination with the constituent elements and their ordering, however, uniquely associates the two passages. Lamarche (*Zacharie*, 140–42) also identifies the similarities

that encompass the reference to the Pierced One. These allusions include repeated references to the house of David (12:7, 8, 10, 12; 13:1) in referring to its glory (12:7–8), its mourning over the Pierced One (12:10–12), and Yhwh's favor extended to David's house and the inhabitants of Jerusalem (12:10; 13:1).[53]

A second account of the death of a messianic figure (13:7–9) follows that of the Pierced One after an intervening section (13:2–6) that addresses the removal of idols and false prophets from the land.[54] There are numerous parallels between the two accounts. Features that identify the individuals with kings in each case include the intensity (12:11) and extent (12:12–14) of the mourning associated with the first, and the identification of the individual as "my shepherd" (13:7) in the second.[55] Each of the accounts (12:10; 13:7) also contain plausible allusions to deaths of Davidic kings (12:11; 13:7).

The verbs utilized in Zech 12:10 and 13:7 both convey lethal actions associated with a sword when directed at humans.[56] The allusion associated with the Pierced One is far more obvious with its reference to Megiddo

---

between the passages and states, "cette doxologie d'Is 42,5 a sans doute inspiré, en parte du moins, Zach 12,1" (142).

53. That "the house of David" and David's name only appear in these instances (12:7—13:1) in the book of Zechariah increases the strength of these messianic allusions. Petterson (*Zechariah*, 264) considers "the focus on the house of David in the immediate context" particularly significant for associating "the one who is pierced . . . with the coming Davidic king."

54. In compact fashion, this short passage parallels the extended section in Isaiah between the first two Servant passages (Isa 42:8—48:22) in which the theme of idols (i.e., false worship) repeatedly emerges.

55. Although the RSV indicates that Yhwh refers to the shepherd in 11:17 as "*my* worthless shepherd," the context suggests (and the MT supports) reading "*the* worthless shepherd" (without the possessive) in 11:17 (cf. BDB, 47; KJV, NET). Though the construct and suffixed forms of the substantivized participle (translated "shepherd") are identical, his characteristics and actions (11:16) are incongruous with Yhwh calling him "*my* shepherd." The absence of a possessive pronoun in the LXX supports this reading.

56. The verb in Zech 12:10 (דקר) only occurs five times with "sword" in the OT (Judg 9:54; 1 Sam 31:4; 1 Chr 10:4; Isa 13:15; Lam 4:9) and in each instance it either narrates or refers to death by the sword. There are more than sixty OT occurrences of the verb used in 13:7 (נבה; "smite" or "strike") with "sword," however, when the terms occur together to describe an action taken against an individual (see Num 21:24; Deut 20:13; Josh 8:24; Judg 1:8) the action conveyed is lethal. Petterson (*Zechariah*, 277) indicates, "striking on its own does not necessarily imply death (e.g., 13:6), but when one is struck with a sword it does, especially when it is an individual who is struck (e.g., 2 Sam. 12:9; Isa. 37:38)."

(cf. 2 Chr 35:22–25; cf. 2 Kgs 23:29–30).[57] Although the potential allusion in 13:7 is more subtle, Yhwh's shepherd (*my* shepherd) evokes a Davidic king.[58] Both accounts narrate the death of a person closely associated with Yhwh.[59] The actions that result in the deaths in both accounts correspond with those performed on evildoers (the false prophet pierced [13:3–6] and the foolish shepherd *contacted* by the sword [11:17]).[60] It is only the perspective of Yhwh that differentiates the deaths of these messianic figures (12:10; 13:7) from the evildoers suffering just punishment in other texts (11:17; 13:3–6) in close proximity. Finally, the similar effects of the deaths in bringing about repentance (Zech 12:10—13:1; 13:9), especially in light of the abovementioned similarities, associates the individuals with one another and suggests that they are complementary accounts of the death of the coming messianic king.[61]

Numerous features within the accounts and the associated passages (3:8–10; 6:10–15; 9:9–10) connect the slain individual (12:10; 13:7) with the Suffering Servant.[62] These include the Suffering Servant and the collec-

---

57. The reference to Megiddo along with the characterization of the magnitude of the mourning over the Pierced One (Zech 12:10) allude to the death of Josiah in Megiddo (2 Chr 35:22–25; cf. 2 Kgs 23:29–30).

58. Petterson (*Zechariah*, 277) indicates that Zedekiah was "the only king ... killed by the sword (Jer. 21:7)."

59. In 12:10, the MT indicates that Yhwh says, "they shall look *to me*," when speaking of the Pierced One and he refers to the individual in 13:7 as "*my* shepherd, *my* associate." Although the term translated as "associate" (עָמִית) is relatively obscure (occurring only here and in Leviticus), its interchangeability (cf. Lev 19: 11, 15, 17) with a more frequent term (רֵעַ; cf. 19:13, 16, 18) that conveys personal closeness provides a basis for the translation (cf. *HALOT*, 2:845; 3:1253–55).

60. The actions of the foolish shepherd (11:16) and the false prophet (13:2–6) identify them as evildoers. The term *contacted* reflects that the verb used in 13:7 (see 119n56) is not present in 11:17 where Yhwh states, "a sword upon your arm and upon your right eye," which will diminish the function of both.

61. Lamarche (*Zacharie*, 106–8) observes numerous parallels between 12:10—13:1 and 13:7–9 which include the importance of the person, their close relationship with Yhwh, the subsequent purifications by water (13:1) and fire (13:9), and repentance manifested (12:10; 13:9) in their turning their eyes "to me" (Yhwh; 12:10) and saying "Yhwh is my God" (13:9). He identifies them as parallel elements (b-b') in a chiasm that extends from 12:1 to 14:15 with the elimination of idols and prophets from the land in 13:2–6 as the pivot.

62. Lamarche (*Zacharie*, 139–54) demonstrates aspects of their complementarity in addressing parallels between Zachariah 9–14 and Isaiah's Suffering Servant passages (144–45). He subsequently observes, "ce morceau [13:7–9] prolonge et explicte le passage qui lui est parallèl, 12,10—13,1" (152) and concludes that the clear structure and

tive figures in Zech 12:10 and 13:7 being slain/smitten (Isa 53:6), suffering in accord with God's will (53:6, 10; Zech 13:7), the *appearance* that they were justly punished as evil doers (Isa 53:9; Zech 12:12, cf. 13:2–6; 13:7; cf. 11:17), and the associated conversion and forgiveness (Isa 53:4–12; Zech 12:10—13:1, 9).[63] The similarities manifested between the two accounts of Yhwh's close associates smitten in Zechariah and the Suffering Servant passages in Isaiah corroborate their identification as complementary accounts of the death of the Messiah. Recognizing these accounts in Zechariah (12:10; 13:7) as complementary reveals the progressive nature of the conversion of the people interwoven between them. They mourn the Pierced One (12:10–14), experience purification from sin and uncleanness (13:1), and profess their faith in Yhwh (13:9). This leads to an eschatological battle (14:1–3), the consequent vision of Jerusalem (and, implicitly, the temple) as the source of unending light and living water (14:4–11), and universal worship of Yhwh (14:16–21).

SIGNIFICANT CONTEXTUAL ELEMENTS IN THE GOSPEL FOR UNDERSTANDING JOHN 19:36-37

In conflating passages from the Law (Exod 12:46; LXX 12:10; Num 9:12) and the Writings (Ps 34:21 [LXX 33:21]) in 19:36 and thematically combining them with the citation from the Prophets (Zech 12:10) in 19:37, John collectively enlists the OT passages and their contexts as witnesses to the testimony provided in the Gospel. He does this through the limited portions of the OT texts presented in 19:36–37. He similarly engages his audience throughout the Gospel by presuming their use of information supplied by him to make the manifold intratextual and intertextual connections in the Gospel. This section will address three aspects of the literary

---

parallels establish, "il s'agit d'un mème personnage qui apparait dans quatre morceaux parallèles (9,9–10; 11,4–17; 12,10—13,1; 13,7–9)" (153).

63. That the form of the command given *directly* by Yhwh (cf. Joel 4:9) in 13:7 for the sword to arise (עוּרִי) only occurs in Isa 51:9 (three occurrences) and 52:1 (two occurrences) prior to the final Suffering Servant passage (52:13—53:12) provides a linguistic connection between the two passages. Block ("Servant," 51) presumes such an association and complementarity as part of his argument for a "Davidic interpretation of Isa. 53." He observes, "the postexilic prophet Zechariah joins his prophetic predecessor in portraying him as one whom the people reject (11:8; 12:10), and as one who is struck in accordance with the will of Yahweh for the ultimate good of the people (13:7–9)."

context of John's Gospel that assist his audience to recognize and properly understand the connections associated with 19:36-37.

Recognition of Jesus as the Lamb, Servant, and Messianic King (1:29-49)

John the Baptist recognized Jesus as "the Lamb [ἀμνός] of God" (1:29, 36) and the Suffering Servant who "takes away the sin [ἁμαρτίαν] of the world" (1:29) when Jesus first appeared in the Gospel.[64] In parallel fashion, the evangelist introduces the beginning of Jesus' hour (12:27) by affirming his identity as the Suffering Servant (12:38-40; cf. Isa 53:1) who, in freely accepting his suffering as *the* Lamb of God (John 1:29, cf. Isa 53:7), the Father would glorify in his being "lifted up" (John 12:32, cf. Isa 52:13). John the Baptist had subsequently attested to Jesus' identity as the Suffering Servant with his eyewitness account of seeing the Spirit descend upon him and remain (John 1:33; cf. Isa 42:1) which led the Baptist to testify that Jesus was "the Chosen One of God" (1:34; cf. Isa 42:1).[65] The Baptist's testimony was the first in a series of messianic titles associated with Jesus that included the Messiah/Anointed (1:41), the "Son of God" and "King of Israel" (1:49). Jesus responded to the final two identifications with his first reference to himself as "the Son of Man" (1:51). The messianic identifications immediately preceded the wedding at Cana (2:1-11) and Jesus' first reference to his hour (2:4). Its culmination affirms each of these aspects of Jesus' identity based on what transpires in his hour and the collective testimony that follows Jesus' death (19:31-34) in light of the scriptures fulfilled (19:36-37).

---

64. Isaiah similarly identifies the Servant with a lamb (ἀμνός; 53:7) who will bear the sins (ἁμαρτίας; 53:11) of many. Brown (*John*, 1:63) indicates, "both [the Lamb of God and the Suffering Servant] fit into John's Christology and are well attested in 1st-century Christianity . . . [and] can probably be found in I Peter [2:22-25]."

65. See 55n63 for the basis for identifying "the *Chosen One* of God" (ὁ ἐκλεκτὸς τοῦ θεοῦ) as the preferred reading in 1:34. The combination of the Baptist's observation (1:33) and testimony (1:34) correspond with characteristics of the Suffering Servant provided at the beginning of the first Suffering Servant passage (Isa 42:1) and affirm the implicit identification made in his initial statement (John 1:29).

EXEGESIS OF JOHN 19:36-37

Fulfillment Realized in Jesus' Hour through the "Lifted Up" Son of Man

The intertextual and intratextual connections throughout Zechariah and in the proximate context of 12:10 identify the Pierced One as the messianic king foretold implicitly in 3:8-10 and 6:10-15, and explicitly in 9:9-10 as well as the Suffering Servant (esp. Isa 52:13—53:12). Since such identifications are not apparent if one views Zech 12:10 in isolation, however, it is not surprising that John provides additional assistance for his audience to recognize the connections. He not only recounts Jesus' acknowledgment of his identity as the messianic king foretold in Zech 9:9-10, conveyed by sitting on the young donkey (John 12:15) in response (12:14) to the crowd's acclaiming him as "the King of Israel" (12:13), but subsequently highlights this connection by referring to the disciples' retrospective recognition of its significance (12:16). John's repeated reference to the "crowd" (12:9, 12, 17, 18, 29, 34) throughout the narrative of Jesus' entry into Jerusalem (12:12-36) along with their intervening dialog with him (12:29-32, 34) implies that they were privy to most (or all) of what took place. But their dissonance (12:34) with Jesus' statement about being "lifted up" (12:32) as the way in which the Father would exalt and glorify the messianic Son of Man (12:23, 28-30) indicates that they did not associate Zech 12:10 with the fulfillment of the messianic expectations reflected in 9:9-10.[66] The crowd's initial excitement (John 12:12-19) and subsequent confusion (12:34) is consistent with both the increased frequency of messianic references and the lack of coherence in messianic expectations displayed by the collective testimony of textual witnesses from the turn of the era.[67]

---

66. Various scholars in the modern era have demonstrated the limitations associated with viewing the Pierced One in 12:10 in isolation and not benefitting from the numerous intertextual and intratextual connections in Zechariah that illuminate his identity (see 115n39). Although the crowd had obviously not identified the messianic Shepherd-King explicitly presented in 9:9-10 (cf. John 12:13-16) and alluded to earlier (Zech 3:8-10; 6:10-15) with the Pierced One in 12:10 and with Isaiah's Suffering Servant, John skillfully conveys such associations to his audience (John 12:38-40; 19:36-37).

67. Collins (*Scepter*, 28) observes, "the noun, term or title 'the Messiah' appears only rarely in the literature of Early Judaism or from roughly 250 B.C.E. to 200 C.E. But it is also true in the whole history of Israel and Pre-Rabbinic Judaism 'the Messiah' occurs with unusual frequency and urgency only during this period, especially from the first century B.C.E. to 135 C.E." Charlesworth ("Messianology," 28) finds a "lack of coherent messianology among the documents in the Pseudepigrapha and among the Dead Sea Scrolls."

Jesus announces the onset of his hour (12:23) in response to a request by Greeks who came to Jerusalem to worship and asked to see him (12:20-22).[68] Jesus' ensuing dialogue with the Father (12:27-28) and consequent reply to the crowd (12:29-33) merges the previously distinct themes of his hour, his "being lifted up," and his "being glorified." John also marks the beginning of Jesus' hour by employing the first of two double fulfillment passages (12:38-40) in the Gospel (cf. 19:36-37).[69] The combined citations from Isa 53:1 (John 12:38) and Isa 6:10 (John 12:40) affirm and provide a scriptural basis for the fulfillment to be realized with the fusing of these themes (i.e., Jesus' being "lifted up" *and* "glorified") in his hour. The citation from Isa 53:1 occurs within the fourth Suffering Servant song (52:13—53:12). That the passage begins (52:13) with the prophecy that God's servant shall be "lifted up" (ὑψωθήσεται) and "glorified" (δοξασθήσεται) affirms Jesus' merging of the two themes (John 12:28-29) as the fulfillment of Scripture and reaffirms the earlier identifications of Jesus with the Suffering Servant (cf. 1:29, 34). That both terms occur in the passive in Isa 52:13 corresponds with Jesus' prophecy and affirm that his being "lifted up" coincides with the Father glorifying his name (John 12:28). That Yhwh indicates that the Suffering Servant's being "lifted up" and glorified will involve his utter disgrace and the confusion of many (Isa 52:14-15) corresponds with the crowd's reaction (John 12:34) to Jesus' allusion to his crucifixion (12:32).

That the crowd questions the identity of this "Son of Man" (12:34) in conjunction with such a shameful death implies that they had heard Jesus' earlier allusion to himself under this title (12:23) and that *they* associated the title "Son of Man" with the Christ (12:34), or the Messiah (1:41; 4:25),

---

68. The perfect tense of ἔρχομαι establishes the definitive arrival of Jesus' hour, in contrast with John's negation of its pluperfect in two prior references (7:30; 8:20) indicating that his hour had not yet come.

69. Moloney ("Scripture," 457-66) observes that John shifts from "a steady pattern in the way the citations are introduced" in the first half of the Gospel (1:23—12:15) in which "they either have no introduction [e.g., 1:23; 12:13] or use a form of the verbal expression ἔστιν γεγραμμένον, 'it is written'" (457) to "OT passages (Isa 53:1; 6:10) . . . introduced by a fulfillment formula" (459). He also convincingly argues, "the use of 'fulfillment' language in the second half of the Gospel, culminating in 19:28-30, shows that the author claims to have brought the story of Israel's Scripture to an end" (466). In light of this observation, John displays an affinity with Zechariah. Whereas the post-exilic prophet conveys continuity with the prophets who proceeded him (see 115n40), John indicates that they bore witness to Jesus (John 1:45) who fulfills (cf. 12:38-40; 19:36-37) and completes the Scripture (19:28-30).

as God's Anointed One.⁷⁰ Jesus had twice before referred to himself as the Son of Man in conjunction with being "lifted up" with no evident recognition by his hearers of a metaphorical reference to his crucifixion (3:14–15; 8:28).⁷¹ This final confluence of the Son of Man with being "lifted up" (12:32) fuses the terms with Jesus' hour and his glorification (12:23–28).⁷² The recognition in 12:34 suggests that the contextual information Jesus provided (e.g., his reference to death [12:24–25] and to being troubled [12:27]) prior to speaking of his being "lifted up" enables the crowd to understand it as a reference to crucifixion and prompts their dissonance created by the image of a crucified "Son of Man" (12:34).⁷³ Although Dan 7:13–14 does not explicitly identify the Son of Man as the Messiah, the attributes "authority" (ἐξουσία), "glory" (δόξα), and everlasting "kingdom" (βασιλεία) granted him by the Ancient of Days are consistent with those of a future messianic king (cf. Zech 9:9–10). That Jesus, identified as the Messiah/Christ (cf. John 1:41; 4:25–26), possesses these same attributes of supreme "authority" (ἐξουσία; 5:27), "glory" (δόξα) from God (8:54), and the "kingdom" (βασιλεία) of God (18:37; cf. 3:3–5), affirms his identity as

---

70. The title "Son of Man" occurs thirteen times in the Gospel (1:51; 3:13–14; 5:27; 6:27, 53, 62; 8:28; 9:35; 12:23, 34[2X]; 13:31). Its two occurrences in 12:34 are the only times that someone other than Jesus employs it.

71. Although there are numerous verses between Jesus' references to himself as the "Son of Man" (12:23) and to his being "lifted up" (12:32) in this final confluence (12:23–32), the crowd's question in 12:34 unambiguously connects them.

72. Jesus' dialogue with the Father about "this hour" (12:27) and the past and future *glorification* of his name (12:28) provide the proximate context for this third confluence and Jesus' final reference to being "lifted up" (12:32). Keener (*John*, 2:881) observes that an ancient audience would have readily grasped Jesus' "being lifted up," even in combination with his being glorified, since "ancient writers could speak of raising one up on a cross." Keener provides the example of Alexander promising to crucify those who had killed Darius by "rewarding" them with their "being lifted up."

73. John's narrative comment about Jesus' statement (12:33) indicating the *kind* of death (i.e., not just that he would die) suggests that death by crucifixion exacerbated the dissonance created by the prediction of the death of the Messiah whom they expected to remain forever (12:34). The crowd's reference to the Law (12:34) concurs with other instances in the Gospel (10:34; 15:25) in which the term simply refers to the OT.

the Son of Man and its use as a title for the Messiah.[74] The crowd's response (12:34) confirms the identification of the "Son of Man" with the Christ.[75]

John's subsequent recognition of the fulfillment of Scripture by those who did not believe in Jesus (12:38) affirms that the messianic Son of Man (12:32–33) will manifest his glory as the Suffering Servant in Isaiah. The citation from Isa 53:1 foretells the difficulty associated with God's power (literally, "his arm") revealed in such a counterintuitive manner (by the crucifixion of his Messiah), which the crowd manifested by their questions (John 12:34). John's combining it with the subsequent scripture from Isa 6:10 (John 12:40), taken from a passage in which Isaiah beheld God's glory (Isa 6:1–13), establishes that God foretold the difficulty that people would experience in perceiving his glory manifest in this manner. It also conveys the necessity that the people recognize it, however, in order that they might "turn back [i.e., repent] for me to heal them" (John 12:40; cf. 3:14–15; Num 21:9).

That Jesus had concluded his statement about the Son of Man being "lifted up" as his glorification with the purpose clause (that through his crucifixion he would "draw all men to himself" [12:32]) seems to have gone unnoticed by the crowd (12:34). This statement, however, is consistent with Daniel's prophecy about the Son of Man, which foretells all nations and races of the earth serving him (7:14).[76] Zechariah 14:16–21 foretells a complementary universal gathering of the nations to worship "the King, Yhwh of Hosts" (14:16), which implicitly provides the purpose of the Son of Man drawing all people to himself (for worship) in the context of the Gospel. Jesus' entry into Jerusalem at the onset of his hour illuminates what

---

74. Charlesworth ("Messianology," 13) indicates that it is inappropriate to assume that all Jews distinguished between "the concept of 'the Messiah' and other concepts, such as 'the Son of Man,' 'the Righteous One,' and 'the Elect One.'" He goes on to observe, "in fact, according to the Book of the Parables of Enoch (= 1En 37–71), which was composed by a Palestinian Jew before 70 C.E., these four concepts were related and at times identical." With regard to scholarly dating of 1 Enoch 37–71 (i.e., the Similitudes or the Book of the Parables of Enoch) see 113n35.

75. The crowd's final question, "who is this Son of Man?" (12:34) reflects the diversity that existed in messianic expectations within first-century Judaism. After considering evidence of common assumptions about the Son of Man manifested in intertestamental texts, Collins (*Scepter*, 191–214) concludes, "we should think of a spectrum of messianic expectations, ranging from the earthly messiah of *Psalms of Solomon* and several Dead Sea Scrolls, through the transcendent messiah of *4 Ezra* to the heavenly figure of the *Similitudes of Enoch*" (214).

76. The semantic range of the verb utilized (λατρεύω) includes both general service and worship.

will follow based on his actions (John 12:14), his words (12:23–36), and the testimony of the OT (12:15, 38–40). Collectively they affirm his identity as the messianic Son of Man (12:32; cf. Dan 7:13–14) and Suffering Servant (12:38–40; cf. Isa 53:1; 6:10) who will glorify the Father (and be glorified; 12:28) by offering himself as the Lamb of God (1:29) in true worship in his hour and enabling such worship for those who believe in him (4:23–24).

Culmination of the Hour (19:25–30) and OT Fulfillment (19:24, 36–37)

John's introduction of the OT citations in 19:36–37 refers to at least two events. The "actions" of the soldiers narrated in 19:32–33 (i.e., the decision not to break Jesus' legs and the piercing of his side) and the consequent flow of the blood and water (19:34) are the immediate referents for the pronominal phrase "these things," which introduces the fulfillment of the scriptures cited. Since 19:31–35 is the continuation of the narrative and the consequence of Jesus' death, which immediately precedes it, however, "these things" (19:36) indirectly alludes to the "things" that took place in the previous narrative segment (19:25–30). John includes it in the fulfillment recognized in 19:36–37 by framing 19:25–34 with parallel occurrences of "these things" (19:24, 36) that both refer to the fulfillment of scripture.

In 19:23–24 the soldiers divided Jesus' garments among themselves (19:23), but decided to cast lots for his tunic rather than tear it (19:24a). John observes that they did "these things" in order to fulfill the Scripture (19:24b; cf. Ps 22:19 [LXX 21:19]). By not tearing his tunic, they attested to Jesus' identity as the true high priest (cf. Exod 28:32; MT 39:23). The following section recounts the culmination of Jesus' hour with the formation of the new community of his own (19:25–27) and establishes that immediately "after this," Jesus recognized "that everything had now been accomplished" (19:28a). The singular neuter pronoun "this" (τοῦτο) establishes the significance of the preceding event in fulfilling the Father's work and connects it with Jesus' final manifestation of his consent and his handing over of the Spirit (19:28b–30). It also implicitly associates "this" event (19:25–27) and those that follow (19:28–30) with its subsequent plural counterpart ("these things;" ταῦτα) in 19:36a, which introduces the next and final recognition of the fulfillment of Scripture in the Gospel (19:36b–37). These narrative elements strengthen the connections between 19:25–30 and 19:31–35 in which the conflated and combined scriptures find their fulfillment (19:36–37) and for which they provide valuable illumination.

FIRST-CENTURY JEWISH WORSHIP AND ITS FULFILLMENT IN JOHN'S GOSPEL

As previously established, John presumes knowledge of first-century Jewish worship and the centrality of its feasts, the temple, and sacrifice to illuminate aspects of the Gospel that establish how Jesus fulfills and transcends it. The following subsections will address the feasts and the preeminence of Passover among them, the centrality of the temple and its sacrificial worship, and the preeminence of the ritual slaughter of the Passover lamb in the sacrificial worship of first-century Judaism.

The Jewish Feasts and the Preeminence of Passover

The feasts sanctified time in first-century Judaism. The Sabbath performed this function on a weekly basis and the annual feasts sanctified time throughout the year, with the pilgrimage feasts as the most prominent and Passover preeminent. As established in chapter 2, the OT, intertestamental literature, and first-century AD witnesses testify to such preeminence and recognize Passover's inherent relationship with the exodus from slavery in Egypt, which enabled the authentic worship of God (Exod 3:12).[77]

Passover's preeminence in the worship of first-century Judaism reflects its essential role in the establishment of the covenant at Sinai and its associated worship. That Yhwh intended the observance of Passover (and the exodus) to culminate in worship at Sinai (Exod 3:12; cf. 24:1–8) attests to its chronological primacy in the liturgical worship of Israel (as the first feast observed) and more importantly its teleological primacy in establishing the authentic worship of Yhwh as practiced through the end of the Second Temple period. Through the Law Yhwh provided instruction for such worship. That Yhwh specified all the essential elements (e.g., the contents of the Tabernacle and the priesthood) for temple worship to Moses at Sinai attests to Passover's foundational role in the establishment of temple worship and its corresponding preeminence in it. Passover both represented and

---

77. The word "authentic" recognizes that it enabled worship of the one true God while distinguishing worship established by the covenant at Sinai from the true worship offered in Jesus' hour (John 4:21–24).

summed up the authentic worship of Yhwh, which its initial observance enabled. John's recurring references to the preeminent feast (2:13, 23; 6:4; 11:55; 12:1; 13:1; 18:28, 39; 19:14) reflect such an understanding of Passover, which illuminates the many ways that Jesus fulfills and transcends first-century Jewish worship.

The Centrality of the Temple and Sacrificial Worship

The OT established the temple as the preeminent venue for worship.[78] Its two fundamental attributes associated with this distinction were that Yhwh had designated it as the place where he (or his name) would dwell among his people (Deut 12:5, 11; 1 Kgs 8:29) and the only place within Judaism for sacrificial worship (Deut 12:5-13; 2 Chr 7:11-16; Ps 132:14). The OT also foretold the centrality of an eschatological temple (Ezek 40:1—47:12) as the place of worship for all nations (Zech 14:16-21) and the source of light (14:7) and life-giving water for the world (14:8; Ezek 47:1-12). Sacrifice would remain central to the worship offered in the future temple (40:38—46:24) including the new sacrifice of a sin offering for the people at the Passover (45:22) proffered by "the one lifted up."[79]

John's Gospel manifests a keen awareness of the temple as the place of worship *par excellence* in Judaism (John 4:21-23; cf. 2:16-21). It also alludes to expectations associated with the future temple in establishing that both Jesus (2:19-21) and his disciples, with whom he would constitute the new temple through the Spirit (14:2-27; 16:7), fulfill them. Correspondingly, Jesus established that the true worship that the Father desired would take place in Spirit and Truth (4:23-24) rather than being confined to a particular place (4:21). He also identified the realization of such worship as the work the Father had given him to accomplish (4:34) and associated it with his hour (4:23).

---

78. The term "venue" allows the versatility of referring to the location of the Jerusalem temple as well as to the true worship initiated by Jesus (4:23-24) not restricted to a specific place (4:21).

79. Ezekiel's vision of the new temple (40:1—47:12) interweaves references to sacrifice throughout the narrative, beginning with a reference to the chamber for washing the burnt offerings in 40:38 and ending with a reference to the place where the ministers would boil the sacrifices in 46:24. The following section will address the prophecy about "the one lifted up" providing the sacrifice (see 131n83).

Sacrificial Worship and Preeminence of the Ritual Slaughter of the Passover Lamb

Chapter 2 demonstrated how the OT and subsequent witnesses collectively attested to the importance of integrating the proper external actions (ritual/liturgical worship) with the appropriate internal disposition (ethical worship) in the sacrificial worship offered in the temple. The initial OT accounts of sacrifice (Gen 4:3–5; 8:20–21) embody the truth that distinctive sacrificial offerings are pleasing to God when integrated with obedience to his commands (ethical worship) in the whole of one's life (cf. 6:22, 7:5, 9, 16). Philo's unique first-century theory (cf. *Spec. Laws* 194–96, 257, 290) on sacrifice conveys such an understanding of proper worship.[80] Sacrificial worship in first-century Judaism, however, bore an inherent limitation regarding the degree of integration possible with the worshiper being distinct from the sacrifice offered.

The OT implicitly establishes that the ritual slaughter of the Passover lamb was not only *a* sacrifice, but *the* preeminent sacrifice in Israel's worship and textual witnesses corroborate the persistence of such an understanding in first-century Judaism. The OT indicates that the ritual slaughter is a sacrifice with the verb used (Exod 12:6) and the explicit reference to "the Passover *sacrifice*" (12:27) in Yhwh's instructions for its observance in Egypt.[81] Yhwh subsequently attests to its preeminence by referring to the slaughter of the Passover lamb as "my sacrifice" (23:18; 34:25). The OT affirms the understanding of the ritual slaughter as a sacrifice with the requirement to perform it in the temple (Deut 16:2; cf. 12:5–14) and the practice of pouring the blood of the victim out at the altar (2 Chr 30:16; 35:11).[82] The great number of sacrifices offered through the ritual slaughter of the lamb also attests to its preeminence in temple worship. Whereas the OT and first-century witnesses attest to the ritual slaughter as the preeminent sacrifice, it had the same fundamental limitation as all other sacrifices

---

80. Whereas Philo (*Spec. Laws* 1.194–290) provides the earliest theory, the initial OT accounts of sacrifice (Gen 4:3–5; 8:20–21) and subsequent texts (e.g., 1 Sam 13:8–14; 15:10–13; Isa 1:10–17; Hos 6:4–10; Pss 40:6–8; 51:15–19; Eccl 4:17—5:1) affirm the fundamental truth embodied in these accounts and expressed in Philo's theory in various ways. The structure of the Law given at Sinai also affirms it (see 112n32).

81. According to Clements ("שחט," 14:564), the verb used in 12:6 generally "refers to the slaughtering of animals in connection with cultic acts." That the context is the gathered assembly affirms its cultic character.

82. Later witnesses attest to the continuation of these practices through the Second Temple period (Jub. 49.20; m. Pesaḥ. 5:5–6; Zebaḥ. 5:8).

with the will of the offerer and the life of the offering insuperably distinct from one another.

Whereas the OT never identifies the ritual slaughter of the Passover lamb as a sin offering, its origins associate it with the preservation of natural life (Exod 12:21-28) and redemption from slavery in Egypt (12:29-42). According to John's Gospel, Jesus established the superior parallels of eternal life (John 3:14-15) and freedom from slavery to sin (8:28-38) for those who believe in the "lifted up" Son of Man. Additionally, although the OT never identifies the ritual slaughter as a sin offering, it associates the observance of Passover in the future temple with such an offering. Ezekiel indicates that the "one lifted up" will make a sin offering for the people (Ezek 45:21-24) on the day of Passover in his vision of worship in the eschatological temple (40:1—47:12).[83] When John the Baptist identifies Jesus as *the* Lamb of God *and* the Suffering Servant (John 1:29) he grants insight into how Jesus will transcend the limitation of sacrificial worship in the Jerusalem temple by freely offering himself in sacrifice in the context of Passover as the future temple.

FULFILLMENT ATTESTED BY JOHN 19:36-37

"For these things happened in order that the scripture might be fulfilled: 'a bone of him shall not be broken.' And again another scripture says: 'they shall look to whom they pierced'" (19:36-37).

The scriptures (19:36-37) in conjunction with their direct referents (19:33-34) illuminate the narrative of Jesus' hour. Together with the contexts presumed by John they corroborate various aspects of Jesus' identity as they demonstrate their implications and attest to his completion of the work the Father has given him (4:34; cf. 5:36; 17:4) in his hour (18:1—19:30; esp. 19:25-30) and its significance for John's audience (19:34-35; cf. 4:23-24).

As the Lamb of God (1:29, 36) handed over for sacrifice (19:14), Jesus fulfills and transcends Passover and the temple worship that it enabled

---

83. BDB (672a) indicates that the term utilized in Ezek 45:22 (נָשִׂיא) literally means, *"one lifted up,* i.e. a chief prince" (emphasis added). Similarly, A. Niehr ("נָשִׂיא," 10:45) states that it "represents a *nomen professionis* deriving from the Proto-Semitic verb *nāśā'*, with the fundamental meaning 'to lift up' or 'to elevate, raise, exalt,' so that it is to be understood as 'one raised up, exalted.'" The water (and blood) flowing from the side of Jesus (John 19:34), earlier identified as the new temple (2:19-22; 7:37-39; cf. Ezek 47:1-12), is another example of the intertextuality of John 19 with Ezekiel 40:1—47:12.

(Exod 3:12; cf. 24:1–8). Whereas the initial Passover led to freedom from physical slavery and the authentic worship of Yhwh through the covenant at Sinai, the Lamb of God grants freedom from slavery to sin (John 8:28–38) and enables the true worship that the Father seeks (4:23).[84] As the Righteous One (19:36; Ps 34:21 [LXX 33:21]; cf. Isa 53:11), Jesus offered himself as a lamb for slaughter (53:7) on behalf of the sheep that had each wandered in its own way (53:6). The soldiers' restraint (John 19:33) in light of the OT testimony (19:36) affirms Jesus' self-identification as *the* Good Shepherd who laid down his life for his sheep (John 10:11, 15; cf. Isa 52:13; 53:5) in obedience to the Father (John 10:18) out of love for him (14:31) and his friends (15:13).[85] In this way, Jesus transcended the Passover sacrifice in fully integrating liturgical and ethical worship with his self-sacrifice as both priest (cf. 19:23–24) and victim in a way not possible in the sacrificial worship offered in the temple in Jerusalem (cf. 4:21).[86] John's conflation of the discrete OT verses in 19:36 affirm John the Baptist's initial recognition of Jesus as the Lamb of God who takes away the sin of the world (1:29).

John 19:37 recognizes the fulfillment of Zech 12:10 in those beholding Jesus as the Pierced One (John 19:34). In light of Zech 12:10 and its context, the soldiers affirm Jesus' messianic identity as the (Righteous) Shoot initially foretold in Jer 23:5 (cf. 33:15) to whom Zechariah alludes (3:8; 6:12). His prophecies progressively reveal the outcomes associated with the messianic king (3:8–10; 6:10–15) and subsequently provide insight into the means (suffering) of their accomplishment (Zech 12:10—13:1; 13:7–9). Jesus' action in response to the crowd's greeting during his entry into Jerusalem (John 12:14) identified him as the messianic king (12:15; cf. Zech 9:9) who would complete the work given him by the Father as the humble Suffering

---

84. Jesus associates his ability to grant freedom with his identity as the Son (8:36) and he associates the recognition of his authority with the recognition of his divinity as the "lifted up" Son of Man (8:28).

85. Isa 52:13 and 53:5 collectively establish that the Servant would lay down his life for the sheep. Block ("Servant," 54–55) remarks, "indeed, commentators in general seem to have missed a significant nuance of Jesus' statement 'I am *the* good shepherd; *the* good shepherd lays down his life for the sheep'" (54; emphasis original). In identifying himself as *the* Good Shepherd, rather than *a* good shepherd, Block observes that Jesus alludes to the fourth Suffering Servant song which is the only passage in the OT with "direct references or allusions to a shepherd who voluntarily gives his life for his sheep" (55).

86. The soldiers attest to Jesus' priestly identity in not tearing his tunic (19:23–24; cf. Exod 28:32; MT 39:23) as does the recognition of the fulfillment of the pierced messianic king (John 19:37) foretold in Zechariah (12:10) who would be both priest and king (6:13).

Servant. Jesus expressed this aspect of his identity within the context of his entry by clearly establishing the means of his glorification (John 12:23–32) and John affirmed the association at the onset of Jesus' hour with his first of two double fulfillment quotations in 12:38–40 (cf. Isa 53:1; 6:10).

Whereas the Gospel explicitly (John 1:49; 19:14–15) and implicitly (18:36; cf. 3:3, 5) attests to Jesus' kingly identity and alludes to him as the true high priest (11:45–53; 18:1–27), it reaffirms both of these aspects of the identity of the reigning Messiah foretold in Zechariah 6:12–13 just before the culmination of his hour (John 19:19–22; 23–24). As king, Jesus definitively establishes his kingdom on earth with the formation of the new community (the Church) at the cross (19:25–27) by the implied consent of his mother and beloved disciple (19:27) to his performative statements (19:25–26) and his handing over of the Spirit to them (19:30).[87] He offered true worship to the Father in laying down his life for his sheep (John 10:11, 15; cf. Isa 53:7) as the Lamb of God (John 1:29) in accord with his priestly identity and enabled true worship in establishing his kingdom on earth by providing the Spirit.[88]

Zechariah foretold that the messianic king would *speak* peace to the nations (Zech 9:10).[89] That the complementary accounts of the death of the Suffering Servant messiah in Zechariah (12:10; 13:7; cf. Isa 53:5) associate his death with the conversion and forgiveness (Zech 12:10—13:1, 9; cf. Isa 53:4–12) that lead to the eschatological vision of Jerusalem (Zech 14:4–11) and universal worship (14:16–21) implicitly connects the peace that the Messiah would initiate with such worship.[90] These connections illuminate

---

87. It was immediately after the manifestation of their consent ("after this" [19:28]) that Jesus recognized "that everything had now been accomplished" (19:28). This led to Jesus' visibly manifesting his final consent in expressing his thirst and consuming the sour wine (19:28–29; cf. 18:11) and stating, "it is accomplished" (19:30) with the completion of the work the Father had given him (4:34; cf. 5:36; 17:4).

88. The Spirit is necessary for believers to enter into his kingdom (3:3, 5) and to offer the worship the Father desires by remaining in them (14:17) and enabling Jesus to dwell in them (14:23) so that they can worship the Father in Spirit and Truth (4:23–24).

89. Whereas the LXX indicates he will initiate peace, the MT states, "he shall *speak* peace to the nations and his kingdom shall be from sea to sea and from [the] river to the ends of the earth" (9:10).

90. Jesus' first action in each of his first two post-resurrection appearances to his gathered disciples is to speak peace (20:19, 26). On the first of these, he breathes the Holy Spirit on them and sends them with the authority to forgive or retain sins (20:22–23). Whereas sin scatters the flock (cf. Isa 53:5–6), the authority to forgive sins provides for its gathering and maintaining its integrity for worship. Swetnam ("Bestowal of the Spirit," 571–72) observes that whereas Jesus hands over the Spirit to the Church in 19:30, "the

the fulfillment realized in Jesus' hour when he completes the work of the messianic king (John 12:14–15; cf. Zech 9:9) as the "lifted up" and glorified Suffering Servant (cf. Isa 52:13; John 12:23–32, 38–40).

Jesus confirmed the connections implicit in Zechariah with his three statements about the Son of Man being "lifted up" (3:14–15; 8:28; 12:23–32) through which he progressively disclosed aspects associated with the OT fulfillment he would realize with the completion of his Father's work (4:34) in his hour (19:28–30).[91] In foretelling the realization of his glorification in his being "lifted up" (12:23–32) Jesus alluded to his identity as the Suffering Servant (Isa 52:13) and John affirmed it with his associated recognition of OT fulfillment (12:38–40). Jesus' first mention of the "lifted up" Son of Man (3:14) implicitly connected eternal life through belief in him (3:15) with repentance by associating the "lifted up" Son of Man with the bronze serpent in the wilderness (cf. Num 21:7–9).[92] That Jesus elsewhere identifies sin and the failure to believe in him with death (John 8:24) implicitly associates the forgiveness of sins with the realization of eternal life for those who (repent and) believe in the "lifted up" Son of Man (3:14–15). Zechariah connects conversion, forgiveness of sins, and belief in God with the complementary accounts of the death of the messianic Servant King (12:10—13:9; cf. Isa 53:4–12).[93] In John 3:14–15, Jesus affirms the necessity of these elements

---

bestowal of the Spirit in John 20,22 would seem to be to a restricted group of disciples, possibly only the 'Twelve' (cf. 20,24) . . . associated with the missioning of the disciples expressed in 20,21" (572).

91. Jesus' repeated references to himself as the Son of Man play an important role in integrating the various OT figures (e.g., the Passover lamb, the Suffering Servant, the Pierced One) that prefigure him with his identity as the Son of God and the different aspects of the work he would accomplish in his hour.

92. The serpent provided the means for freeing the people from the punitive effects of the snakebites for all who repented from their earlier questioning of Yhwh's goodness (21:4–5). They expressed their trust in him by looking to the serpent (21:9). In an analogous way, the "lifted up" Son of Man, as the Suffering Servant, eliminates the punitive effects of iniquities in making many righteous by taking away the sins (Isa 53:5–11; cf. John 1:29) of those who believe in him (3:14–15). They express such belief by remaining in him (6:56) and his word (8:31).

93. The death accounts (Zech 12:10; 13:7) and the associated material (12:11—13:6, 8–9) interweave evidence of repentance and conversion (12:11–14; 13:3–6) as well as explicit (13:1–2) and implicit (13:8) references to purification and forgiveness. They culminate with the manifestation of belief in Yhwh (13:9).

to realize the eternal life that the "lifted up" Son of Man makes available to those who believe in him.[94]

In Jesus' third reference to the "lifted up" Son of Man (12:32) he indicated that he would draw all people to himself.[95] Jesus' statement recounted by the proclamation of John's Gospel in the context of early Christian worship, which the "lifted up" Son of Man enabled, provides the necessary framework for his audience to recognize the ongoing fulfillment that follows the death of the Pierced One (Zech 12:10) and shepherd-king (13:7). The complementary death references and the associated conversion (12:10—13:9) leads to the worship of "*the King*, Yhwh of Hosts" (14:16; cf. John 19:14-15, 19-22) by people from all the nations. That Zechariah foretells such worship occurring "on that day" (14:20-21; cf. 14:6-8) associates it with the provision of continuous light (14:7) and life-giving water (14:8) from Jerusalem and, by implication, the temple. That Jesus had foretold the fulfillment of those prophecies in him (John 7:37-38; 8:12), the first of which John connected with Jesus' provision of the Spirit in his hour (7:39), facilitates the audience's recognition of their fulfillment in the "lifted up" Son of Man.[96]

Jesus' remaining reference to the "lifted up" Son of Man (John 8:28), the second in the narrative of the Gospel, is essential for recognizing the fulfillment of the worship of the King (Zech 14:16) and Jesus as the new temple (John 2:19-21; cf. 14:7-8) since it concerns the perception of his divinity.[97] The soldiers' actions in light of the OT testimony provided in John

---

94. The allusive way in which Jesus and the Gospel convey these connections present in Zechariah corresponds with the prophet's style. John's audience manifests their belief when they gather for liturgical worship and in their ethical worship offered by keeping Jesus' commandments (14:15).

95. That Jesus, as the "lifted up" Son of Man (12:23, 32) states, "I will draw [ἑλκύσω] everyone to myself" (12:32) conveys his divinity. Earlier, he attributed such action to the Father who would draw (ἑλκύσῃ) believers to Jesus (6:44). *BDAG* (318) indicates that the figurative meaning of ἕλκω is "to draw a pers. in the direction of values for inner life."

96. That Jesus had foretold their fulfillment in the context of Tabernacles (John 7:1—10:21), which Zechariah (14:18) also associates with "that day" (14:13, 20, 21), strengthens the connection.

97. Jesus stated, "when you lift up the Son of Man, then you will know that I AM" (8:28). He refers to his divinity elsewhere with unqualified "I AM" statements (8:24, 58), but 13:19 is the only other place that he uses such a statement to refer to the manifestation of his divinity through a particular event. In that instance, he refers to the future fulfillment of the OT in the betrayal of Judas (13:18), which would simply manifest his identity to the limited group present at the supper (cf. 13:2). That Jesus' "I AM" statements at his arrest (18:5, 6, 8) occur in response to the soldiers' seeking "Jesus the Nazarene" (18:4-8)

19:36-37 attest to his divinity. By ignoring their implied orders (19:31-32) and not breaking any of his bones, the soldiers attested to Jesus' innocence as the Righteous One (19:36; cf. Ps 34:21 [LXX 33:21]; Isa 53:11) who had no deceit in his mouth (53:9). Their restraint established that Jesus was innocent of the Jewish authorities' ultimate charge, "that he made himself the Son of God" (John 19:7) and so affirmed his divinity (cf. 5:17-18; 10:30-39).

That one of the soldiers pierced Jesus instead (19:34) more subtly attests to his divinity based on the testimony implicit in the more common vocalization associated with the consonantal text of Zech 12:10 (and manifested by the MT) which indicates that Yhwh states "they shall look *to me* whom they pierced." Perceptive members of the audience familiar with the MT *Vorlage* (ideally) or a literal translation of it would be able to *discover* this testimony to Jesus' divinity with the fulfillment of Zech 12:10.[98] At the same time, all members of the audience could recognize OT fulfillment in their looking to Jesus, the Pierced One, and believing in him (John 19:35). That those gathered for worship to hear the Gospel believe in Jesus as God (cf. John 1:1; 20:28) establishes their participation in fulfilling this sense of Zech 12:10 whether or not they are fully aware of its presence in John's source text.[99]

Technically, the plural subject of the looking (i.e., "they") is ambiguous and can include Jesus' disciples who were present (19:25-26, 35, 38-39), the soldiers (19:33-34), and any of the Jewish authorities (19:31) present for the piercing.[100] It also includes those who indirectly "look" through reports from those present (e.g., a report from the soldiers to Pilate) and John's

---

allow for the possibility that such statements are qualified. Additionally, they make no mention of others coming to know Jesus' divinity.

98. Familiarity with either the MT *Vorlage* or a literal Greek rendering of it in accord with the MT vocalization (e.g., Theodotion's translation) would enable members of John's audience to recognize an affirmation of Jesus' divinity in the fulfillment of Zech 12:10. Such a Greek translation conveys Jesus' divinity (in stating "look *to me*"), but it also suggests that John substantially changed it (manifesting only two of five terms). Knowledge of the Hebrew text, however, facilitates the true *discovery* characteristic of John's allusive style (see 109-110nn24-29) since the same consonantal Hebrew text supports John's translation *and* allows one to *discover* testimony to Jesus' divinity (depending on the vocalization).

99. The multivalence of Zech 12:10 and John 19:37 allows members of evangelist's audience to comprehend various aspects of the fulfillment of Zech 12:10 (in the soldier's piercing of Jesus' side and the blood and water flowing out) without it being necessary for them to recognize all of them.

100. In stating that the "one who has seen [ἑωρακώς] has testified... in order that you may *also* believe" (19:35), John identifies the eyewitness as a disciple of Jesus (at least

audience through the testimony of the eyewitness (19:35). The fulfillment recognized through the soldier's actions and the consequent flow of blood and water (19:34) along with the importance of belief in John's Gospel (20:31) indicate the primary referent is the audience as the ones who have "seen" and have come to believe through the testimony of the eyewitness (19:35).[101] The eyewitness testimony implicitly bears witness to all of the events following Jesus' death as OT fulfillment (19:31-34) and particularly to the flow of blood and water that immediately precedes it (19:34). The blood and water that flow forth from the "lifted up" Son of Man convey multiple dimensions of meaning. On the one hand, they attest to the true worship offered by Jesus in his hour, and on the other, they testify to the way he enables worship in Spirit and Truth for those who believe in him.

The presumed contexts of the OT and sacrificial temple worship understand life to be in the blood (Lev 17:14) as the means by which the blood atones (17:11).[102] The blood flowing forth from the side of the Pierced One attests to the *completed* sacrifice of the Lamb of God who bore the sins of the world as the Suffering Servant (cf. John 1:29; Isa 53:5-8).[103] In freely laying down his life for his sheep and bearing their sins, Jesus fulfilled Ezekiel's prophecy that the "one lifted up" would make a sin offering for the people on Passover (45:22). That he offered himself (rather than a bull) as a guilt offering (Isa 53:10), the "lifted up" Son of Man (John 3:14-15) made *the* Passover sacrifice that would make many righteous (Isa 53:11). As the Chosen One of God (John 1:34) upon whom the Spirit came down

---

by the time he wrote the Gospel) so the verses associated with "Jesus' disciples" include 19:35.

101. Obermann (*Erfüllung*, 318) states, "der ἑωρακώς stellvertretend für die Gläubigen insgesamt steht." The audience has expressed their belief in Jesus and they continue to manifest it through their ethical and liturgical worship. Consequently, their gathering together "to worship the King" (Zech 14:16; cf. John 19:14-15, 19-22) is in itself part of the ongoing fulfillment of Scripture. Heil (*John*, 138) observes, "the audience, those who already believe, will continuously 'look upon the one they have pierced' as an object of worship."

102. One of the five other occurrence of "blood" in John's Gospel (aside from 19:34) associates it with life in referring to natural birth (1:13). Carnazzo (*Seeing Blood and Water*, 32) explains, "conception was thought to be the result of the compaction of the mother's life-giving blood around the father's seed (Wis 7:2)."

103. The manipulation of blood (generally pouring or sprinkling) to bring it in contact with the altar was an integral part of sacrificial worship in the temple (e.g., Lev 1:3-17; 4:1-35; 7:1-7). The corresponding removal of blood from the sacrifice was necessary to allow the consumption of the sacrificial victim (17:14), which was an essential part of the ritual worship associated with the Passover lamb.

and remained (1:33) he offered the fully integrated worship that the Father desires in Spirit and Truth (4:23-24) by offering himself as the sacrifice in obedience to the Father (10:18) out of love for him (14:31). The water flowing along with the blood corresponds with the effects of the sacrifice and fulfills the prophecy that Yhwh would open "a fountain for [purification from] sin and uncleanness" (Zech 13:1) on the day they look on the Pierced One and mourn exceedingly (12:10-14), implicitly conveying repentance.[104] These effects are consistent with the cleansing quality of water (as one of its two fundamental attributes) reflected in the OT.[105] Consequently, the blood attests to atonement for sins through Jesus' sacrificial self-offering and the water reflects the means by which those who believe in the Son of Man would realize the purification from sin (i.e., baptism). That Yhwh also foretells pouring out a spirit (12:10) prior to opening the fountain (13:1) corresponds with the order of Jesus' handing over the Spirit (John 19:30) to the Church (19:25-27) prior to the fountain being opened from his side (19:34).

In light of the presumed contexts of the OT and the Gospel in the proximate context of early Christian worship, the blood and water coming out from Jesus' side (19:34) affirms his identity as the new Temple (John 2:19-21) and also attests to the fulfillment of his role as the temple builder (Zech 6:13, 15). As mentioned above, the actions of the soldiers (19:32-33) in light of the OT witnesses (19:36-37) bore witness to his innocence (cf. 19:7) and, consequently, his divinity (8:28), establishing that he transcends the temple's essential characteristic (cf. Num 10:35-36; 2 Chr 6:41; Ps 132:8) by possessing the divine presence in an unparalleled manner (John 1:1; 10:30, 38). The blood and, especially, the water flowing from his side confirms his identity as the new temple with the provision of the living water (7:37-39) of the Holy Spirit, fulfilling the expectations for the eschatological temple in a superabundant way (Zech 14:8; Ezek 47:1-12;

---

104. Whereas the prophecy about the fountain is present in the MT, there is much variation among the LXX witnesses. Although some of the major witnesses exclude any reference to a fountain, others manifest it with some variation among the extant witnesses. Ziegler (*Duodecim prophetae*, 321) considers the shorter reading (i.e., without the fountain) original. That Theodotion includes the opening of a fountain attests to the MT *Vorlage*.

105. Carnazzo (*Seeing Blood and Water*, 27-29) observes, "in the Scriptures of Israel, water is portrayed primarily as a natural cleansing mechanism and the essential life-sustaining quencher of thirst" (27). He provides numerous examples of evidence from the OT and subsequently shows how the NT reflects these fundamental characteristics in its "symbolic uses of water" (28).

Joel 4:18). In the proximate context of worship, the audience would readily associate the water with the Holy Spirit and baptism, and the blood with the Eucharist.[106] That they came out together reflects the Spirit's integral role in imparting (or sustaining) eternal life through the sacraments.[107]

Jesus' handing over the Spirit (19:30) to the Church in his hour (19:25–27) and to individual believers through the sacraments (19:34) attest to his fulfillment of the Messiah's role in building the new temple (Zech 6:13, 15). Jesus had indicated that his disciples would constitute the new temple as the dwelling (μονή) of the Father and of Jesus (John 14:2–3; 23) through the Spirit who remains *in* them (14:16–17; 16:7).[108] The Spirit gives new birth to individual believers in baptism, making them children of God (1:13) and remains with them (cf. 1:33; 14:17) as the living water (7:38–39) and source of eternal life (4:14). The Eucharist sustains this gift of eternal life within the individual believers (6:54) enabling them to remain in Jesus as he remains in them (6:56). The Spirit dwelling in his disciples (14:17) along with Jesus, the Truth (14:6), making his home in them (14:23) enables those who believe in him to worship in Spirit and Truth (4:23–24), thus transcending temple worship.

The blood and water flowing forth from the side of the "lifted up" Son of Man (19:34) manifest the origins of the sacraments and reflect the inherent relationship of the worship (and eternal life) they enable with the true worship offered by Jesus in his hour. The gift of the Spirit in Jesus' hour (19:30) received by individual believers through the sacraments empowers the community to participate in Jesus' fully integrated self-sacrificial worship when they gather for liturgical worship and, especially, in their

---

106. The Gospel associates water with baptism (John 1:26, 31, 33; 3:5, 23) and the Spirit (4:10, 11, 14, 15; 7:38). Four of the five other occurrences of "blood" (6:53–56) in the Gospel take place within the climax of the Bread of Life Discourse (6:51–58) where they clearly refer to the Eucharist. Carnazzo (*Seeing Blood and Water*, 78) indicates, "the overwhelmingly dominant interpretation of this verse in the history of exegesis is that there is some relation between John 19:34 and the sacraments of the intended audience." He also provides a list of modern scholars who have suggested the possibility of such an interpretation (78n50).

107. Jesus conveys the Spirit's essential role in baptism by speaking initially about birth by water and the Spirit (3:5) and then proceeding to simply refer to being "born of the Spirit" (3:6, 8) in his dialogue with Nicodemus. Regarding its fundamental role in imparting eternal life through the consumption of the Eucharist, Jesus states "it is the Spirit that gives life" (6:63) in the conclusion of the Bread of Life Discourse.

108. Through the indwelling divine presence, Jesus' disciples transcend the fundamental characteristic associated with the Jerusalem temple (cf. Ezek 43:7, 1 Kgs 8:12–50; 2 Chr 6:1–39).

sacramental worship through which he continues to constitute the new temple (through baptism) and fortify it (through the Eucharist). The Spirit, the other Advocate sent by Jesus (16:7) and the Father (14:16), also enables his disciples to offer integral ethical worship in keeping his commandments (14:21–23) including his new commandment to love one another as he loves them (13:34; 15:12) by enabling them to abide in Jesus (15:4; cf. 6:56) and his love (15:9–10).[109] Thus, "these things" that happened after Jesus' death (19:32–34) in light of the OT witnesses presented in 19:36–37 collectively testify to the fulfillment of the OT and the completion of the work of the Father (4:34) in Jesus' hour through the perfect sacrificial worship offered by the "lifted up" Son of Man (3:14–15; 8:28; 12:23–32). At the same time, they attest to the ongoing fulfillment realized through worship offered in Spirit and Truth by his disciples (4:23–24) which Jesus enabled in his hour through the gifts of the Spirit (19:30) to the Church (19:25–27) at the culmination of his hour and to individual believers through the sacraments (19:34).

SUMMARY

This chapter demonstrated the fulfillment attested by John 19:36–37. It began with an analysis of the text that included a discussion of John's sources for the scriptures cited and his presentation of them. The following section addressed the original contexts of John's OT sources that the evangelist presumes and draws upon in recognizing the fulfillment of the portions of them presented in 19:36–37. The third section identified significant contextual elements from the Gospel that provide information to assist John's audience in understanding his final fulfillment citations (19:36–37) and the testimony provided by them and the corresponding actions (19:33–34) that the scriptures illuminate in establishing their significance. The fourth section reviewed significant elements associated with first-century Jewish worship. The final section synthesized the foregoing analysis in light of the proximate context of early Christian worship to address the fulfillment attested by 19:36–37.

It demonstrated how 19:36–37 in conjunction with its direct referents in 19:33–34 corroborate various aspects of Jesus' identity and attest to the

---

109. Prior to Jesus' second mention of his new commandment in 15:12 (cf. 13:34) he implies that abiding in his love is both the means for and the result of keeping his commandments (15:9–10).

completion of the work the Father had given him (4:34) and its significance for John's audience. The scriptures cited (19:36-37) in interpreting the soldiers' "actions" and their consequences (19:33-34) attest to Jesus' identity as the Lamb of God, Suffering Servant, messianic shepherd-king (Zech 9:9-10; 13:7), and Pierced One (12:10) as aspects of his self-identification as the Son of Man (John 1:51; cf. Dan 7:13-14). Jesus' self-references to the "lifted up" Son of Man (3:14-15; 8:28; 12:23-32) integrate the various OT figures that convey aspects of the messianic fulfillment realized by him in his hour as well as the recognition of his divinity. John 19:36-37 in conjunction with its direct referents (19:33-34) in the context of the Gospel and the other contexts presumed by the evangelist illuminate the significance of "these things" that took place in the culmination of Jesus' hour.

Through the discrete OT passages utilized, their original contexts, the Gospel's intratextual and intertextual connections, and the presumed contexts of first-century Jewish and early Christian worship, 19:36-37 attests that Jesus fulfills the OT and transcends temple worship (4:21-22) in the completion of the Father's work (4:34) with the true worship offered and enabled in Jesus' hour. John 19:36-37 and its corresponding referents (19:33-34) attest to such fulfillment and transcendence realized in the perfect self-sacrificial worship offered by the "lifted up" Son of Man (3:14-15; 8:28; 12:23-32). They also bear witness to their ongoing realization in the worship offered in Spirit and Truth by Jesus' disciples (4:23-24) enabled through his gift of the Spirit to the Church (19:25-27) at the culmination of his hour (19:28-30) and to individual believers through the sacraments (19:34). Chapter 6 will summarize and synthesize the results of this study.

6

Summary and Synthesis

THIS STUDY INVESTIGATED THE fulfillment attested by John 19:36–37. It is not possible to overstate the significance of these last two fulfillment citations in the Gospel (which arguably presents itself as the completion of Scripture), with the evangelist's recognizing their fulfillment in the culmination of Jesus' hour. In providing no explanatory remarks to assist his audience in comprehending the fulfillment attested, however, John requires them to rely entirely upon the external contexts he presumes and the internal context he provides. This study has investigated these contexts and utilized them to gain greater insight into the fulfillment attested by 19:36–37 in light of the Gospel's proximate context of early Christian worship. The current chapter provides a summary of the study and a synthesis of its results.

SUMMARY OF THE STUDY

Chapter 1 began by recognizing the importance implicitly conferred by John on 19:36–37 and that, in providing no explanatory information, he requires his audience to rely on the external contexts he presumes and the literary context he provides. It established that this study would examine these contexts and subsequently use information from them in light of the Gospel's proximate context of early Christian worship to gain greater insight into the fulfillment attested by 19:36–37. The chapter proceeded to provide preliminary information based on recent scholarship and concluded with an overview of the study.

Chapter 2 addressed the context of worship in first-century Judaism and identified the temple, the feasts, and sacrificial worship as fundamental aspects of it. God established the temple as the place in which he would dwell in a unique way among his people (Num 10:35–36; 2 Chr 6:41; Ps 132:8, 14) and the only place for sacrificial worship (Deut 12:5–13; 16:2; 26:2; 2 Chr 7:11–16). First-century Jewish witnesses reflect the temple's centrality (cf. *Ant.* 3.179–87, 224–57; *J.W.* 5.17; 4.262; *Spec. Laws* 1.66–345) and the NT corroborates their testimony (cf. Matt 24:1; Mark 13:1; Luke 21:5). John's account of Jesus referring to his body as the temple (John 2:19–21), which he would raise up when "destroyed," offers the most effective illustration of the temple's significance in first-century Jewish worship based on the way that echoes of it continued to reverberate (Matt 26:61; 27:40; Mark 14:58; 15:29; Acts 6:13–14).

The feasts sanctified time in Second Temple Judaism, with the pilgrimage feasts as the most prominent and Passover preeminent. The inherent relationship between Passover and the exodus (Exod 12:1—13:16) and their foundational role in enabling the authentic worship of God (3:12) made it the preeminent feast and representative of the temple worship it enabled.[1] The worship associated with the ritual observance of Tabernacles (namely, the water drawing/libation rituals and the associated illumination of the temple courts) manifested aspects of the eschatological temple (Zech 14:7–8; cf. Ezek 47:1–12) and the universal worship associated with it (Zech 14:16–21).

Whereas the importance of sacrificial worship in Judaism was not unique in the ancient world, its restriction of sacrifice to one location and the ritual slaughter of Passover were distinctive as was the purpose of sacrifice implicit in the OT and later explicated by Philo. The truth embodied in the initial OT accounts of sacrifice in the Primordial History (Gen 4:3–5; 8:20–21; cf. 6:22; 7:5, 9, 16) and subsequent OT passages (e.g., 1 Sam 13:8–14; 15:10–13; Isa 1:10–17; Hos 6:4–10), affirming the importance of integrating external actions (liturgical worship) and internal disposition

---

1. As previously established, first-century texts (cf. Matt 26:17–19; Mark 14:1, 12; *J.W.* 2.280; 6.423–25; *Spec Laws* 2.145–49) offer testimony consistent with the explicit (cf. Lev 23:4–8; Deut 16:1–8; 2 Chr 30:1–19; 35: 1–19; Ezra 6:19–22) and implicit (cf. Exod 34:18–26; Num 28:16–25; Jos 5:10–12) testimony of the OT, attesting Passover's preeminence through the end of the Second Temple era.

(ethical worship), provide a biblical foundation for Philo's theory.[2] The OT similarly provides bases for identifying the Passover ritual slaughter as the preeminent sacrifice (Exod 12:27; 23:18; 34:25), and first-century witnesses attest to the persistence of such an understanding through the Second Temple period.[3]

Chapter 3 provided internal and external evidence to support the recognition of early Christian worship as John's proximate context. Consideration of the Didache, the *First Apology* of Justin Martyr, and a letter from the Roman governor Pliny the Younger to the emperor Trajan, as the earliest extant witnesses on Christian liturgy, provided valuable insight into fundamental characteristics of early Christian worship. Their combined witness, extending from the mid-first through the mid-second century AD, attests to the integration of ethical and liturgical worship as an essential feature of early Christian worship. They also bear witness to the fundamental role of baptism, the centrality of the Eucharist, and the reading of Scripture (OT and NT) and homilies in liturgical worship as well as to its ordering, with sacramental worship following didactic worship.

In light of the features attested by these earliest witnesses on the liturgy, the NT texts manifested substantial evidence for recognizing its fittingness for the liturgy and its apparent use in early Christian worship (1 Thess 5:27; Col 4:16).[4] Whereas such characteristics apply to the NT texts in general, the Gospels offer evidence that their purpose and provenance was the liturgy. Collectively their structure and content reflect the eucharistic mold into which their authentic witness to the words and deeds of Jesus have been cast. Structural elements of the Synoptics include their loosely

---

2. In clarification, the reference to ethical worship here, applied in a restricted sense, refers to the proper internal disposition associated with the external actions of ritual sacrifices. In general, as indicated in various places in this study, ethical worship entails manifesting the internal disposition to love and honor God through external actions (as well as living the whole of one's life) in obedience to his commands (see Gen 6:22; 7:5, 9, 16; John 14:15).

3. Philo implicitly affirms the sacrificial nature of the ritual (*Decal.* 159; *Moses* 2.224-25; *Spec. Laws* 2.148) and refers to it as a sacrifice (2.226; *Alleg. Interp.* 3.94, 165; *Moses* 2.226, 228). Similarly, Josephus repeatedly attests to it as a sacrifice (*Ant.* 2.311-14; 3.248; 17.213). Paul presumes its sacrificial character in 1 Cor 5:7. Yhwh qualitatively distinguishes the Passover slaughter by referring to it as "my sacrifice" (Exod 23:18; 34:15) and the numbers associated with it in the first-century (*J. W.* 2.280; 6.423-25) quantitatively attest to its distinction as the preeminent sacrifice in temple worship.

4. The references listed explicitly specify the public proclamation of those particular NT texts.

SUMMARY AND SYNTHESIS

connected episodes that recount Jesus' public ministry in which he comes, and people approach to petition or question him.[5] Their content manifests the fundamental role of baptism and the centrality of the Eucharist in sacramental worship, and it provides invaluable material for didactic worship in teaching the audience about Jesus and inspiring them to worship him (cf. John 20:26–29).

John's Gospel displays its theme of worship from the beginning (1:1–18) and consistently conveys it throughout its length. The evangelist introduces the hour of Jesus early in his public ministry (2:4) and subsequently associates it with the true worship (4:21, 23) that Jesus would offer and enable (4:23–24) as the work the Father has given him (4:34). In the culmination of his hour (19:25–30), Jesus offers true worship in freely laying down his life for his own (10:17–18b) out of love for his Father (10:18c; 14:31) and his friends (13:1; 15:13–15) and he enables it through the gift of the Spirit (19:30) for those who believe in him. The events following his death (19:31–35) and the associated eyewitness (19:35) and OT (19:36–37) testimonies attest to these realities that complete the Scripture and the work the Father has given him (19:28–30).

Chapter 4 addressed practices utilized by ancient author-exegetes to incorporate Scripture into their works, implicitly invoking the authority of OT texts as they interpreted them. Such exegetical practices flourished from the third century BC through the first century AD. That this period corresponded with the translation and revision of the LXX and the earliest textual witnesses of the Targums, each interpretations in themselves, attests to the level of interest in and openness to such interpretive actions performed on Scripture. Rabbinical lists, with the tradition underlying the earliest dating from the first century BC, categorized some of the exegetical methods manifested in ancient texts from this period.

Seven such methods are relevant to John's use of the OT in 19:36–37. Three of them are principles for associating OT texts that authors incorporated into their works, three are operations that they performed on the texts to incorporate them, and the final method exhibits characteristics of both. The study described and compared these methods based on the type of classifications presented in the rabbinic literature.[6] The following sec-

---

5. Although John's Gospel does not manifest this same pattern, it identifies Jesus as the "one who comes" in more prominent ways (1:15, 27; 3:31; 6:14; 11:27; 20:19–23, 24–29; 21:1–14).

6. Although there are no extant lists from the intertestamental era, the rabbinic literature provides useful and representative classifications for methods displayed in texts

tion provided examples of their application in the DSS, the NT, and other ancient witnesses to illustrate their use and complementarity. The examples assisted with the subsequent identification of potential evidence of those exegetical methods operative in 19:36-37.

Chapter 5 analyzed the text of 19:36-37 and evaluated the scriptural passages to which John refers and their textual traditions as well as his presentation of them. The combination of the content, word order, and verb form of the Scripture provided in 19:36 indicate that the evangelist conflated the pentateuchal bone-breaking prohibition that applied to the Passover lamb (Exod 12:46; LXX Exod 12:10; Num 9:12) with a passage from the Psalms (LXX 33:21 [MT 34:21]) that attests to God's providential care for the righteous. John's narration of what took place after Jesus' death (19:31-35) in light of the conflated OT passages (19:36) affirms his identity as the Lamb of God and the Righteous One, an allusion to the Suffering Servant (Isa 53:11), affirming John the Baptist's testimony when Jesus first appeared in the Gospel (John 1:29). The evangelist thematically combines the conflated Scripture in 19:36, using an intervening introductory phrase, with his OT citation in 19:37 that refers to the mysterious Pierced One of Zech 12:10. The content and form of the Scripture provided, in light of scholarly analyses of other OT citations in the Gospel, suggest that John translated it directly from the Hebrew (with the MT *Vorlage* arguably providing a consonantal textual basis for his unique translation).

John 19:36-37 implicitly draws upon the original contexts of its OT sources. Exodus 12:46 evokes the feast of Passover as well as the whole of the worship that it and the exodus enabled. The Psalm (LXX 33:21 [MT 34:21]) attests to Jesus as the Righteous One, which in the context of first-century Judaism identifies him as the Messiah. It also provides a significant linguistic basis for associating his messianic identity with the Suffering Servant (Isa 53:11). The context of Zech 12:10 (and the book's intratextual connections and extensive intertextuality with other OT texts) affirms Jesus' identity as the messianic king (9:9-10; cf. John 12:13-16) who will gather Yhwh's flock by removing iniquity (Zech 3:9; cf. Isa 53:6, 11) and assemble people from afar for worship as a temple builder (Zech 6:12-13, 15), priest, and king (6:13). Numerous intertextual connections and broader parallels with Isaiah's Suffering Servant passages associate Zechariah's death accounts of messianic figures (12:10; 13:7) and their effects (12:10—13:1; 13:9) with one another and with Isaiah's Suffering Servant (Isa 53:4-12).

---

from that period and earlier (in the OT).

John assists his audience in properly comprehending the testimony of the conflated and thematically combined OT witnesses in 19:36–37 with contextual elements provided earlier in the Gospel. Particularly significant contextual elements are the progression of titles associated with Jesus' identity (1:29–51), his self-references to the "lifted up" Son of Man (3:14–15; 8:28; 12:23–34), and the narrative structure of the culmination of his hour (19:25–30) and the events that follow it (19:31–35), which bear witness to the fulfillment realized in conjunction with the Scriptures fulfilled (19:36–37). In this way, the Gospel implicitly affirms the connections present in Zechariah that identify the coming messianic king (9:9–10) with the Pierced One (12:10) and Isaiah's Suffering Servant (52:13—53:12; cf. John 12:38–40) with all of them finding their fulfillment in the "lifted up" Son of Man.

In the context of Passover (cf. 13:1; 19:14, 31), the Gospel establishes that Jesus transcended the feast and the temple worship it enabled by freely offering himself in fully integrated self-sacrificial worship in obedience to the Father (10:18) out of love for him (14:31) and his friends (15:13). In the proximate context of early Christian worship, it also demonstrates how Jesus enabled his disciples to participate in the true worship he offered with his handing over the Spirit to the Church (19:30) and to individual believers through the sacraments (19:34) accomplishing the work the Father had given him (4:34).

SYNTHESIS OF THE RESULTS

The fulfillment attested by 19:36–37 in light of the contexts presumed by the Gospel and those evoked by the Scriptures and John's presentation of them (including the location in which he places them) is expansive. Since Jesus provides progressive and complementary insights into aspects of the fulfillment he would accomplish in his hour in completing the work given him by the Father (4:34) with his three self-references to the "lifted up" Son of Man (3:14–15; 8:28; 12:23–32), this synthesis will utilize them for its bases.

The Gospel establishes that Jesus transcends the worship enabled by Passover by offering himself as the Lamb of God and Suffering Servant in fully integrated self-sacrificial worship in the context of the feast (cf. 13:1; 19:14, 31). The effects realized by those who (repent and) believe in the "lifted up" Son of Man (3:14–15; cf. Num 21:7–9) attest to the superiority of the worship Jesus offered and enabled. Whereas the OT associates the worship of Passover with the preservation of natural life (Exod 12:21-28) and redemption from slavery in Egypt (12:29-42), Jesus grants eternal life (John 3:14-15) and freedom from slavery to sin (8:28-38) for those who believe in him. The blood and the water (19:34) attest to Jesus' completed sacrifice and its surpassing effects. The blood attests to the atonement for sins realized (cf. Lev 17:11) as well as the eternal life sustained by the Eucharist (John 6:54). The water reflects baptism as the means by which those who believe in the Son of Man would realize purification from sin (cf. Zech 13:1) and new life (John 3:3-8). As the "one lifted up" (Ezek 45:22) in the context of Passover, Jesus provides himself as the Lamb of God for the sin offering and affirms his identity as the messianic shepherd-king (Zech 3:8-10; 6:10-15; 9:9-10) and priest (6:13). He gathers those sheep scattered by sin (Isa 53:6, 11) into one flock by laying down his life (John 10:11) in sacrifice as the Suffering Servant (Isa 53:12). In offering fully integrated worship as priest and victim, Jesus transcends the sacrificial worship enabled by Passover.

In attesting to Jesus' innocence by ignoring their orders to break his legs and piercing his side instead (John 19:31-34), the soldiers bore witness to his identity as the Righteous One (19:36; cf. Ps 34:21 [LXX 33:21]; Isa 53:11) and, consequently, to the divinity (cf. John 19:7) of the "lifted up" Son of Man (8:28).[7] This attestation affirms Jesus' identity as the true temple (John 2:19-21; cf. Num 10:35-36; 2 Chr 6:41; Ps 132:8) as does his gift of the living water of the Spirit (7:37-39; cf. Ezek 47:1-10; Zech 14:8) to the Church (19:25-27) in the culmination of his hour (19:30) and to the individual believers through baptism and the Eucharist (19:34). His provision of the Spirit also identifies him as the messianic temple builder (Zech 6:13, 15), constituting his disciples as the new temple (John 14:2-3, 23). Through the indwelling Spirit (14:16-17; 16:7) they transcend the fundamental characteristic associated with the Jerusalem temple (cf. Ezek 43:7, 1 Kgs 8:12-50; 2 Chr 6:1-39).

That the Spirit enables Jesus, the Truth (John 14:6), to remain in his disciples (14:23) allows them to offer true worship (4:23-24). In drawing all people to himself for such worship (12:32), the "lifted up" Son of Man (12:23-32) fulfills the universal worship foretold by the OT (Zech 14:16-21)

---

7. As previously established, the common vocalization of the MT *Vorlage* for the scripture from Zech 12:10 that John presents in 19:37 provides corroborating testimony to Jesus' divinity.

SUMMARY AND SYNTHESIS

following the death of the Pierced One (12:10) and shepherd-king (13:7) and the associated conversion (12:10—13:9). That Jesus remains in his disciples through the indwelling Spirit provides for the *ongoing* realization of the effects of the sin offering provided by the one "lifted up" on Passover (Ezek 45:22) with their participation in his sacrifice through their worship in Spirit and Truth (John 4:23-24) enabled by the sacraments (19:34).

CONCLUSION

This chapter provided a summary of the contents of the present study, which sought greater insight into the fulfillment attested by 19:36-37, and a synthesis of its results. It demonstrated that these final OT fulfillment citations in conjunction with the things that happened following Jesus' death (19:31-34) establish that he offered and enabled (19:25-30, 34) the true worship prefigured in the worship of Israel and collectively foretold by the OT as well as by Jesus himself (4:21-24) as the work given him by the Father (4:34). The recognition of the combined testimony of the OT (19:36-37) and "these things" that happened following Jesus' death (19:32-34) illuminate the culmination of his hour and attest to the fulfillment that he accomplished through perfect worship.

Bibliography

Abegg, Martin, Jr. "A Liturgy." In *The Dead Sea Scrolls: A New Translation*, translated by Michael Wise et al., 476. San Francisco: HarperOne, 2005.
Alexander, T. D. *From Paradise to the Promised Land: An Introduction to the Pentateuch*. 3rd ed. Grand Rapids: Baker Academic, 2012.
———. "The Passover Sacrifice." In *Sacrifice in the Bible*, edited by Roger T. Beckwith and Martin Selman, 1–24. Grand Rapids: Baker, 1995.
Allen, Leslie C. *Ezekiel 20–48*. WBC 29. Nashville: Thomas Nelson, 1990.
Attridge, Harold W. "Historiography." In *Jewish Writings of the Second Temple Period: Apocrypha, Pseudepigrapha, Qumran, Sectarian Writings, Philo, Josephus*, edited by Michael E. Stone, 157–84. Philadelphia: Fortress, 1984.
Aune, David E. "Worship, Early Christian." In *ABD* 6.973–89.
Avemarie, Friedrich. "Interpreting Scripture through Scripture: Exegesis Based on Lexematic Association in the Dead Sea Scrolls and the Pauline Epistles." In *Echoes from the Caves: Qumran and the New Testament*, edited by Florentino García Martínez, 83–102. STDJ 85. Boston: Brill, 2009.
Baillet, Maurice. *Discoveries in the Judean Desert VII: Qumrân Grotte 4; III (4Q482–4Q520)*. Oxford: Clarendon, 1982.
Bakhos, Carol. "Midrash, Midrashim." In *EDEJ* 944–49.
Barrett, C. K. *The Acts of the Apostles: A Shorter Commentary*. New York: T. & T. Clark, 2002.
Bartos, Michael, and Bernard M. Levinson. "'This is the Manner of the Remission': Implicit Legal Exegesis in 11QMelchizedek as a Response to the Formation of the Torah." *JBL* (2013) 351–71.
Bauckham, Richard. *Gospel of Glory: Major Themes in Johannine Theology*. Grand Rapids: Baker Academic, 2015.
Baumgarten, Joseph. "Recent Qumran Discoveries and Halakhah in the Hellenistic-Roman Period." In *Jewish Civilization in the Hellenistic-Roman Period*, edited by Shemaryahu Talmon, 147–58. Philadelphia: Trinity, 1991.
Beasley-Murray, George R. *John*. WBC 36. Waco, TX: Word, 1987.
Bienaimé, Germain. *Moïse et le Don de l'Eau dans la Tradition juive ancienne: Targum et Midrash*. AnBib 98. Rome: Biblical Institute, 1984.
Block, Daniel I. *For the Glory of God: Recovering a Biblical Theology of Worship*. Grand Rapids: Baker Academic, 2014.

———. "My Servant David: Ancient Israel's Vision of the Messiah." In *Israel's Messiah in the Bible and the Dead Sea Scrolls*, edited by Richard S. Hess and M. Daniel Carrol R., 17–56. Grand Rapids: Baker, 2003.

Boda, Mark J. *The Book of Zechariah*. NICOT. Grand Rapids: Eerdmans, 2016.

Borchert, Gerald L. *Worship in the New Testament: Divine Mystery and Human Response*. St. Louis: Chalice, 2008.

Boxall, Ian. *The Revelation of Saint John*. BNTC. Peabody, MA: Hendrickson, 2006.

Bradshaw, Paul F. *The Search for the Origins of Christian Worship: Sources and Methods for the Study of Early Liturgy*. 2nd ed. Oxford: Oxford University Press, 2002.

Brooke, George J. "Biblical Interpretation in the Qumran Scrolls and in the New Testament." In *The Dead Sea Scrolls Fifty Years after their Discovery: Proceedings of the Jerusalem Congress, July 20–25, 1997*, edited by Lawrence H. Schiffman, et al., 60–73. Jerusalem: Israel Exploration Society in cooperation with The Shrine of the Book, Israel Museum, 2000.

———. *Exegesis at Qumran: 4Q Florilegium in its Jewish Context*. JSOTSup 29. Sheffield: JSOT, 1985.

Brown, Raymond E. *The Death of the Messiah: From Gethsemane to the Grave. A Commentary on the Passion Narratives in the Four Gospels*. 2 vols. New York: Doubleday, 1994.

———. *The Gospel According to John*. 2 vols. AB 29/29A. New York: Doubleday, 1966, 1970.

———. *An Introduction to the Gospel of John*. New York: Doubleday, 2003.

Bultmann, Rudolf. *The Gospel of John*. Translated by G. R. Beasley-Murray et al. Philadelphia: Westminster, 1971.

———. *The History of the Synoptic Tradition*. Translated by John Marsh. Rev. ed. Peabody, MA: Hendrickson, 1963.

Bynum, Wm. Randolph. *The Fourth Gospel and the Scriptures: Illuminating the Form and Meaning of Scriptural Citation in John 19:37*. Leiden: Brill, 2012.

Byrne, Brendan. *Life Abounding: A Reading of John's Gospel*. Collegeville, MN: Liturgical, 2014.

Carnazzo, Sebastian A. *Seeing Blood and Water: A Narrative-Critical Study of John 19:34*. Eugene, OR: Pickwick, 2012.

Cavicchia, Alessandro. "'Guarderanno a Colui che hanno trafitto': Studio di ermeneutica cristologica su Zac 12,10 in Gv 19,37." *Anton* 87 (2012) 205–57, 423–74.

Charbonneau, André. "Jésus en croix (Jn 19,16b–42), Jésus élevé (3,14ss; 8,28s; 12,31ss)." *Science et Esprit* 45 (1993) 5–23, 161–80.

Charles, R. H. *Pseudepigrapha of the Old Testament*. Vol. 2. Oxford: Clarendon, 1913.

Charlesworth, James H. "The Date and Provenance of the *Parables of Enoch*." In *The Parables of Enoch: A Paradigm Shift*, edited by James H. Charlesworth and Darrell L. Bock, 37–113. New York: Bloomsbury, 2013.

———. "From Messianology to Christology: Problems and Perspectives." In *The Messiah: Developments in Earliest Judaism and Christianity*, edited by James H. Charlesworth, 13–28. Minneapolis: Augsburg Fortress, 1992.

———, ed. *The Messiah: Developments in Earliest Judaism and Christianity*. Minneapolis: Augsburg Fortress, 1992.

Ciccarino, Christopher M. "Christ Our Passover Has Been Sacrificed." PhD diss., Pontifical Gregorian University, 2008.

Clements, R. E. "שחט." In *TDOT* 14:563–66.

Cockerill, Gareth. *The Epistle to the Hebrews*. NICNT. Grand Rapids: Eerdmans, 2012.
Coloe, Mary. "Raising the Johannine Temple (John 19:19–37)." *ABR* 48 (2000) 47–58.
Collins, John J. *The Apocalyptic Imagination: An Introduction to Jewish Apocalyptic Literature*. 3rd ed. Grand Rapids: Eerdmans, 2016.
———. *The Scepter and the Star: Messianism in Light of the Dead Sea Scrolls*. 2nd ed. Grand Rapids: Eerdmans, 2010.
Collins, Raymond F. *Introduction to the New Testament*. New York: Doubleday, 1987.
Cook, Edward. "The Damascus Document (CD)." In *The Dead Sea Scrolls: A New Translation*, translated by Michael Wise et al., 49–78. San Francisco: HarperOne, 2005.
———. "A Liturgy of Thanksgiving." In *The Dead Sea Scrolls: A New Translation*, translated by Michael Wise et al., 518–19. San Francisco: HarperOne, 2005.
Cook, Edward, and Michael Wise. "An Aramaic Translation of the Book of Job." In *The Dead Sea Scrolls: A New Translation*, translated by Michael Wise et al., 577–88. San Francisco: HarperOne, 2005.
Cullmann, Oscar. *Early Christian Worship*. Lima, OH: Wyndham Hall, 1953.
Culpepper, R. A. "The Theology of the Johannine Passion Narrative: John 19:16b–30." *Neot* 31 (1997) 21–37.
Daube, David. "Rabbinic Methods of Interpretation and Hellenistic Rhetoric." *HUCA* 22 (1949) 239–64.
Dauer, Anton. "Das Wort des Gekreuzigten an seine Mutter und den 'Jünger, den er liebte.'" *BZ* 12 (1968) 80–93.
De la Potterie, Ignace. *The Hour of Jesus: The Passion and Resurrection of Jesus according to John*. Slough, UK: St. Paul, 1989.
Dibelius, Martin. *From Tradition to Gospel*. New York: Scribner's, 1965.
Dimant, Devorah. "Pesharim." In *EDEJ* 1050–56.
Dines, Jennifer M. "The Minor Prophets." In *The T. & T. Clark Companion to the Septuagint*, edited by James K. Aitken, 438–55. London: T. & T. Clark, 2015.
Dodd, C. H. *According to the Scriptures: The Sub-Structure of New Testament Theology*. New York: Scribner's, 1953.
Draper, Jonathan A. "The Apostolic Fathers: The Didache." *ExpTim* 117 (2006) 177–81.
Dunn, James D. G. *Jesus Remembered*. CIM 1. Grand Rapids: Eerdmans, 2003.
———. *The Partings of the Ways: Between Christianity and Judaism and Their Significance for the Character of Christianity*. 2nd ed. London: SCM, 2006.
Eberhart, Christian A. "Sacrifice? Holy Smokes! Reflections on Cult Terminology for Understanding Sacrifice in the Bible." In *Ritual and Metaphor: Sacrifice in the Bible*, edited by Christian A. Eberhart, 17–32. SBLRBS 68. Atlanta: SBL, 2011.
Esposito, Thomas. *Jesus' Meals with Pharisees and Their Liturgical Roots*. AnBib 209. Rome: Gregorian & Biblical, 2015.
Eve, Eric. *Behind the Gospels: Understanding the Oral Tradition*. London: SPCK, 2013.
Falk, Daniel K. "Festivals and Holy Days." In *EDEJ* 636–45.
Falls, Thomas B. *Saint Justin Martyr: The First Apology, the Second Apology, Dialogue with Trypho, Exhortation to the Greeks, Discourse to the Greeks, the Monarchy of the Rule of God*. FC 6. Washington, DC: Catholic University of America Press, 1965.
Farkasfalvy, Denis. *Inspiration and Interpretation: A Theological Introduction to Sacred Scripture*. Washington, DC: Catholic University of America Press, 2010.
Feuillet, A. *Études Johanniques*. MLSB 4. Paris: Desclé de Brouwer, 1962.
Fishbane, Michael. *Biblical Interpretation in Ancient Israel*. Oxford: Clarendon, 1985.

Fitzmyer, Joseph A. *First Corinthians: A New Translation with Introduction and Commentary*. AB 32. New Haven: Yale University Press, 2008.

Garrow, Alan J. P. *The Gospel of Matthew's Dependence on the Didache*. JSNTSup 254. New York: T. & T. Clark, 2004.

Gilders, William K. "Jewish Sacrifice: Its Nature and Function (According to Philo)." In *Ancient Mediterranean Sacrifice*, edited by Jennifer Wright Knust and Zsuzsanna Várhelyi, 94–105. Oxford: Oxford University Press, 2011.

Gordley, Matthew. "The Johannine Prologue and Jewish Didactic Hymn Traditions: A New Case for Reading the Prologue as a Hymn." *JBL* 128 (2009) 781–802.

Grobel, Kendrick. "Interpretation, History and Principles of." In *IDB* 2:718–24.

Gruber, Margareta. "Der Quelle zu trinken geben: Eine intratextuelle Lektüre von Joh 4,1–42; 7,37–39 und 19,28–37, verbunden mit einer methodischen Überlegung zum Modell-Leser." In *Der Bibelkanon in der Bibelauslegung: Methodenreflexionen und Beispielexegesen*, edited by Egbert Ballhorn and Georg Steins, 314–30. Stuttgart: Kohlhammer, 2007.

Hartley, John E. *Leviticus*. WBC 4. Nashville: Thomas Nelson, 1992.

Hauck, F. "μονή." In *TDNT* 4:579–80.

Hays, Richard B. *Echoes of Scripture in the Gospels*. Waco, TX: Baylor University Press, 2016.

Heil, John Paul. *The Book of Revelation: Worship for Life in the Spirit of Prophecy*. Eugene, OR: Cascade, 2014.

———. *The Gospel of John: Worship for Divine Life Eternal*. Eugene, OR: Cascade, 2015.

———. "Jesus as the Unique High Priest in the Gospel of John." *CBQ* 57 (1995) 729–45.

Henniger, Joseph. *Les Fêtes de Printemps chez les Sémites et la Pâque israélite*. Paris: Librairie Lecoffre, 1975.

Henrici, Peter. "'Do this in Remembrance of Me:' The Sacrifice of Christ and the Sacrifice of the Faithful." *Comm* 12 (1985) 146–57.

Heschel, Abraham Joshua. *The Sabbath*. New York: Farrar, Straus and Giroux, 2005.

Hoskins, Paul M. "Deliverance from Death by the True Passover Lamb: A Significant Aspect of the Fulfillment of the Passover in the Gospel of John." *JETS* 52 (2009) 285–99.

Humann, Roger J. "The Function and Form of the Explicit Old Testament Quotations in the Gospel of John." *LTR* 1 (1988–89) 31–54.

Instone-Brewer, David. *Techniques and Assumptions in Jewish Exegesis before 70 CE*. TSAJ 30. Tübingen: J.C.B. Mohr, 1992.

Jacobs, Louis. "The Qal Va-Homer Argument in the Old Testament." *BSOAS* 35 (1972) 221–27.

———. "Shavuot." *EncJud* 18:422–23.

Jacobs, Louis, and David Derovan. "Hermeneutics." *EncJud* 9:25–29.

Jassen, Alex P. *Scripture and Law in the Dead Sea Scrolls*. New York: Cambridge University Press, 2014.

Jenson, Philip P. "The Levitical Sacrificial System." In *Sacrifice in the Bible*, edited by Roger T. Beckwith and Martin Selman, 25–40. Grand Rapids: Baker, 1995.

Johnson, Luke Timothy. *The Acts of the Apostles*. SacPag 5. Collegeville, MN: Liturgical, 1992.

Keener, Craig S. *The Gospel of John: A Commentary*. 2 vols. Peabody, MA: Hendrickson, 2003.

Kereszty, Roch A. *Wedding Feast of the Lamb: Eucharistic Theology from a Historical, Biblical and Systematic Perspective.* Chicago: Hillenbrand, 2004.

Kerr, Alan. *The Temple of Jesus' Body: The Temple Theme in the Gospel of John.* Sheffield: Sheffield Academic, 2002.

Köstenberger, Andreas J. *John.* BECNT. Grand Rapids: Baker Academic, 2004.

Kubiś, Adam. *The Book of Zechariah in the Gospel of John.* EBib Nouvelle série 64. Pendé, France: J. Gabalda, 2012.

Kugel, James L. "Early Jewish Biblical Interpretation." In *EDEJ* 121–41.

Lamarche, Paul. *Zacharie IX–XIV: Structure Littéraire et Messianisme.* Ebib. Paris: Librairie Lecoffre, 1961.

Lee, Dorothy. *Hallowed in Truth and Love: Spirituality in the Johannine Literature.* Eugene, OR: Wipf & Stock, 2012.

———. "In the Spirit of Truth: Worship and Prayer in the Gospel of John and the Early Fathers." *VC* 58 (2004) 277–97.

———. "Paschal Imagery in the Gospel of John: A Narrative and Symbolic Reading." *Pacifica* 24 (2011) 13–28.

Levine, Lee I. "Temple, Jerusalem." In *EDEJ* 1281–91.

Lieberman, Saul. *Hellenism in Jewish Palestine: Studies in the Literary Transmission [of] Beliefs and Manners of Palestine in the I Century B.C.E.—IV Century C.E.* 2nd ed. TSJTSA 18. New York: Jewish Theological Seminary, 1962.

Longenecker, Richard N. *Biblical Exegesis in the Apostolic Period.* 2nd ed. Grand Rapids: Eerdmans, 1999.

Manns, Frédéric. "Zacharie 12,10 relu en Jean 19,37." *Liber Annuus* 56 (2006) 301–10.

Martínez, Florentino García, and Eibert J. C. Tigchelaar, eds. *The Dead Sea Scrolls Study Edition: Volume 1 (1Q1–4Q273).* Grand Rapids: Eerdmans, 2000.

Martínez, Florentino García, et al., eds. *Qumran Cave 11. II: 11Q2–18, 11Q20–31.* DJD 23. New York: Oxford University Press, 1998.

McGowan, Andrew B. *Ancient Christian Worship: Early Practices in Social, Historical and Theological Perspective.* Grand Rapids: Baker, 2014.

Menken, Martinus J. J. "'He Has Blinded Their Eyes . . .' (John 12:40)." In *Old Testament Quotations in the Fourth Gospel: Studies in Textual Form,* 99–122. CBET 15. Kampen: Kok Pharos, 1996.

———. "Jewish Feasts in the Gospel of John." In *Studies in John's Gospel and Epistles: Collected Essays,* 187–207. CBET 77. Leuven: Peeters, 2015.

———. "The Old Testament Quotation in Jn 19,36: Sources, Redaction, Background." In *The Four Gospels 1992: Festschrift Frans Neirynck,* edited by F. Van Segbroeck et. al., 3:2101–18. Leuven: Leuven University Press, 1992.

———. *Old Testament Quotations in the Fourth Gospel: Studies in Textual Form.* CBET 15. Kampen: Kok Pharos, 1996.

———. "The Origin of the Old Testament Quotation in John 7:38." *NovT* 38 (1996) 159–74.

———. "The Textual Form and the Meaning of the Quotation from Zechariah 12:10 in John 19:37." *CBQ* 55 (1993) 494–511.

Michel, Otto. "οἶκος, οἰκία." In *TDNT* 5:119–34.

Moloney, Francis J. *The Gospel of John.* SP 4. Collegeville, MN: Liturgical, 1998.

———. "The Gospel of John as Scripture." *CBQ* 67 (2005) 454–68.

Neusner, Jacob. *The Mishnah: A New Translation.* New Haven: Yale University Press, 1988.

Nickelsburg, George W. E., and James C. VanderKam. *1 Enoch: The Hermeneia Translation.* Minneapolis: Fortress, 2012.

Niehr, A. "נֶשִׁי." In *TDOT* 10:44–53.

Nielsen, Jesper Tang. "The Narrative Structures of Glory and Glorification in the Fourth Gospel." *NTS* 56 (2010) 343–66.

Obermann, Andreas. *Die christologische Erfüllung der Schrift im Johannesevangelium: Eine Untersuchung zur johanneischen Hermeneutik anhand der Schriftzitate.* Wissen schaftliche Untersuchungen zum Neuen Testament 83. Tübingen: J.C.B. Mohr, 1996.

O'Brien, Peter. *The Letter to the Hebrews.* PNTC. Grand Rapids: Eerdmans, 2010.

Pardee, Nancy. *The Genre and Development of the Didache: A Text-Linguistic Analysis.* WUNT 2/339. Tübingen: Mohr Siebeck, 2012.

Petterson, Anthony R. *Behold Your King: The Hope for the House of David in the Book of Zechariah.* London: T. & T. Clark, 2009.

———. *Haggai, Zechariah and Malachi.* ApOTC 25. Downers Grove, IL: InterVarsity, 2015.

Plummer, Alfred. *The Gospel According to St. John.* Cambridge: Cambridge University Press, 1923.

Porter, Stanley E. *John, His Gospel, and Jesus: In Pursuit of the Johannine Voice.* Grand Rapids: Eerdmans, 2015.

Propp, William H. C. *Exodus 1–18, A New Translation with Introduction and Commentary.* AB 2. New York: Doubleday, 1999.

Quek, Tze-Ming. "A Text-Critical Study of John 1.34." *NTS* 55 (2009) 22–34.

Rouwhorst, Gerard. "Christlicher Gottesdienst und der Gottesdienst Israels: Forschungsgeschichte, historische Interaktionen, Theologie." In *Gottesdienst der Kirche: Handbuch der Liturgiewissenschaft.* Vol. 2 of *Theologie des Gottesdienstes.* Part 2, *Christliche und jüdische Liturgie,* edited by Martin Klöckener et al., 491–572. Regensburg: Pustet, 2008.

Rubenstein, Jeffrey L. *The History of Sukkot in the Second Temple and Rabbinic Periods.* BJS 302. Atlanta: Scholars, 1995.

Salvesen, Alison. "Exodus." In *The T. & T. Clark Companion to the Septuagint,* edited by James K. Aitken, 29–42. London: T. & T. Clark, 2015.

Sanders, E. P. "Did the Pharisees Eat Ordinary Food in Purity?" In *Jewish Law from Jesus to the Mishnah: Five Studies,* 183–353. Minneapolis: Augsburg Fortress, 2016.

———. *Judaism: Practice and Belief, 63 BCE–66 CE.* Minneapolis: Augsburg Fortress, 2016.

Sandt, H. W. M. van de. "Why Does the Didache Conceive of the Eucharist as a Holy Meal?" *VC* 65 (2011) 1–20.

Schlund, Christine. *"Kein Knochen soll gebrochen werden:" Studien zu Bedeutung und Funktion des Pesachfests in Texten des frühen Judentums und im Johannesevangelium.* Neukirchen-Vluyn: Neukirchener, 2005.

Schrenk, Gottlob. "δικαιόω." In *TDNT* 2:215–19.

Schuchard, Bruce G. *Scripture within Scripture: The Interrelationship of Form and Function in the Explicit Old Testament Citations in the Gospel of John.* SBLDS 133. Atlanta: Scholars, 1992.

Schürer, Emil. *The History of the Jewish People in the Age of Jesus Christ (175 B.C.–A.D. 135): A New English Version.* Vol. 2. Edited by Geza Vermes et al. Edinburgh: T. & T. Clark, 1979.

Selman, Martin J. "Sacrifice in the Ancient Near East." In *Sacrifice in the Bible*, edited by Roger T. Beckwith and Martin J. Selman, 88–104. Grand Rapids: Baker, 1995.

Smith, Ralph L. *Micah-Malachi*. WBC 32. Nashville: Thomas Nelson, 1984.

Stanley, Christopher. *Paul and the Language of Scripture: Citation Technique in the Pauline Epistles and Contemporary Literature*. Cambridge: Cambridge University Press, 1992.

Stern, Menahem, ed. *Greek and Latin Authors on Jews and Judaism: Edited with Introductions and Commentary*. Vol. 1, *From Herodotus to Plutarch*. Jerusalem: The Israel Academy of Sciences and Humanities, 1976.

Strathmann, H. "λειτουργέω." In *TDNT* 4:215–31.

Swetnam, James. "Bestowal of the Spirit in the Fourth Gospel." *Bib* 74 (1993) 556–76.

Tov, Emmanuel. *Textual Criticism of the Hebrew Bible: Third Edition Revised and Expanded*. Minneapolis: Augsburg Fortress, 2012.

VanderKam, James C. *The Book of Jubilees*. Sheffield: Sheffield Academic, 2001.

Van Seters, John. "The Place of the Yahwist in the History of Passover and Massot." *ZAW* 95 (1983) 167–82.

Wellhausen, Julius. *Prolegomenon to the History of Ancient Israel*. Translated by J. Sutherland and Allan Menzies. Whitefish, MT: Kessinger, 2010.

Wheaton, Gerry. *The Role of Jewish Feasts in John's Gospel*. SNTSMS 162. New York: Cambridge University Press, 2015.

Whiston, William, trans. *The Works of Josephus: Complete and Unabridged*. Peabody, MA: Hendrickson, 1987.

Williams, Wynne, trans. *Pliny: Correspondence with Trajan from Bythinia (Epistles X)*. Warminster, UK: Aris & Phillips, 1990.

Wise, Michael. "The Coming of Melchizedek." In *The Dead Sea Scrolls: A New Translation*, translated by Michael Wise et al., 590–93. San Francisco: HarperOne, 2005.

———. "The Last Days: A Commentary on Selected Verses." In *The Dead Sea Scrolls: A New Translation*, translated by Michael Wise et al., 254–58. San Francisco: HarperOne, 2005.

Wise, Michael, et al., trans. *The Dead Sea Scrolls: A New Translation*. San Francisco: HarperOne, 2005.

Wolters, Al. *Zechariah*. HCOT. Leuven: Peeters, 2014.

Yee, Gail. *Jewish Feasts in John's Gospel*. Wilmington, DE: Michael Glazier 1989.

Yonge, C. D., trans. *The Works of Philo: Complete and Unabridged*. Peabody, MA: Hendrickson, 1995.

Ziegler, Joseph, ed. *Duodecim prophetae*. SVTGAAS 13. Göttingen: Vandenhoek & Ruprecht, 1984.

Index of Names

Abegg, Martin, Jr., 5n20, 27n67
Alexander, T. D., 18n34, 19n35, 19n36, 19n38, 20n40, 20n42, 36n103, 37n104, 37n106
Allen, Leslie C., 20n42
Attridge, Harold W., 31n81
Aune, David E., 41n3, 41n4
Avemarie, Friedrich, 81n9, 86n29, 86n30

Bakhos, Carol, 86n28, 87n33, 88n35
Barrett, C. K., 46n26
Bartos, Michael, 95n58, 96n63
Bauckham, Richard, 55n62
Baumgarten, Joseph, 26n65
Beasley-Murray, George R., 28n73, 30n80, 60n78, 69n107, 70n109
Bienaimé, Germain, 29n74
Block, Daniel I., 16n25, 17n29, 116n46, 121n63, 132n85
Boda, Mark J., 5n21, 115n40, 115n41, 115n42
Borchert, Gerald, 6, 6n25
Boxall, Ian, 48n36
Bradshaw, Paul F., 41n3, 45n21, 48n37, 51n47
Brooke, George J., 82n15, 83n19
Brown, Raymond E., 3n7, 12n10, 16n24, 28n73, 55n58, 55n60, 56n65, 57n69, 58n72, 59n75, 60n75, 62n81, 63n86, 69n107, 75n129, 104n6, 105n7, 122n65
Bultmann, Rudolf, 49, 49n38, 55n62
Bynum, Wm. Randolph, 3n10, 98n68, 99n73, 107n16, 107n17

Byrne, Brendan, 28n73, 55n60, 65n95, 66n95

Carnazzo, Sebastian A., 36n101, 137n102, 138n105, 139n106
Cavicchia, Alessandro, 3n10, 107n16, 107n17
Charbonneau, André, 73n124
Charles, R. H., 11n6, 95n57
Charlesworth, James H., 4n14, 113n35, 123n67, 126n74
Ciccarino, Christopher M., 18n34, 21n46
Clements, R. E., 37n105, 130n81
Cockerill, Gareth, 46n28
Collins, John J., 113n35, 123n67, 126n75
Collins, Raymond F., 49n38
Coloe, Mary, 66n98, 67n99
Cook, Edward, 5n20, 30n78, 79n4, 94n54
Cullmann, Oscar, 6, 6n24, 46n26, 51n47
Culpepper, R. A., 72n118

Daube, David, 82n14, 83n20, 84n22, 87n34
Dauer, Anton, 72n118
De la Potterie, Ignace, 75n130
Derovan, David, 96n63, 97n66
Dibelius, Martin, 49, 49n38
Dimant, Devorah, 80n5
Dines, Jennifer M., 99n73
Dodd, C. H., 91n46
Draper, Jonathan A., 6n22, 41n4
Dunn, James D. G., 15n21, 52n51

INDEX OF NAMES

Eberhart, Christian A., 33n89, 35n99, 36n102, 36n103, 37n104
Esposito, Thomas, 53n55
Eve, Eric, 6n23, 49n38, 49n39, 49n40, 50n44

Falk, Daniel K., 23n55, 24n58, 27n68
Falls, Thomas B., 42n10, 43n15
Farkasfalvy, Denis, 6n23, 49n39, 50n43, 50n44, 51n46, 52n49
Feuillet, A., 68n105
Fishbane, Michael, 82n17, 82n18
Fitzmyer, Joseph A., 20n42, 21n42

Garrow, Alan J. P., 6n22, 41n4
Gilders, William K., 32n86, 32n87, 33n89, 33n90
Gordley, Matthew, 44n16, 54n57, 55n60
Grobel, Kendrick, 79n4
Gruber, Margareta, 58n71, 68n104, 70n111, 74n128, 76n133

Hartley, John E., 23n53, 23n54
Hauck, F., 67n99
Hays, Richard, 2–3, 3n5, 3n6, 3n7, 10n1, 10n2, 50n41, 50n42, 57n67, 63n87, 64n91, 79n2, 80n5, 109n24, 110n29, 115n42
Heil, John Paul, 6, 7n26, 16n26, 28n73, 30n80, 48n36, 52n50, 54n56, 55n59, 55n62, 56n63, 56n66, 58n70, 59n73, 60n76, 61n79, 61n80, 62n82, 62n83, 63n86, 64n88, 65n92, 65n93, 69n108, 70n110, 70n111, 71n112, 71n114, 71n115, 72n117, 73n121
Henniger, Joseph, 36n101
Henrici, Peter, 45n24
Heschel, Abraham Joshua, 15n22
Hoskins, Paul M., 3n11
Humann, Roger J., 108n19

Instone-Brewer, David, 5n19, 81n12, 81n13, 82n15, 85n25, 85n26, 86n31, 87n31, 88n35, 88n36, 89n38, 91n45

Jacobs, Louis, 24n56, 96n63, 97n65, 97n66
Jassen, Alex P., 92n49
Jenson, Philip P., 36n100
Johnson, Luke Timothy, 46n26

Keener, Craig S., 28n73, 125n72
Kereszty, Roch A., 50n41
Kerr, Alan, 61n80
Köstenberger, Andreas J., 28n73, 30n80, 55n62, 65n93, 69n107
Kubiś, Adam, 3n10, 107n16, 107n17
Kugel, James L., 80n6, 81n8

Lamarche, Paul, 116n43, 116n44, 118n52, 120n61, 120n62
Lee, Dorothy A., 3n11, 6, 6n25, 57n68
Levine, Lee I., 11n8, 13n15, 14n19
Levinson, Bernard M., 95n58, 96n63
Lieberman, Saul, 85n27, 86n28, 87n32
Longenecker, Richard N., 81n8, 82n17, 82n18

Manns, Frédéric, 83n19
Martínez, Florentino García, 93n52, 97n64
McGowan, Andrew B., 43n12, 43n15, 46n25, 46n26, 46n27, 47n31, 49n38
Menken, Martinus J. J., 3, 3n8, 3n9, 58n72, 61n80, 63n84, 78n1, 84n24, 98n68, 99n73, 99n74, 105n7, 106n12, 107n16, 107n17, 108–9, 108n18, 108n19, 108n20, 108n21, 108n22, 108n23, 109n24
Michel, Otto, 66n98
Milik, J. T., 113n35
Moloney, Francis, 2, 2n4, 16n24, 30n80, 58n72, 60n75, 60n76, 60n77, 64n90, 65n93, 65n94, 66n96, 71n113, 73n123, 74n126, 75n132, 103n4, 124n69

Neusner, Jacob, 30n79, 63n84
Nickelsburg, George W. E., 113n35
Niehr, A., 131n83
Nielsen, Jesper Tang, 64n89

INDEX OF NAMES

Obermann, Andreas, 74n126, 74n127, 137n101
O'Brien, Peter, 46n28

Pardee, Nancy, 6n22, 41n4
Petterson, Anthony R., 5n21, 115n39, 118n51, 119n53, 119n56, 120n58
Plummer, Alfred, 108n19
Porter, Stanley E., 3n11, 55n62, 64n90
Propp, William H. C., 112n33

Quek, Tze-Ming, 55n63

Rouwhorst, Gerard, 47n31
Rubenstein, Jeffrey L., 5n18, 25n60, 26n64, 28n71, 28n72, 29n74, 29n76, 30n78, 30n79

Salvesen, Alison, 105n9
Sanders, E. P., 4n15, 4n16, 4n17, 11n6, 13n12, 14n17, 14n18, 14n20, 16n25, 22n47, 24n58, 27n65, 32n88
Sandt, H. W. M. van de, 42n5
Schlund, Christine, 3n11
Schrenk, Gottlob, 114n36
Schuchard, Bruce G., 98n68, 107n16, 107n17
Schürer, Emil, 4n17, 14n16, 14n17, 14n19, 29n77, 33n91, 83n21

Selman, Martin J., 32n88, 33n89, 34n96
Seters, John Van, 19n37
Smith, Ralph L., 56n65
Stanley, Christopher, 5n20, 79n2, 83n21, 88n36, 88n37, 89n39, 90n41, 90n42, 90n43, 90n44
Stern, Menahem, 28n70
Strathmann, H., 16n27
Swetnam, James, 75n130, 75n131, 133n90

Tigchelaar, Eibert J. C., 93n52, 97n64
Tov, Emmanuel, 79n3

VanderKam, James C., 11n6, 113n35

Wellhausen, Julius, 19n37
Wheaton, Gerry, 4n12
Whiston, William, 28n69
Williams, Wynne, 43n13
Wise, Michael, 5n20, 79n4, 81n10, 81n11, 97n64
Wolters, Al, 5n21, 115n41
Woude, van der, 97n64

Yee, Gail, 4n12, 16n24
Yonge, C. D., 33n92

Ziegler, Joseph, 138n104

Index of Ancient Documents

OLD TESTAMENT

Genesis

1-2	34
1:1—2:3	16
1:26-27	34
1:28	34
1:28-29	34n95
1:29	34
2:3	16
2:7, 21-23	34
2:9-10, 15-16	34
2:15-17	34, 34n95
2:19-20	34
3:1-19	34
4:3-5	34, 130, 130n80, 143
4:5	35n97
6:9	35
6:22	35, 130, 143, 144n2
7:5, 9, 16	35, 130, 143, 144n2
7:11	29
8:1-2	29
8:20	35
8:20-21	34, 130, 130n80, 143
8:21	35, 35n98
12:7—21:10	91n47
22:1-18	34n93
22:15-18	34n93
29:32	8on6
37:31	37n105
49:3	8on6

Exodus

3:1—4:15	112
3:12	19, 39, 112n31, 128, 143
3:12, 18	111
3:12b	17
3:18	112n31
4:17—12:50	112
4:23	112n31
4:31	69n107, 112n31
5:3	17
5:3, 8, 17	112n31
5:6-9	17
6:12	88
6:14	8on6
7:16, 26	112n31
8:4, 21, 22, 23, 24, 25	112n31
8:16	112n31
9:1, 13	112n31
10:3, 7-8, 11, 24, 26	112n31
11:1	112
11:8	112n31
12	37, 38, 111
12:1—13:16	19, 39, 143
12:1-28, 43-50	111, 112n33
12:6	37, 37n105, 130, 130n81
12:7	21n44
12:9	8on6
12:9 LXX	56n66
12:10	105n9, 111

Exodus (*continued*)

12:10 LXX	3, 98, 105, 105n10, 111, 121, 146
12–13	19n36
12:21	112n31
12:21–28	131, 148
12:21–32	112
12:27	37, 112n31, 130, 144
12:29–42	111, 131, 148
12:31	112n31
12:46	3, 98, 105, 105n8, 106, 106n11, 106n13, 111, 121, 146
12:51	111
15:17–18	92, 92n51, 93
17:1	84n22
17:6	93
20:1—23:33	112
20:2–6, 23–26	112n32
20:5	112n31
20:6b	93, 93n53, 94n54
20:7–17	112n32
20:8	16
20:8–11	16
20:25	112n31
21:1—22:27	112n32
22:28–29	112n32
22:30	112n32
23:1–12, 20–22	112n32
23:4	112n31
23:5	97, 97n66
23:12	15
23:13–19, 24–26, 32–33	112n32
23:14–16	24
23:14–17	13
23:16	23, 24
23:17	37n106
23:18	37, 37n106, 38, 39, 130, 144, 144n3
23:24–25	112n31
24:1	112n31
24:1–8	112, 128, 132
24:5	112n31
24:6	20, 20n41, 21n44
24:8	20n41
28:6	71n115
28:6, 32	71
28:9–12, 21	72n117
28:29	72n117
28:32	71, 71n115, 127, 132n86
28:32 MT	71n116
29:16, 20	20
29:16, 21	21n44
30:6–10	14n17
30:10	36n101
30:14–15	14n19
31:13	18n32
32:1–20	112
33:10	69n107
34:15	144n3
34:18–25	24, 24n57
34:18–26	19, 143n1
34:20–21	113
34:21	15, 16
34:22	23, 23n51, 24
34:22–23	13
34:23	37n106
34:25	37, 37n106, 38, 39, 130, 144
35:3	16
36:10, 12	71n115
36:10, 12, 15, 29, 34 LXX	71
36:13–14, 21	72n117
36:15	71n115
36:29 LXX	71, 71n115
36:34	71n115
38:21	84n22
38:32 LXX	71n116
39:7, 21, 31, 36, 39	71
39:23 MT	71, 71n116, 127, 132n86
40:34–35	54
40:35	55n58

Leviticus

1:3–17	137n103
1:5	37n107
1:5, 11	20
1–7	35, 35n99
3:2, 8, 13	20
4:1–35	137n103
4:3, 5, 16	116n44

INDEX OF ANCIENT DOCUMENTS

4:25, 34	36n101	**Numbers**	
5:9	36n101	1:20	80n6
5:11–13	36n100	3:51	84n22
6:25	116n44	6:3	74n125
7:1–7	137n103	7:1	63n84
16:15–21	36n101	9:6–8	105
17:11	20, 36, 36n101, 39, 148	9:9–12	105
17:14	137, 137n103	9:12	3, 98, 105, 105n8, 111, 121, 146
19	16n25		
19:2	44	9:12 LXX	111
19:3, 30	18n32	9:23	84n22
19:11, 15, 17	120n59	10:35–36	11, 138, 143, 148
19:13, 16, 18	120n59	12:18	99n74
19:30	16n24	15:1–12	36n100
23:1–44	15, 24	18:17	20
23:3	15	21	65n91
23:4–7	20	21:4–5	134n92
23:4–8	19, 143n1	21:7–9	134, 147
23:5–8	15	21:9	126, 134n92
23:9–10, 15–16	23n52	21:16–20	29n74
23:9–11	23n53	21:24	119n56
23:13	36n100	28:1—29:40	15
23:15–16	23n51	28:3–8	17
23:15–17, 20	23	28:9–10	17
23:16–20	23	28:9—29:40	24n57
23:21	23	28:16–25	19, 20, 143n1
23:33–43	15	28:17–18	21n42
23:34	24	28:22	20n42, 21n42
23:37–40	27	28:26	23, 23n51
23:40	25, 27, 28	28:26–31	23
23:42–43	25, 39	29:12–34	25
24:8	17		
25	96n60, 96n61, 97n64	**Deuteronomy**	
25:8–13	95n58	4:39	93
25:8–55	95n59	5:12–15	16
25:13	95, 96, 96n60, 96n63, 97n64	5:13–15	15
		6:4–5	16n25
25:13, 39–55	95	7:8	94, 95
25:13–31	95	7:9	93, 93n53, 94n54
25:25, 35, 39	96n60	7:18	95n57
26:2	16n24, 18n32	9:5	94
26:14	35n98	10:11–12	16n25
26:31	35n98	12:5, 11	129
27:24	97n64	12:5–13	11n3, 129, 143
		12:5–14	130
		15	96n60

Deuteronomy (*continued*)

15:1, 2, 9	96n61
15:1–3	96, 96n60
15:1–18	95n59
15:2	95, 95n58, 96, 96n63
15:12	96, 96n60
16:1–8	19, 19n38, 143n1
16:2	11n3, 130, 143
16:7	80n6
16:10	23, 23n51
16:10–15	29
16:11	29
16:13–16	24
16:16	24
16:16–17	13
20:13	119n56
22:4	97, 97n66
25:1	113, 114n36
26:2	11n3, 143
29:3	89n40
30:4–5	63n86
31:10	96n61

Joshua

5:10–12	19, 20, 20n39, 143n1
8:17	25
8:24	119n56
22:9	84n22

Judges

1:8	119n56
2:17	57n69
8:27, 33	57n69
9:54	119n56

Ruth

2:14	74n125

1 Samuel

2:29	38n110
13:8–14	34n94, 130n80, 143
15:10–13	34n94, 130n80, 143
16:6	116n44
24:7, 11	116n44

26:9–23	116n44
31:4	119n56

2 Samuel

5:2	117n47
7	92n51
7:1–7	92
7:7	117n47
7:10–11a	92
7:11	92, 92n51, 93
7:11b–17	93
7:12–17	116, 116n44
7:13	117
12:9	119n56
24:17	117n47

1 Kings

5:5	117
8	25n60
8:2	25
8:2–66	24, 25
8:3–11	11n4
8:10–12	54–55
8:12	55n58
8:12–50	67n100, 139n108, 148
8:27	88
8:29	129
8:32	113, 114n36
8:65	25

2 Kingdoms

19:19 LXX	16n27

2 Kings

16:13, 15	20, 21n44
17:24–31	57n69
23:29–30	120, 120n57

1 Chronicles

5:1	80, 80n6
9:32	17
10:4	119n56
12:30	94n55
23:30	17n30

INDEX OF ANCIENT DOCUMENTS

23:31	17n30	1:43, 51	62
24:4	14n18	4:36	31, 31n82
		4:36–59	31
2 Chronicles		4:41–42	31n82
5:2—7:8	24, 25	4:41–51	31n82
5:3	25	4:44–47	31n82
6:1–39	67n100, 139n108, 148	4:48	31n82, 31n83, 62
6:23	113, 114n36	4:54, 59	31, 62
6:41	11, 138, 143, 148	4:54–56	31n82
7:8	25	5:1	31, 62
7:9	25n59	10:1–8	62
7:11–16	11n3, 129, 143	10:21	24
8:13	24		
15:16	16n27	**2 Maccabees**	4n16, 11, 11n6
29:22	20	1:1—2:18	31
30:1–19	19, 20, 20n39, 143n1	1:9	25, 31, 31n84
30:16	20, 20n41, 37, 130	1:9—2:18	25
35:1–19	19, 20, 20n39, 143n1	1:41–66	31
35:11	20, 20n41, 21n44, 37, 130	2:1–8	11n5
		2:9–12	31
35:13	80, 80n6	3:19–32	31n81
35:22–25	120, 120n57	8:24–27	18
		9:4–28	63n85
Ezra		9:12	63n85
3:1	82n16	10:1–8	31
3:1–6	25n60	10:5	32
3:4	24	10:6	32
6:19–22	19, 20, 20n39, 143n1	10:7	32
		12:32	23n52
Nehemiah		12:36–39	18
2:13	31		
8:1–12	82n16	**Job**	
8:8	80n4	3:22	100, 110n28, 114
8:13–18	25	5:26	100, 110n28, 114
8:14–17	24	6:19	99n74
8:16	25	15:22	100, 110n28, 114
13:15–22	16	29:29	100, 110n28, 114
Tobit		**Psalms**	
2:1	23n52	2:2–8	116, 116n44
		5:10	94
1 Maccabees	4n16, 11, 11n6, 31n81	5:10 LXX	89n39
		21:16 LXX	74n125
1:41–60	62	21:19 LXX	72, 127
		22	72

Psalms (continued)

22:19	127
22:28	63n86
31:7	94n55
33 LXX	112
33:15 MT	113
33:20 LXX	98
33:20–21 LXX	114
33:21	98
33:21 LXX	3, 98, 98n69, 105, 106, 106n12, 106n13, 107, 111, 114, 121, 132, 136, 146, 148
34	112
34:2–4	112
34:2–7	113n34
34:5–7	113
34:8	113n34
34:8–15	113
34:9–10	113n34
34:13–15	113n34
34:16	113n34
34:16–19	113n34
34:16–23	113
34:18 MT	113n34
34:20	113
34:20–21	113, 113n34
34:20–23	113n34
34:21	3, 98, 105, 105n7, 114, 121, 132, 136, 148
34:21 MT	106, 106n13, 111, 146
34:22–23	113n34
40:6–8	34n94, 130n80
40:10 LXX	66n97
41	66n97
41:3 LXX	74n125
48:2–3, 9–10	11
51:15–19	34n94, 130n80
62:2 LXX	74n125
68	74n127
68 LXX	74
68:2–13 LXX	74
68:20–22 LXX	74
68:22 LXX	74, 74n125
68:23–29 LXX	74
72:1–17	116
86:9	63n86
89	116n44
89:2–5, 28–38	116n44
89:2–5, 29–38	116
89:39, 52	116n44
92	17n30
92:1	17n30
106:36–39	57n69
132:8	11, 138, 148
132:8, 14	143
132:14	11n3, 129
139:4 LXX	89n39, 94
140:4 MT	94

Proverbs

25:20	74n125
27:18	94n55
31:24	56n65

Ecclesiastes

4:17—5:1	34n94, 130n80

Wisdom

7:2	137n102

Isaiah

1:10–17	34n94, 130n80, 143
2:2–5	61, 63n86, 64
2:3	11
4:2	116n45
5:23	113, 114n36
6:1–13	126
6:10	64n91, 108, 124, 124n69, 126, 127, 133
9:1–6	116
13:15	119n56
29:10	89n40
37:38	119n56
38:11	99n74
40:1—55:13	118
42:1	56n63, 63, 98, 122, 122n65
42:1–4	116n43
42:1–7	115, 118
42:5	118, 118n52, 119n52
42:8—48:22	119n54

INDEX OF ANCIENT DOCUMENTS

43:5–7	63n86	22:1–30	117
49:1–3	116n43	23:5	113n35, 116, 116n45, 117, 132
49:1–6	115, 118	23:5–6	113, 113n35
50:4–9	115, 118	23:6	113n35, 116
51:9	121n63	31:8–11	63n86
52:1	121n63	33:15	116, 116n45, 132
52:13	65n91, 122, 124, 132, 132n85, 134		
52:13—53:12	55, 65n91, 114n36, 115, 118, 118n50, 121n63, 123, 124, 147	**Lamentations**	
		4:9	119n56
52:14–15	124		
53	113	**Ezekiel**	
53:1	65n91, 122, 124, 124n69, 126, 127, 133	3:12	132
		20:12, 13, 16, 20, 21, 24	18n32
53:1 LXX	64n91	22:8, 26	18n32
53:3–11	116	23:1–49	57n69
53:4–12	56, 121, 133, 134, 146	23:38	18n32
53:5	132, 132n85, 133	34:23–31	117n47
53:5, 10	114n36	37:21–28	117n47
53:5–6	133n90	39:1	38n110
53:5–8	137	39:17	38n110
53:5–11	134n92	39:19	38n110
53:5–12	116n43	39:20	38n110
53:6	121	40:1—47:12	20, 129, 129n79, 131, 131n83
53:6, 11	117, 146, 148		
53:7	55, 99n72, 122, 122n64, 132, 133	40:38	129n79
		40:38—46:24	129
53:8	63n87	43:7	67n100, 139n108, 148
53:9	99, 114n38, 121, 136	43:18	20
53:10	137	44:12	16n27
53:11	99, 113, 114n36, 117, 122n64, 132, 136, 137, 146, 148	44:24	18n32
		45:19	36n101
53:12	148	45:21–24	20, 20n42, 21n42, 131
56:4	18n32	45:22	129, 131n83, 137, 148
58:1–14	17	46:24	129n79
58:13–14	18	47:1–10	148
58:14	17	47:1–12	26, 29n74, 61, 129, 131n83, 138, 143
66:18–21	63n86		
66:23	64	47:9–10	26n63
		47:12	26n63

Jeremiah

Daniel

3:1–10, 20	57n69	7	65n91
3:17–18	63n86	7:13–14	65n91, 125, 127, 141
21:7	120n58		

Hosea

2:1–23	57n69
4:10	94n55
4:12	57n69
6:4–10	34n94, 130n80, 143
12:8	56n65

Joel

4:9	121n63
4:18	26n63, 61, 139

Amos

8:4–6	17n28
8:5	16

Micah

4:2	11

Zephaniah

1:11	56n65

Zechariah

1:1–6	115, 115n40
2:14	117n49
2:15	117n49
2:46 LXX	117
3:8	116, 116n45, 132
3:8–10	115–16, 117, 117n49, 118, 120, 123, 123n66, 132, 148
3:9	116, 146
3:10	117, 117n49
6:10	117n49
6:10–15	118, 120, 123, 123n66, 132, 148
6:12	116n45, 117, 132
6:12–13	133
6:12–13, 15	146
6:12–15	116, 117, 117n49, 118
6:13	117, 132n86, 146, 148
6:13,15	138, 139, 148
6:15	117
8:20–23	117n49
9:9	113, 116, 117n49, 118n50, 132, 134
9:9–10	116, 116n43, 117n49, 118, 120, 121n62, 123, 123n66, 125, 141, 146, 147, 148
9:10	116, 133
9:10 MT	133n89
9–14	116n43, 120n62
9:16	117n49
11:4–14	116n43
11:4–17	121n62
11:7, 11	56n65
11:8	121n63
11:11	117n49
11:16	119n55, 120n60
11:17	119n55, 120, 120n60, 121
12:1	118, 118n52, 119n52, 120n61
12:3—14:20	117n49
12:7, 8, 10, 12	119
12:7—13:1	119n53
12:10	3, 3n8, 4n11, 5, 99, 99n74, 107, 108n18, 109, 110, 110n29, 111, 111n30, 114–21, 119n56, 120n57, 120n61, 121n63, 123, 123n66, 132, 132n86, 133, 134n93, 135, 136, 136n98, 136n99, 138, 141, 146, 147, 148n7, 149
12:10 LXX	107n15
12:10 MT	120n59
12:10–12	119
12:10–13	116n43
12:10—13:1	118, 120, 120n61, 120n62, 121n62, 132, 146
12:10—13:1, 9	121, 133
12:10—13:9	134, 135, 149
12:10–14	121, 138
12:11	119
12:11—13:6, 8–9	134n93
12:11–14	134n93

12:12	121	53:6, 10	121
12:12–14	119		
13:1	119, 120n61, 121, 138, 148	**APOCRYPHA**	
13:1–2	134n93	**Psalms of Solomon**	**126n75**
13:2–6	119, 120n60, 120n61, 121	17:32	113
13:3–6	120, 134n93		
13:6	119n56	**PSEUDEPIGRAPHA**	
13:7	119, 119n56, 120, 120n59, 120n60, 121, 121n63, 133, 134n93, 135, 141, 146, 149	**1 Enoch**	
		37–71	113n35, 126n74
		38:2	113
		53:6	113
13:7–9	116, 116n43, 118, 119, 120n61, 120n62, 121n62, 121n63, 132	**4 Ezra**	**126n75**
13:8	134n93		
13:9	120, 120n61, 121, 134n93, 146	**Jubilees**	**11, 11n6**
14	25, 25n61, 26, 26n62, 26n64	6.15–17	23n55
		6.17	23n55
14:1–3	121	16.20–31	27
14:4–11	121, 133	16.31	27
14:6–8	135	49	22n48
14:6–21	25, 26, 28, 30	49:13–14	105n10
14:7	30, 39, 61, 129, 135	49.20	20n41, 37, 130n82
14:7–8	143		
14:8	26, 39, 61, 129, 138, 148	**Pseudo-Philo**	
		LAB 13.7	28
14:8–10	26		
14:13, 20, 21	135n96	***Similitudes of Enoch***	**126n75**
14:15	120n61		
14:16	61, 126, 135, 137n101		
14:16–17	64	**DEAD SEA SCROLLS**	**5N20, 92N49**
14:16–19	25, 29		
14:16–21	24, 39, 117n49, 121, 126, 129, 133, 143, 148		
14:17	26, 26n62		
14:18	135n96	**1QS**	
14:18–19	26n62	1:18—2:25	23n55
14:20	26n62		
14:20–21	26, 135	**4Q174**	**81n11**
14:21	26n62, 56n65	4QFlorilegium	81n10, 92
14:21 LXX	56n65	I, 2–3	82, 93, 93n52
14:21a	56n65	I, 2b–3a	93
17:11	137	I, 10	92n51
45:22	149		

INDEX OF ANCIENT DOCUMENTS

4Q252		
Frag. 1 V, 3-4		113

4Q266		
11, 16-18		23n55

4Q270		
7 II, 11-12		23n55

4Q409		
1 I, 10-11		27

4Q502		27, 30
fragment 24		30n78

11Q13	95, 96
II, 2-3	82, 96-97
II, 2-6	96, 111
II, 2a	96
II, 2b-3	96
II, 3	96
II, 4	96n62
II, 4-6	96
II, 5-6	96n62

CD	
20:21	93n53

XX	
21	93

CD-A	
VIII	
14-15	82, 94, 95
16b-18a	95

CD-B	
XX	
21	94n54
21-22a	82, 93, 94

Community Rule from Qumran

1QS	
8:5-10	14

Damascus Document	94n54

DJD
fragment 99, Baillet
7.494	27n68

Hebrew Copper Scroll
3Q15	83n21

Melchizedek scroll	95n58

Qumran

11QT
27:10—28:11	27n68
42:7-17	27n68

Job targum	80n4

ANCIENT JEWISH WRITERS

Hillel
Seven rules	5n19
Josephus	4, 4n16, 28

Against Apion
1.209	17
2.108	14n18
2.175	17

Jewish Antiquities
2.311	38n108
2.311-14	22, 38, 144n3
2.312	38n108
2.313	38n108
3.179-87, 224-57	13, 143

INDEX OF ANCIENT DOCUMENTS

3.226–27	22n47
3.244–47	27
3.248	22, 38, 144n3
3.252–53	24
7.165	14n18
8.100	28n69
8.100–123, 225–31	28n69
9.288	57n69
10:37–38	63n85
12.316–26	32
12.325	32n85
13.252	23n54
14.110	14n19
14.226–27, 257–58	17
14.337	23
14.60–64	18
14.65–68	18
17.213	22, 38, 144n3
18.254	23
18.311–13	14n19
20.106–7	22
20.211, 219	12n9
20.211–19	12
20.219	14n17

Jewish War

1.145–46	18
1.253	23–24
1.48	18
1.73	28n69
2.10	22
2.280	13, 13n15, 22, 143n1, 144n3
2.392	18n31
2.42	24
3.248–51	22n49
4.262	13, 143
5.17	13, 143
6.299	24
6.422–26	13n13
6.423–25	13, 13n15, 22, 143n1, 144n3
7.401	22, 22n50
20.515–16	13

Philo   4
Allegorical Interpretation

3.154	21
3.4	82, 93
3.94, 165	37, 144n3

Cherubim

27	81n11

Decalogue

159	22, 37, 144n3
160	23

Heir

255	21

Moses

2.215–16	17
2.224–25	22, 37, 144n3
2.226, 228	37, 144n3

Special Laws

1.194	33
1.194–290	130n80
1.195	33
1.196	33
1.205	36n101
1.257	33
1.290	34
1.66–345	143
1.69–70	13n13
2.145–49	13, 143n1
2.148	37, 144n3
2.176–78	24
2.176–87	24
2.179	24
2.180–81	24
2.226	37, 144n3
194–196, 257, 290	130

Special Laws 2

2.145–49	22
2.145–61	22
2.150–55	22n48
2.150–61	22

173

RABBINIC WORKS

Mishnah

'Abot

1:1	82n16

Megillah

3:6	62n84

Pesahim

5:5–6	20n41, 37, 130n82
7:11–12	105n10

Sukkah — 26n65

3:1	27
3:1–11	28
4:1	28
5:1–5	29, 30, 62
5:3	29, 30

Zebahim

3:1	22n47
3:6	105n10
5:8	20n41, 37

Tannaitic Midrash

Sipra Leviticus	96n63
Sipre Deuteronomy	96n63

Tosefta

Pesahim

4:13	86

Sanhedrin

7:11	81, 86

Sukkah — 26n65

2:7—3:1	28
2:10—3:1	27
3:3–15	29n74
3:15	29n74
4:1	30

4:1, 5	29

Zebahim

5:8	130n82

NEW TESTAMENT

Matthew — 6, 79n2

3:13–17	49
5:17	44
5:18–48	44
5:23–24	45
6:24–28	45
7:21–23	45
10:38–39	45n20
12:3, 5	47n30
12:5–6	12
12:10	97
12:10–12	88, 97
12:12	97n65
14:13–21	46n27, 52
14:19	52
14:20	53
15:32–38	46n27, 52
15:36	52
15:37	53
16:24–25	45n20
17:24–27	14n19
21:12–13	12
21:23	12
23:16–22	12
24:1	11n7, 143
24:38	66n97
26:17–19	21, 21n43, 143n1
26:20	53n53
26:26	52n51, 53
26:26–29	46, 49
26:61	12, 143
27:40	12, 143
28:19–20	45

Mark — 79n2

1:9–11	49
6:4	53
6:32–44	46n27, 52
6:41	52

INDEX OF ANCIENT DOCUMENTS

8:1–10	46n27, 52	22:17–19	49
8:6	52, 52n51	22:19	52n51, 53
8:7	52n51	22:19–20	46
8:8	53	24:25–27	47
8:19	53n54	24:27	46, 83n19
8:34–35	45n20	24:30	46, 53
10:38–39	50	24:35	46
11:15–17	12		
12:10	47n30	**John**	34n93, 79n2
12:35	12	1:1	54, 136, 138
13:1	11n7, 143	1:1–2	55n59
14:1, 12	21, 21n43, 143n1	1:1–18	8, 54, 145
14:12	13	1:9	55n62
14:18	53n53	1:9, 11, 15, 27	55n61
14:22	52n51, 53	1:11	73, 73n120
14:22–25	46, 49	1:12	55, 63n86, 73, 73n120
14:58	12, 143	1:13	137n102, 139
15:29	12, 143	1:14	54, 56, 57n67
16:15–16	45	1:14, 49	62n82
		1:15, 27	52, 145n5
Luke	79n2	1:17–18	63
1:1–4	49	1:18	55, 69
2:41–42	13	1:19–51	56n63
3:21–22	49	1:22–34	55n63
4:16–17	17	1:23	124n69
6:27–36, 43–49	45	1:23—12:15	124n69
7:36–50	53n55	1:26, 31, 33	139n106
9:10–17	46n27	1:29	21, 55, 61, 63n87, 70, 98, 99, 99n72, 122, 122n65, 127, 131, 132, 133, 134n92, 137, 146
9:10–27	52		
9:16	52		
9:17	53		
9:23–24	45n20	1:29, 32–34	100
11:37–54	53n55	1:29, 34	124
12:50	50	1:29, 36	21n45, 56, 60, 63, 65n93, 70n110, 76n133, 98, 100, 122, 131
13:15–16	97, 97n65, 97n66		
14:1–24	53n55		
14:5	97n65		
14:5–6	97, 97n66	1:29–49	122
16:29–31	47	1:29–51	147
17:27–31	47	1:31–34	49, 50
19:45–46	12	1:32–33	55
19:47	12	1:33	56, 60, 122, 122n65, 138, 139
21:5	11n7, 143		
22:1	21	1:34	55, 55n63, 60, 61n79, 63, 98, 98n70, 122, 122n65, 137
22:1–14	21n43		
22:7–13	13		

175

John (continued)

Reference	Pages
1:36	99n72
1:38, 41	78
1:41	100, 122, 124, 125
1:45	44n19, 47, 62, 70, 124n69
1:49	56n63, 70, 117n48, 122, 133
1:50–51	109
1:51	57n67, 122, 125n70, 141
2	4n13
2:1–11	122
2:1–12	72
2:3–5, 10	56
2:4	56, 65n93, 72, 72n119, 77, 122, 145
2:4—19:27	2n3, 39n111
2:5–11	56
2:6–11	56
2:11	56
2:13	4, 56, 64n88
2:13, 23	65n93, 129
2:13–17	12n9
2:13–22	12n10, 57n67
2:14	12n10, 59n73
2:14–16	12
2:15–22	59n73
2:16	56n65
2:16–17	66n98
2:16–21	129
2:17	56, 70, 74n127, 78n1, 109n24
2:18	56
2:18–22	12, 28n73
2:19	12, 56, 59n73
2:19, 21	12n10
2:19–21	12n10, 62, 129, 135, 138, 143, 148
2:19–22	30, 41n2, 61, 131n83
2:20	12, 12n9, 12n10
2:20–21	12n11
2:21	62n82
2:21–22	57
3	4n13
3:3	69
3:3, 5	66n96, 69, 70n109, 133, 133n88
3:3, 7, 31	71
3:3–5	57, 125
3:3–6	60, 73n120
3:3–8	41n2, 148
3:3–21	50
3:5	69, 139n107
3:5, 23	139n106
3:5–6	67
3:6, 8	139n107
3:6–21	57
3:13–14	125n70
3:13–15	65n91
3:14	2n3, 39n111, 56n64, 134
3:14–15	125, 126, 131, 134, 134n92, 137, 140, 141, 147, 148
3:15	134
3:16	61n79
3:22–26	57
3:31	52, 145n5
4:1–2	57
4:1–15	68n104
4:1–42	57n68, 70n111
4:6	70
4:7	57, 58, 74n128
4:7–26	57, 58, 73n124
4:10, 11, 14, 15	139n106
4:10–11, 13–15	70n111
4:10–14	67
4:10–15	57
4:13–15	60
4:14	74n128, 139
4:16, 20	57n69
4:16–19	57n69
4:18, 22	57n69
4:19–20	57
4:20	67n99
4:20–24	69n107
4:21	57n67, 112, 129, 129n78, 132
4:21, 23	65n93, 145
4:21–22	62, 141
4:21–23	129
4:21–24	128n77, 149

INDEX OF ANCIENT DOCUMENTS

4:21–25	57, 58	5:21	67n101
4:22	62	5:27	125, 125n70
4:22–23	112	5:30	62n82
4:23	62n84, 70, 129, 132	5:33–34	59
4:23–24	39, 56, 57, 61, 62, 62n82, 63, 67, 67n99, 69, 70n111, 77, 127, 129, 129n78, 131, 133n88, 138, 139, 140, 141, 145, 148, 149	5:36	68, 73n123, 74, 74n128, 104, 131, 133n87
		5:39, 46	47
		5:45–46	62
		5:46	70
		6:1–13	52
4:23f	76n133	6:1–15	46n27, 59
4:25	124	6:1–71	58
4:25–26	100, 125	6:4	4, 59n74, 60, 64n88, 65n93, 129
4:27	58		
4:27, 30–33	58	6:11	52, 53n53, 59
4:28–30	58	6:12, 13	53
4:29	57n69	6:14	52, 145n5
4:31, 38	58	6:15	70
4:34	58, 58n71, 62n82, 68, 73n123, 74, 74n128, 77, 104, 129, 131, 133n87, 134, 140, 141, 145, 147, 149	6:22–71	59, 60n75
		6:23	59, 60n75
		6:27, 53, 62	125n70
		6:30–31	59
		6:31	78n1
4:35–38	67n102	6:31–58	66n97
4:35–42	68n104	6:32	55n62
4:36	67n102	6:32–33	67n101
4:39	67n102	6:35	59, 60
4:39, 41–42	70n111	6:35, 48	60
4:39–42	58	6:35–50	59n75
4:42	58n70, 62n82	6:35–58	59
4:45	65n93	6:35–59	59n75
5:1	58	6:38	62n82, 68
5:1, 9	65n93	6:40	69
5:1–9	58	6:44	135n95
5:1—10:42	4, 16n24, 58	6:45	108n19
5:1–47	58	6:51	59
5:2	78	6:51, 58	66
5:9–18	58	6:51–58	50, 60, 139n106
5:14	58, 59n73, 65	6:53–56	60, 139n106
5:14–16	62	6:53–58	61
5:15	59	6:54	60n76, 139, 148
5:15–16	58	6:54, 56, 57, 58	60
5:16	59	6:54, 56–58	66n97
5:17–18	114n38, 136	6:56	68, 134n92, 139, 140
5:18	114n38	6:60	60n77
5:19–29	18n33, 58	6:63	60n77, 61, 67, 139n107
5:20–38	58	6:63a	60

John (continued)

6:63b	60n78
6:64	61n79, 66
6:69	60, 61n79, 62n82
6:71	61n79
7:1—10:21	58, 61, 135n96
7:2	65n93
7:2—10:21	58n72
7:14	12, 126
7:18	78n1
7:30	64n88, 65n93, 124n68
7:37	61
7:37—10:21	58n72
7:37-38	5, 61, 135
7:37-39	4, 4n13, 25, 25n61, 27n66, 28n73, 60, 61, 67, 70n111, 73n124, 131n83, 138, 148
7:38	61n80, 70n111, 74n128, 78n1, 139n106
7:38-39	61, 139
7:39	2n3, 39n111, 56n64, 60, 61, 64n89, 70n111, 135
8:8	70
8:12	4, 4n13, 5, 25, 25n61, 27n66, 30, 61, 62, 135
8:20	64n88, 65n93, 124n68
8:24	134
8:24, 58	135n97
8:28	2n3, 39n111, 56n64, 68n103, 114, 114n38, 125, 125n70, 132n84, 134, 135, 135n97, 138, 140, 141, 147, 148
8:28-38	131, 132, 148
8:31	134n92
8:36	132n84
8:54	64n89, 125
8:59—9:1	58n72
9:1—10:21	58n72
9:1-41	58n72, 62
9:5	62
9:6-12	62
9:13-34	62
9:17	62
9:24-41	61
9:31	62, 62n82, 63
9:34	68n103
9:35	125n70
9:35-41	62n82
9:38	59, 62
9:41	59n73, 62n82, 65
9:41—10:1	58n72
10:1-21	58n72, 73n120
10:3, 4, 12	65, 73n120
10:3-4, 11-12, 15	65n93
10:3-4, 27	72, 73n120
10:10	32n86
10:11	148
10:11, 15	132, 133
10:11-15	69n108
10:12	63n86
10:14-16	69
10:14-18	63, 70
10:15	73
10:15-16	72
10:16	63n86
10:17	65
10:17-18	62, 65n95, 69
10:17-18b	145
10:17-19b	73
10:18	65, 69, 72, 75, 132, 138, 147
10:18c	73, 145
10:22	31n83, 65n93
10:22-40	62
10:22-42	32, 58
10:26	73, 73n120
10:30	63, 114n38
10:30, 38	138
10:30-39	136
10:31	63
10:33	114n38
10:34	125n73
10:36	62, 63, 68, 98
10:37-38	63n85, 68
11:3, 35	53n53
11:4	63, 64n89
11:22	63
11:27	52, 145n5
11:41-44	63
11:45-53	71n114, 117n48, 133
11:48	63n87

INDEX OF ANCIENT DOCUMENTS

11:50	72n117	12:28b	64
11:50–52	63, 69n108, 72	12:29–32, 34	123
11:52	63n86, 72n117	12:29–33	124
11:55	63n87, 64n88, 129	12:31–33	64, 65n91
11:55–57	65n93	12:32	122, 123, 124, 125, 125n71, 125n72, 126, 127, 135, 135n95, 148
12:1	64, 65n93, 129		
12:2	53n53		
12:9, 12, 17, 18, 29, 34	123	12:32, 34	2n3, 39n111, 56n64
12:12–19	123	12:32–33	126
12:12–36	123	12:33	125n73
12:13	124n69	12:34	123, 124, 125, 125n71, 125n73, 126, 126n75
12:13, 15	70, 108n19, 123		
12:13–16	123n66, 146	12:37, 39	64
12:14	116, 123, 127, 132	12:37–38a	2n3
12:14–15	134	12:37–41	65n91
12:15	116, 123, 132	12:38	64n90, 64n91, 74, 74n126, 124, 126
12:15, 38–40	127		
12:15, 40	78n1	12:38, 40	109n24
12:16	64n90, 123	12:38–40	2n3, 64, 122, 123n66, 124, 124n69, 127, 133, 134, 147
12:16, 23, 28	2n3, 39n111, 56n64, 64n89		
12:20	64	12:39	2n3
12:20–22	64, 124	12:40	64n91, 108, 108n19, 109, 109n24, 124, 126
12:21	64		
12:22–23	64	12:41	64
12:23	64, 64n88, 72, 124, 125n71	12:41–43	2n3
		12:42	64
12:23, 24	125n70	12:43	64, 65n92
12:23, 27	65n93, 116	13:1	65, 65n93, 70, 72, 73, 73n120, 73n123, 129, 145, 147
12:23, 28–30	123		
12:23, 32	135n95		
12:23–24	147	13:1—17:26	65
12:23–26	64	13:1a	65n93
12:23–28	125	13:2–5	65
12:23–32	125n71, 133, 134, 140, 141, 147, 148	13:3–35	65
		13:5	66
12:23–32, 38–40	134	13:6–9	65
12:23–36	127	13:8	66, 66n96
12:24	67n102, 68n104	13:10	66
12:24–25	125	13:12–15	65, 65n95
12:27	122, 125, 125n72	13:18	60n76, 66, 66n97, 74, 74n126, 78n1, 108n19, 109, 109n24, 135n97
12:27–28	64, 124		
12:27–32	64		
12:27–38a	64	13:19	135n97
12:28	114n37, 124, 125n72, 127	13:23	53n53
		13:23, 28	53n53
12:28–29	124	13:31	64n89, 125n70

John (continued)

13:31, 32	2n3, 39n111, 56n64, 64n89
13:32	64n89
13:34	140, 140n109
13:34–35	45n20, 65, 67, 68
13:35	68
14:2	66, 66n98
14:2, 23	66n98, 67n99
14:2–3, 23	139, 148
14:2–27	129
14:3, 27	67
14:4–6	68
14:5–6	67
14:6	40n1, 67, 68n106, 139, 148
14:6–7	57n67
14:7–8	135
14:7–11	110
14:10	67
14:13	64n89
14:15	135n94, 144n2
14:16	56, 67, 68, 140
14:16–17	139, 148
14:17	68, 133n88, 139
14:20	117n49
14:21	56, 72
14:21–23	68, 140
14:23	40n1, 66, 67, 133n88, 139, 148
14:26	67, 67n103
14:31	73, 75, 132, 138, 145, 147
15:1	55n62
15:1–11	68, 68n105
15:2, 4, 5, 8, 16	68n104
15:2–8, 16	67
15:4	140
15:4, 5, 6, 7, 9, 10	68n105
15:8	64n89, 68n104
15:9–10	140, 140n109
15:10	72
15:12	68, 140, 140n109
15:12–14	65
15:12–16	68
15:12–17	45n20, 67, 68
15:13	75, 132, 147
15:13–15	73, 145
15:16	68
15:22–24	59n73
15:25	74, 74n126, 74n127, 109n24, 125n73
15:26–27	68
15:27	68
16:2–4	68
16:7	67, 68, 129, 139, 140, 148
16:12–15	67
16:13	67, 67n103
16:13–15	67n103
16:14	2n3, 39n111, 56n64, 64n89
16:14–15	67
16:15	68n103
16:21	72, 72n119
16:21–22	72n119
16:23, 26	117n49
16:32	72
17:1	65, 72
17:1, 4, 5, 10	69
17:1, 5	2n3, 39n111, 56n64, 64n89
17:1, 5, 10	64n89
17:1–26	69
17:2–5	69
17:3	98
17:4	104, 131, 133n87
17:4, 23	73n123, 74
17:4, 36	74n128
17:5, 22, 24	69
17:10	64n89
17:17	68n106
17:17, 19	68, 68n106
17:19	68n106
17:21	68n106
17:21–23	69
18:1—19:30	104, 131
18:1–27	71n114, 133
18:4–8	135n97
18:5, 6, 8	135n97
18:5, 7	67n99
18:6	69
18:7–9	69
18:7–11	69

INDEX OF ANCIENT DOCUMENTS

18:11	69, 70, 73, 73n124, 133n87	19:27b	72
18:28, 39	129	19:28	65n94, 73, 73n122, 73n123, 73n124, 74n126, 74n127, 74n128, 75n129, 77, 133n87
18:33	69		
18:33, 37, 39	71n113		
18:36	69, 71, 133		
18:37	125	19:28, 30	65n94
18:38	98	19:28–29	133n87
19	131n83	19:28–30	69n108, 73n123, 76, 77, 124n69, 127, 134, 141, 145
19:4, 6	98		
19:7	114, 114n38, 136, 138, 148		
		19:28–35	70n111
19:13	70, 78	19:28a	127
19:14	4, 7, 70, 129, 131	19:28b–30	127
19:14, 15	71n113	19:29	74
19:14, 31	147	19:29–30	74n125
19:14, 36	55	19:30	56, 70n111, 74, 75, 133, 133n87, 133n90, 138, 139, 140, 145, 147, 148
19:14–15	133		
19:14–15, 19–22	117n48, 135, 137n101		
19:14–16	4, 4n13	19:30, 34	77
19:19	67n99	19:31	136
19:19–20	70, 71n112	19:31, 42	4, 7
19:19–22	70, 133	19:31–32	136
19:20a	71n113	19:31–33	97, 114n37
19:20b	71n113	19:31–34	1, 76n133, 103, 103n1, 122, 137, 148, 149
19:23	71, 127		
19:23–24	71, 71n114, 72, 117n48, 127, 132, 132n86, 133	19:31–35	1n1, 2, 75, 103, 127, 145, 146, 147
19:24	109n24	19:32	103
19:24, 36	127	19:32–33	114, 127, 138
19:24, 36, 37	74, 74n126	19:32–34	111, 140, 149
19:24, 36–37	127–28	19:33	103, 104, 132
19:24a	127	19:33–34	102, 104, 110, 131, 136, 140, 141
19:24b	127		
19:25	72	19:34	6, 66n96, 70n111, 75, 98, 103, 103n3, 104, 109n26, 127, 131n83, 132, 136, 137, 137n102, 138, 139, 139n106, 140, 141, 147, 148, 149
19:25–26	133		
19:25–26, 35, 38–39	136		
19:25–27	72n118, 73n122, 76, 127, 133, 138, 139, 140, 141, 148		
19:25–30	1n1, 2, 104, 127–28, 131, 145, 147	19:34–35	49–50, 50n41, 131
		19:34a	104
19:25–30, 34	149	19:34b	104n6
19:25–34	127	19:34ba	104
19:26	72, 72n119	19:35	70n111, 75, 98, 103, 103n1, 103n4, 109n26, 136, 136n100, 137, 137n100, 145
19:26–27	72n119		
19:26–27a	72		
19:27	72, 73, 73n123, 77, 133		

John (continued)

19:36	3, 3n8, 3n9, 21n45, 78n1, 98, 98n69, 100, 104n5, 104n6, 105, 105n8, 106, 106n11, 106n12, 106n13, 107, 110, 111, 114, 121, 127, 132, 136, 146, 148
19:36–37	1, 25, 25n61, 27n66, 32, 64n90, 75, 77, 78–101, 104, 110, 122, 123n66, 124, 124n69, 127, 128, 138, 140, 145
19:36a	127
19:36b–37	127
19:37	3, 3n8, 3n9, 4n11, 5, 99, 99n73, 99n74, 100, 103n3, 104, 104n6, 107, 107n15, 107n16, 107n18, 108, 108n19, 109, 109n24, 109n26, 110, 111, 114, 115, 121, 132, 132n86, 136n99, 146, 148n7
19:37a	104
20:8	109
20:16	78
20:19, 26	52, 133n90
20:19–23, 24–29	52, 145n5
20:21	134n90
20:22	134n90
20:22–23	52, 133n90
20:24	134n90
20:26–29	145
20:27–29	52
20:28	52n50, 136
20:29	109
20:30–31	49, 70
20:31	137
21:1–14	52, 145n5
21:6–7	52
21:13	52
21:19	64n89
21:24–25	49, 70
28:3–8	15n23
28:9–10	15n23
28:11–15	15n23
28:16—29:38	15n23

Acts

2:1	23
2:5–10	13n13
2:5–11	13
2:37–41	45
2:37–42	6
2:42	47n29, 51
2:42, 46–47a	41
2:42–46	46
2:42–47	45
2:46	53
2:46–47	13
3:1—4:22	13
5:17–25	13
6:13	12n11
6:13–14	12n11, 143
6:14	12
8:12–17, 26–40	45
8:26–40	45n22
9:18	45
10:43	47
10:44–48	45, 45n22
12:1–11	21
13:14–15, 27	17
13:15	47n30
13:26–44	47
15:21	17
16:14–15, 33	45, 45n22
18:28	47
19:1–7	45, 45n22
20:7	51
20:7, 11	53
20:7–11	47n29, 51
20:7–12	46
20:16	23
21:26–30	13
27:34–36	46n27
27:35	53

Romans

3:10–18	89n39
3:13	89, 89n39, 94
6:1–11	45n20
6:3–4	45

INDEX OF ANCIENT DOCUMENTS

6:3–11	6, 45
6:18	45n20
7:4–6	45n20
9:1—11:36	89n40
10:6, 8	91n48
10:19–21	88
11:8	89, 89n40
12:4–8	15n21
15:4	47
16:16	46

1 Corinthians

1:23	65n95
2:2	49
3:16–17	15, 45
5:7	21, 21n42, 21n45, 38, 38n109, 144n3
6:9–20	45
6:19	45, 45n23
10:1–11	47
10:16	53
10:16–22	45n24
11:17, 18, 20, 33–34	45
11:17–22	45
11:17–33	47n29, 51
11:20–32	45n24
11:23–25	46
11:23–26	6
11:23–34	45
12:12–27	45
12:13	45
12:13–31	15n21
14:1–40	45
14:23, 26	45
14:26–31	47, 47n31
16:2	45
16:8	23
16:20	46
16:22	47, 48, 48n34, 48n35, 51

2 Corinthians

3:12–16	83n19
3:14	47n30
4:5	49
6;16	15
6:16	45, 45n23
7:1	44
13:12	46

Galatians

3:6—4:31	91n47, 111
3:25—4:7	45

Ephesians

2:20–22	15
2:21–22	45, 45n23
4	15n21

Philippians

2:8	65n95

Colossians

1:18	44
2:2	45n20
2:8—4:6	45
2:12	45
3:3	45n20
4:16	46, 47n29, 144

1 Thessalonians

5:26	46
5:27	46, 46n29, 144

1 Timothy

4:13	47, 47n30

2 Timothy

4:13	47, 47n31

Hebrews

1:1–2	83n19
11:11, 15	15n21
11:28	21
12:2	65n95
12:22–23	15n21
13:10–14	15n21

James

1:26–27	45

1 Peter

1:16	44
1:17–19	21
2:4–5	15
2:5	45, 45n23
2:20–25	45n20
2:22	114n38
2:22–25	122n64
3:18–22	6, 45
4:10–12	83n19
4:11	45
5:14	46

1 John

3:16	45n20

Revelation

1:3	46–47
1:4–9	48n36
1:7	48
1:10	45, 48
5:6–13	21
21:22	15n21
22:16–21	48n36
22:20	47–48, 48n35, 48n36, 51

APOCRYPHA (NEW TESTAMENT)

Didache   5, 6, 41, 41n3, 144

1–6	44n17
1.1—6.3	44n18
7:1–3	44n17
7:1–4	44
7.1	41
7.1–3	41
7.4—8.3	42
9:1—10:7	44
9.1, 2, 3	42n5
9.1, 5	42n5
9.1—10.7	42, 42n7
9.2	42n5, 68n105
9.3, 4	42n5
9.5	42n5, 44n18
10.1, 2, 4, 7	42n5
10.6	42, 47, 47n33, 47n34, 48n34, 48n35
10.7	42n6
11.1—13.7	42, 42n7
12.1—13.7	44n18
14.1, 3	42n7
14.1–3	41n4, 42, 42n5
14.2	42n7
14.4—16.8	44n18
15:1, 4, 5	68n105

Letter of Aristeas   11, 11n6

40	14n19
83–99	13
95	14n18
$155	82, 95

EARLY CHRISTIAN WRITINGS

Justin Martyr

First Apology   5, 6, 41, 41n3, 42, 144

1.1	42n9
15	44n18
17	44n18
27	44n18
43	44n18
44	44n18
46.1	42n8
52–53	44n18
52.12	107n18
57	44n18
61	42, 44, 44n17, 44n18
61–67	42
62–64	42n11
65	43, 44n18, 46n25
65, 67	50n45
65.1	42n11
65.1–2	50

65.3	42n11
66	43, 44
66–67	44n18
66.1	44n18
66.3	43n12, 107n18
67	43, 44n17, 44n18, 48
67:3	47n30
67.3	43, 51, 107n18
67.4–5	43
67.4–6	43
67.5	50, 51

GRECO-ROMAN WRITINGS

Aristotle
Rhetoric

2.23.2–4	83n20
2.23.4	87

Cicero
Inv.

1.13.17	83n20

Top.

4.23	83n20

Plato
Politics

295	83n20

Pliny the Younger 5, 41, 144
Epistulae

X 96.7	43, 43n13, 54n57

Plutarch 28
Quaestiones Convivales

IV, 6.2	28n70

Polybius
Histories

3.32.5	87n32
16.29.5	87n32

www.ingramcontent.com/pod-product-compliance
Lightning Source LLC
Chambersburg PA
CBHW051743230426
43670CB00012B/2138